POETRY

POETRY

Second Edition

John Strachan and Richard Terry

EDINBURGH UNIVERSITY PRESS

© John Strachan and Richard Terry, 2000, 2011

Edinburgh University Press Ltd
22 George Square, Edinburgh

First edition published by
Edinburgh University Press in 2000

Typeset in Bembo
by Norman Tilley Graphics, and
printed and bound in Great Britain
by CPI Antony Rowe, Chippenham and Eastbourne

A CIP record for this book is available
from the British Library

ISBN 978 0 7486 4407 0 (hardback)
ISBN 978 0 7486 4401 8 (paperback)

The right of John Strachan and Richard Terry
to be identified as authors of this work
has been asserted in accordance with
the Copyright, Designs and Patents Act 1988.

Contents

Preface to the second edition   viii
Acknowledgements   ix

Introduction   1

1 *The key words of poetry*   7
   1.1   What is poetry?   8
   1.2   The key words of English poetic history   13
   1.3   Exercises   20

2 *The shape of poetry*   23
   2.1   The aesthetics of print   23
   2.2   Pictograms and concrete poems   24
   2.3   Visible but unreadable   28
   2.4   Layout and punctuation   30
   2.5   The poetic stanza and stanzaic form   33
   2.6   Exercises   44

3 *The sound of poetry*   47
   3.1   Poetic sound effects: an overview   47
   3.2   Onomatopoeia   51
   3.3   Sound-patterning   54
   3.4   Rhyme   56
   3.5   The 'orthodox' rhyme   59
   3.6   Some 'unorthodox' rhymes   60

	3.7	Some indeterminacies of rhyme	65
	3.8	Rhyme and meaning	67
	3.9	Exercises	69

4	*Metre and rhythm*	72
	4.1	Complexities in the study of metre	73
	4.2	The key metrical units	74
	4.3	Metrical regularity and variance	77
	4.4	'Missing' and 'extra' syllables	79
	4.5	Feet	80
	4.6	Iambic metre	80
	4.7	Trochaic metre	88
	4.8	Dactylic metre	92
	4.9	Anapaestic metre	94
	4.10	Occasional feet	95
	4.11	Metrical verse lines	97
	4.12	Free verse	104
	4.13	Exercises	108

5	*Comparisons and associations*	111
	5.1	Literal v. figurative	111
	5.2	Metaphor and simile	112
	5.3	Metonymy and synecdoche	115
	5.4	Tenor, vehicle and ground	118
	5.5	Conceits and extended similes	123
	5.6	Dead and dying metaphors	127
	5.7	Riddle poems	132
	5.8	Exercises	134

6	*The words of poetry*	137
	6.1	Linguistic diversity	137
	6.2	Poetic diction	140
	6.3	Poetry of the everyday language	145
	6.4	Creating your own language	147
	6.5	Diction and argots	149
	6.6	Poems about language	153
	6.7	Poetic intertextuality	156
	6.8	Forms of allusion	159
	6.9	Creative quotation and poetic imitation	164
	6.10	The Queen's (and other people's) English	168
	6.11	Exercises	172

7 *Writing poetry*   174
   7.1   Why write poetry?   175
   7.2   Write a poem   180
   7.3   Feedback on your poetry: creative writing classes, poetry
           workshops and writers' groups   183
   7.4   Publishing your poetry   186
   7.5   Poets on poetry   189
   7.6   Forty practical tips on writing poetry   194
   7.7   Exercises   198

A glossary of poetical terms   201
Metre exercise: answers   227
Further reading   232
Index   236

Preface to the second edition

This new edition of *Poetry* has been revised and expanded from the book's first edition, which was published in 2000. Some changes to the text are small; others are substantial. Though the first five chapters of the book have been revised, most of the alterations to the text here are minor and the most important changes to the study are in its final chapters. We have introduced three new subsections to Chapter 6, 'The words of poetry', on poetic inter-textuality, forms of allusion, and creative quotation and poetic imitation. We have also added a number of entries to the Glossary of poetical terms and brought in a new section, 'Further reading', which offers summary bibliographies for the book's seven chapters and Glossary.

The most substantial additions in this edition are the inclusion of exercises at the end of each chapter – which can be undertaken in the classroom or in private study – and a new chapter, 'Writing poetry'. The decade since the first publication of *Poetry* has seen a rapid development of creative writing courses in British universities, most of which attend to poetry, and the concluding chapter here reflects the importance of this development, discussing why poets write and offering advice on composing poetry. This is now the only introductory book of its kind to include analysis of both the study and the writing of poetry. The volume's emphasis has always been a practical one. In its new edition, alongside its consideration of how poetry works, there is a detailed attention to how poems are written.

Acknowledgements

We would like to express thanks to Jackie Jones, Carol Macdonald and James Dale for the help received from Edinburgh University Press during the preparation of the original and second editions of this book. Our thanks also go to our students, past and present, who contributed greatly to our sense of what a textbook on the study of poetry might best contain.

The authors are grateful to the copyright holders for permission to quote extracts from the following poems: John Agard and Serpent's Tail Ltd for 'Listen Mr Oxford Don', from John Agard, *Mangoes and Bullets* (1985); John Ashbery and Carcanet Press Limited for lines from 'The Dong with the Luminous Nose', from *Wakefulness* (1998): © 1988, 1998, 1999 by John Ashbery; reprinted also by permission of Georges Borchardt, Inc., on behalf of the author; Colette Bryce and Picador for 'Wish You Were', from Colette Bryce, *The Heel of Bernadette* (2000); W. W. Norton & Company Ltd for 'l(a)' and 'o sweet spontaneous', from E. E. Cummings, *Complete Poems 1904–1962*, edited by George J. Firmage, by permission of W. W. Norton & Company Ltd © 1991 by the Trustees for the E. E. Cummings Trust and George James Firmage; Carol Ann Duffy and Picador for 'Mrs Sisyphus', from Carol Ann Duffy, *The World's Wife* (1999); Faber and Faber and Harcourt Inc. for 'The Hollow Men', from T. S. Eliot, *Collected Poems 1909–1962* (1962); Penguin Putnam Inc., Laurence Pollinger Ltd and the Estate of Frieda Lawrence Ravagli for 'Gloire de Dijon', from *The Complete Poems of D. H. Lawrence* (1957); Tom Leonard and Galloping Dog Press for 'Just ti Let Yi No', from Tom Leonard, *Intimate Voices: Selected Work 1965–1983* (1984); Carcanet Press Limited for 'The Loch Ness Monster's Song', from Edwin Morgan, *Collected Poems* (1982); Faber and Faber and HarperCollins for 'You're', from Sylvia Plath, *Collected Poems*

(1981); Craig Raine and Oxford University Press for 'A Martian Sends a Postcard Home', from Craig Raine, *A Martian Sends a Postcard Home* (1979); Oxford University Press for 'Naming of Parts', from Henry Reed, *Collected Poems*, edited by Jon Stallworthy (1991), reprinted by permission of Oxford University Press; Faber and Faber and Random House for 'The Pylons', from Stephen Spender, *Collected Poems* (1955); J. M. Dent for 'The Force that through the Green Fuse Drives the Flower' and 'Do not Go Gentle into that Good Night', from Dylan Thomas, *Collected Poems* (1952); and New Directions Publishing Corporation for the same items from *The Poems of Dylan Thomas*, © 1952 by Dylan Thomas, reprinted by permission of New Directions Publishing Corp; Carcanet Press Limited for 'Death' and 'This is Just to Say', from William Carlos Williams, *Collected Poems*; and New Directions Publishing Corporation for the same items from William Carlos Williams, *Collected Poems: 1909–39*, Volume I, © 1938 by New Directions Publishing Corp. reprinted by permission of New Directions Publishing Corp.

Every effort has been made to trace and correspond with copyright holders. If any have been inadvertently overlooked, the publishers will be pleased to make the necessary arrangement at the first opportunity.

Introduction

The purpose of this book can be expressed in one sentence. It is intended as an accessible survey of those technical aspects of poetry which students of English literature often see as daunting. It attempts to demystify the study of poetry, aiming to explain the issues in a lively and informative fashion. In effect, *Poetry* is intended as a route map though the poetic maze, with chapters on such essential but often complex issues as rhythm and metre, the use of metaphor in poetry, poetic sound effects and the visual appearance of poetry. Crucially, the book aims to make the jargon of poetry less intimidating, offering clear explanations of poetic terminology allied to close readings which demonstrate how poetry actually works in practice to students studying and writing verse.

This study's organising principle is tripartite, consisting of the introduction of terminology, exposition and illustration. Our hope is that the text will thus provide a stimulating blend of different types of discussion. Throughout, poetic terms are introduced, explained and demonstrated by citation and analysis. The latter aspect is perhaps the most crucial to the reader. The study of poetic devices, like the study of the terminology of all intellectual disciplines, is best addressed by examples of how poets have actually used these devices. Consequently, each chapter contains several sustained set-piece readings of poems that are presented as illustrations of the critical readings readers can learn to perform for themselves. It is our hope that this book will allow students to move away from the feeling that the formal aspects of poetry are matters which make sense only to a few initiates, and that they will, as a consequence, feel comfortable with these issues in a manner which will directly and practically inform their wider reading, studying and writing of English poetry. If this book can prompt a sense amongst its readers that the technical analysis of poetry is both valuable and something which is well within their intellectual grasp, then its purpose will have been achieved.

II

In his meditative satire *Table Talk* (published in 1782), the poet William Cowper (1731–1800) worried that his great early eighteenth-century predecessor Alexander Pope, with his carefully contrived and regular verse, had 'made poetry a mere mechanic art'. Here Cowper stands at the cusp of the Romantic period and, indeed, seems to anticipate the Romantic view of poetry, with its distrust of an undue emphasis upon the technical aspects of verse and attendant privileging of the concepts of originality, spontaneity and self-expression. Indeed, by the end of the eighteenth century, Cowper's great admirer William Wordsworth (1770–1850) manifests an anxiety that the formal examination of a work of art somehow threatens to mutilate and destroy its effect: 'we murder to dissect'. Such an attitude has its post-Romantic devotees to this day, amongst those readers of poetry who maintain that there is something cold, overly scientific, about the academic study of literature and that poetry is an art primarily to be enjoyed on an emotional level. A fine poem, according to this line of argument, is, after all, a thing of beauty, appealing to the heart rather than the head; and close, formal analysis serves only to break the butterfly on the wheel. We would not wish to deny the emotional power of verse and acknowledge, furthermore, that the affective potency of good poetry does have something intangible about it, often seeming to deny and defy any attempt to catch its essence. However, and whatever high Romantic argument might suggest, we would also argue that poetry is a contrived and highly wrought cultural product which is heavily dependent upon formal and generic conventions which have developed and evolved through many centuries. This book's purpose is to explore these formal and technical aspects of English verse in an accessible and entertaining manner. In essence, *Poetry* examines the 'mechanic art' of verse, addressing what one might call the nuts and bolts which lock the poetic work of art together. Such an attention to the 'mechanic' is not to deny the 'art' of poetry, any more than an understanding of the machinery of a Ferrari distracts from its status as a thing of beauty – a mechanically tooled thing of beauty, but a thing of beauty nonetheless. Indeed, we would argue that an understanding of the formal underpinning of a poem actually serves to deepen one's appreciation of its status as a work of art: the pleasure and exhilaration which one can feel in reading a fine poem are sensations which should actually be heightened by an appreciation of the skill of its construction.

On a more pragmatic level, it is undeniable that a knowledge of the poetic terminology addressed in this book and the critical skills which it seeks to demonstrate by example are of great utility to the principal audience for this book, the undergraduate student of English. This is a book which aims to give such readers the tools to work on the formal organisation of poetry with confidence. It discusses form both through definition and through example; each chapter's introduction of technical terminology is allied to close readings which demonstrate how poets have *used* these techniques. These illustrations take the form of examples drawn from a wide range of English poetry from the Renaissance to the present day, from the sixteenth-century work of Edmund Spenser (c. 1552–1599) to the contemporary Afro-Caribbean voice of John Agard (b. 1949) – the adjective 'English' is here used with reference to language rather more than to nationality. English poetry is a tradition which continues to develop and mutate in exciting new forms to this day, a rich and diverse set of writings which in recent decades has demonstrated the capacity to assimilate new voices from a multitude of different circumstances (social, sexual, racial). Consequently, the critical skills which this book seeks to demonstrate are not, to use Wordsworth's term, skills of dissection, as the analysis of English poetry does not involve the student conducting an autopsy upon a deceased patient, but rather what one might call the diagnosis of a poetic body which is still healthy and vibrant today.

This book is based on the authors' practical experience of teaching poetry at undergraduate level. Indeed, it is heavily influenced by discussions with our first-year students about the difficulties raised by the study of poetry and, most crucially, by what students see as the key critical skills necessary to that study. We have commonly found that our students initially find the formal study of poetry, with its seemingly impenetrable jargon and preponderance of Greek words, somewhat daunting and this book seeks to dispel this impression. It does not seek to deny that, for example, the discourse of prosody or the varieties of figurative language are intellectually challenging. However, it does assert that these are matters which can be understood by the student, rather than remaining the province of those initiated into the academic and poetic communities. This book attempts to fill the gaps in knowledge identified by our students, readers who feel little apprehension about being required to answer assignment questions about the themes and contexts of poetry (whether social, political or sexual), but who tend to find the technical aspects of poetry somewhat alienating. In other words, assessing what poetry *says* seems to hold few terrors for the typical student, but the question of *how* these meanings are delivered is rather more problematical. Consequently, our book is an attempt to offer an accessible and clearly-written textbook for both the student and the general reader seeking to understand how poetry *works*. It guides the reader who is, for example, uncertain about the distinction between free verse and blank verse or bemused by the difference between a metaphor and a metonym through the problems raised by the study of poetry.

III

This book is divided into seven chapters which address different aspects of the study and writing of poetry, and a concluding Glossary of poetical terms, with each chapter including practical exercises based on its content. It opens and closes by considering matters of definition. The opening chapter's examination of certain key poetic terms which are inescapable in the study of English poetry and its history is intended to offer a more in-depth and expansive treatment of these crucial terms than is available in the Glossary's more concise format. Thus the first chapter, 'The key words of poetry', begins from the starting question 'What is poetry?', a deceptively simple question and one which poets and critics have provided with a series of different answers. From this it then moves on to a historical overview of the matters at issue in the rest of the volume in a discussion of the large taxonomic labels which are used in literary history and university survey courses on English poetry: 'medieval', 'Renaissance', 'neoclassicism', 'Romanticism' and so on. The detailed consideration of the history of English poetry is outside the province of this book and is not attempted here. Nonetheless, this chapter's focus upon those vexed definitional questions which underpin the historical study of English poetry, quite apart from complementing the attention to terminology and definition evident throughout this volume, also serves as a reminder that poetry should be read with a sense of its historical circumstance and significance.

Poems are not simply things that we *read*, but also things that we *see*, and Chapter 2, 'The shape of poetry', considers the visuality of poetry, looking at the different ways in which poets exploit the medium of the printed page. For centuries, poets have exploited the visual medium of print by composing poems that are self-consciously configured on the page and this chapter addresses the ways that poetry recommends itself to the reading eye; whilst some poets have written 'shape' poems which represent visually their own subject-matter, others, while not arranging their poems pictorially, have organised them spatially in an equally self-conscious way, employing the various resources of typography to complement their thematic preoccupations. One particularly important convention in the visual appearance of poetry is the stanza, and the chapter concludes by considering different sorts of stanzaic form which have been used by poets down the centuries. Chapter 3, 'The sound of poetry', complements the argument of the previous chapter by considering poetry not as something that is *seen* but as something that is *heard* and addressing all aspects of poetic sound effects excluding metre and rhythm (which are treated separately in Chapter 4). As with the visual medium, poets also exploit the medium of sound and perhaps the most obvious of such exploitations is through introducing rhyme. Consequently, this chapter considers different types of rhyme and examines how poets can exploit these for particular effect. Rhyme is a sound repetition normally falling at the end of the line, but poetry also uses similar patterns of repetition internal to the line, repetitions that we call alliteration and this device is also examined here. Finally, through a reflection upon the phenomenon of 'sound poems', the chapter examines the question of whether or not sound itself, as a pure entity, can convey meaning.

Chapter 4, 'Metre and rhythm', also attends to sound-patterning, building on the arguments of the previous chapter in an examination of the crucial role of poetic metre in English verse. This chapter addresses that aspect of poetry which many students find particularly terrifying: prosody, the analysis of the rhythmical patterning – the arrangement of poetic lines into stressed and unstressed syllables – evident in almost all pre-twentieth-century English verse. As well as introducing students to the full range of metrical forms, it also reminds them that verse scansion is something of a subjective activity: scanning a poem is not so much a matter of identifying a pre-existent pattern but of working out what the words are trying to say and how the lines would have to be scanned to bear out this meaning. The chapter also demonstrates how stress is important in all spoken language, and how poetry can be seen as merely a specialised kind of spoken or speakable language (a theme also taken up later in the book, in Chapter 6).

Poets often use words to mean something other than what they literally mean and Chapter 5, 'Comparisons and associations', considers the use of figurative language in poetry. It distinguishes between the overt and covert comparison (simile and metaphor), and uses the nomenclature of 'tenor', 'vehicle' and 'ground' as a way of exploring how both sorts of comparison work. It also looks at specialist sorts of figurative construct such as the 'symbol' and 'conceit', both of which have great importance in English poetry. Chapter 6, 'The words of poetry', considers the ways in which poets negotiate the relationship between their own poetic language and the language of everyday speech and writing. Every time poets write a poem, they must position their work in relation to the language at large and this chapter considers a wide gamut of issues to do with the nature of poetic language. Whilst there have been poets (such as Wordsworth) who have deliberately tried to denude their poetry of ostensible poeticality, others have used poetic idioms deliberately divorced from normal language, from the 'poetic diction' of some eighteenth-century poets to more recent poets' tendency to slew their language towards archaism, dialect or individually fashioned poetic argots.

Chapter 7, 'Writing poetry', moves from the study of poetry to the writing of poetry. It examines *why* poets write, in discussing the creative motivations of a number of twentieth-century American poets (Robert Frost, Anne Sexton, William Stafford and Adrienne Rich), and then offers detailed practical advice on writing poetry, on creative writing courses, poetry workshops and writers' groups, and on publishing poetry.

The final part of the book, the Glossary of poetical terms, records, and gives illustrations of, all the specialist vocabulary used in the book as part of a wide-ranging glossary of poetic devices. It offers a systematic lexicon of poetical terminology, providing at-a-glance answers to definitional questions about poetry, from the most commonplace devices used by poets (metaphor, simile and symbol) to the rather more obscure and arcane (anacrusis, cretic, wrenched accent). The latter are included for the sake of comprehensiveness, ensuring that the Glossary will remain a useful tool for students, at whatever stage in their academic career they might be.

IV

This is a book primarily concerned with the formal organisation of poetry. Nonetheless, it should be acknowledged that poetry cannot adequately be discussed solely in terms of itself, in terms of form alone. Poetic language is but a specialised form of linguistic usage and, like all language users, poets use language for effect, using words to communicate, to entertain, to persuade. Any attempt to study the form of poetry divorced from the examination of its meanings and content, and of the various contexts in which it participates, is an arid and inadequate discipline. That said, however, an attention to poetic form remains a crucial part of the study of poetry. Furthermore, we think it fair to argue that the focus of contemporary pre-university study of poetry has, perhaps, moved rather too far away from an attention to formal structure, leaving undergraduate readers feeling ill-equipped for the task of stylistic analysis. The critic L. C. Knights once wrote that literary criticism is an 'exploration, in the first place, of words in a certain arrangement'; however, the emphasis in much school – and some university – teaching has shifted away from this first principle, stressing what poetry *means* rather than attending to the way in which these meanings are achieved. Poetic content is important and the reader who neglects it is indulging in pointless intellectual manoeuvring. However, the theme of this book, the poetic arrangement of words, is still central to the study of poetry. We hope that this volume will give its readers critical skills to complement those which they employ in their study of poetry's more thematic concerns. Form complements content and an understanding of how poetry works is crucial to its study and to an appreciation of the extraordinary vigour and versatility of English verse.

1

The key words of poetry

'Sir, what is poetry?'
'Why Sir, it is much easier to say what it is not. We all *know* what light is; but it is not easy to *tell* what it is.'

(Boswell's Life of Johnson)

In the study of literature, the questions which seem most straightforward are often the most complex ones to answer. In particular, innocent-sounding questions of definition such as 'What is poetry?' or 'What is Romanticism?' can be addressed in an almost bewildering number of ways, as the scholarly quarrels over the definition of these words demonstrate. Much critical ink is spilt as to what a key poetic term might mean and how it might best be applied, often leaving the reader new to these complexities somewhat bemused. Consequently, this is a chapter which deals with the definitions of a series of central words which resound through the study of poetry and its history, words whose meanings are not easy to pin down. Indeed, it is fair to say that issues pertaining to the definition of terminology have often bedevilled literary debate, leaving the student reader somewhat impatient at this seeming critical inability even to approach first base, let alone proceed with the game. Nonetheless, much as one might want to abandon large overarching labels and stick to the specifics of verse (individual poems, individual poets), these are words which are inescapable in the study of poetry. The student needs working definitions of the terms which resonate through critical writing about English poetry – from 'poetry' itself to 'medieval', 'Renaissance', 'Augustan', 'Romantic', 'Victorian' and 'modernist' – and this chapter attempts to offer such definitions. It is intended to provide a fuller discussion of the most central historical terminology used in the study of English poetry than is available in the concise

Glossary of poetical terms which ends this volume. And in effect, in its discussion of the large taxonomic labels which are used in literary history and university survey courses on English poetry, it also offers a historical overview of the matters at issue in the rest of this book. As a consequence, this chapter's focus upon those definitional questions which underpin the historical study of English poetry, quite apart from complementing the attention to terminology and definition evident throughout this volume, also serves as a reminder that poetry should be read with a sense of its historical circumstance and significance.

1.1   WHAT IS POETRY?

We shall begin our discussion with the most central – and arguably the most contentious – word of them all, 'poetry'. This section is an attempt to offer a working definition of poetry as it is understood today and also to look at the earlier critical senses of the word in English poetical history. What is poetry? The critic who attempts to answer this vexatious question should be seen as either brave or foolhardy. Defining a cultural form as ancient as poetry, a cultural form which has been used in so many different ways throughout human history, is a project to tax the most ingenious critic. Almost every definition which can be formulated seems instantly to prompt examples of counter-definitional poetry. Nonetheless, the attendant difficulties have not prevented critics from venturing definitions. Critics and poets, from Aristotle onwards, have come up with a number of different accounts of the nature of poetry, responses which have evolved throughout poetical history. Certainly a significant number of the most notable poets and critics in the English tradition have offered definitions: Sidney, Wordsworth, Coleridge, Shelley, Hazlitt, Arnold, Ruskin and T. S. Eliot amongst them. However, it must be acknowledged that very few of them have agreed with one another, testimony to the fact that the answer to our question depends, of course, on who is doing the answering and when. Like many other words, 'poetry' is a term which has seen its meaning change and evolve with time. Thus, for instance, our contemporary sense of the nature of poetry is in some ways different from the sense of the word most common in the seventeenth century. So we approach the issue in two ways: first, we attempt a definition of poetry as it is currently understood and, secondly, we examine the different responses to the question 'What is poetry?' which have been offered by certain key poets and critics in English poetic history.

Those in search of guidance as to the meaning of a given word generally turn first to the *Oxford English Dictionary* (*OED*). The dictionary gives the most usual current definition of the word 'poetry' as 'The art or work of the poet'.

From this incontrovertible pronouncement, it goes on to define the formal characteristics of poetry: 'Composition in verse or metrical language, or in some equivalent patterned arrangement of language; usually also with choice of elevated words and figurative uses, and option of a syntactical order, differing more or less from those of ordinary speech or prose writing.' The *OED* is right to insert the qualificatory 'usually' in its argument that poetry is characterised by elevated language and syntactical variation from everyday language and writing, as it is perfectly possible to produce poetry which lacks both characteristics (as, for example, the plain and unadorned style of some of Wordsworth's ballads demonstrates). Consequently, we take the central characteristic of poetry, with the significant exception of free verse (see below), to be what the *OED* calls 'patterning'. Poetry has a pattern, and in English poetry, the particular nature of that patterning is characterised by sound. Poetry is a cultural form where the placing of the words is driven by their sound as well as by their sense or meaning. And English poetry – free verse excepted – has a regularity of rhythm which is found in the recurring sound-patterns evident as one listens to a poem. These rhythms – metre is the more precise term – best define poetry. Poetry is but a specialised form of language, and all language has rhythm; the key distinction is that poetry has a discernible rhythmic regularity. What sets poetry apart is the consistency of its patterning. Poets can – and do – deviate from their 'base metre' for poetic effect (see Chapter 4 below), but it is regularity of sound effect which is one of the key distinctions, perhaps *the* key distinction, between poetry and prose. Whilst the unsystematic cadence of prose lacks consistency of rhythm, the attentive listener to a poem can recognise a more or less regular rhythmical ('metrical') pattern.

We would illustrate our distinction between verse and prose by briefly turning to S. T. Coleridge's (1772–1834) 'The Rime of the Ancient Mariner'. In this work, Coleridge's poetry is accompanied by marginal notes which gloss the action of the poem in prose. This is a stanza from Part IV of the poem, with its accompanying prose marginal:

(Poetry)   The moving Moon went up the sky,
           And no where did abide;
           Softly she was going up,
           And a star or two beside.

(Prose)   In his loneliness and fixedness he yearneth towards the journeying Moon,
           and the stars that still sojourn, yet still move onward; and every where the
           blue sky belongs to them, and is their appointed rest, and their native
           country and their own natural homes, which they enter unannounced,
           as lords that are certainly expected and yet there is a silent joy at their
           arrival.

Here the *OED*'s need to qualify its assertion that poetry involves language different from that used in everyday speech and writing is well illustrated, as it is the prose, with its consciously archaic medieval usages ('yearneth') and rhetoric which owes much to the King James Bible, which is self-evidently divorced from commonplace language. The poem, in contrast, surrenders its meaning in a linguistically sparse and unadorned manner. It is the poem's form rather than its content which signals its status as poetry: its use of a four-line 'stanza', its sound recurrence in the form of rhyme in lines 2 and 4 and in the narrow range of syllable count which varies little throughout the poem. The regularity of rhyme, line-numbers, sound-patterning and syllable count evident throughout Coleridge's long poem is nowhere apparent in his prose glosses. Coleridge's prose has a grand rhetorical ebb and flow, but not one which manifests a regularity of rhythmic effect. This is a defining difference between poetry and prose. Furthermore, in its simplest form, another central difference is that Coleridge's poetry is set in lines where the endings are determined by the *poet* rather than, as with the prose, by the compositorial decision of the *printer* of the poem. Stripping out the notion of poetry's linguistic difference from conventional language – which, as we have seen, is no prerequisite – from our basic definition of poetry, and concentrating on the way in which the poet decides on the placing of the line-end and employs a recognisable pattern of sound, we might offer the following definition of poetry as 'language set in lines which manifest a measurable sound–pattern evident in varying degrees of regularity'. Though the remark quoted above as the epigraph to our chapter demonstrates Samuel Johnson's (1709–1784) unease about the problematical task of defining poetry, the Doctor was professionally obliged to define the word for his great *Dictionary of the English Language* (1755). And his definition of poetry remains a succinct and valuable one today: 'Poetry: metrical composition; the art or practice of writing poems.'

Though metre, as Dr Johnson's formulation demonstrates, is at the core of poetry, it should be acknowledged that the twentieth century saw the emergence of 'free verse' (see Chapter 4 below) where poets who see metre as overly restrictive have employed verse where the traditional rules of metrics, and in particular the conventions of rhyme and metre, do not apply. Nonmetrical verse, the unruly child of conventional metre, does not conform to a regular or recurring poetic metre. This raises problems for the person who is attempting to define poetry, and if we require a definition of poetry which can encapsulate free verse, then we might have to resort to such a bald formulation as 'language printed in lines on a page' and make the distinction between prose and poetry in terms of the argument that prose does not manifest such a pattern. That said, a pedant might reply that *all* printed language is set on a page in lines (this very page for instance). However, though prose is set on the page in lines, the reader of prose ignores these line-ends and attaches no weight of meaning to them, concentrating instead on punctuation: full stops, semi-colons and so on. Things are different in poetry, where the reading eye grants interpretive weight to each line-end.

We shall now turn our attention to the historical development of definitions of poetry and to poet-critics' definitions of the term. Whilst there is nothing contentious about Johnson's mid-eighteenth-century emphasis upon the narrow notion of poetry as metrical writing, there is also another ancient sense of the word which is of critical importance. This is the wider notion of poetry as the term used to characterise creative and imaginative writing in a number of genres: the fable, the drama, the prose pastoral as well as metrical verse. The most notable formulation of this concept is found in Sir Philip Sidney's (1554–1586) *The Defence of Poesie* (1579–80), which declares that 'verse … [is] but an ornament and no cause to Poetry: sith there have been many most excellent Poets, that never versified'. Sidney's was no eccentric view; Dryden (1631–1700) was given to labelling almost any literary work a 'poem' and the poet James Beattie (1735–1803) praises Fielding's novel *Tom Jones* and Shakespeare's play *The Merry Wives of Windsor* as 'the two finest Comic poems, the one Epic, the other Dramatical, now in the world'. Here poetry is being used, somewhat indiscriminately, as a catch-all term of praise, as the best kind of creative activity. 'Poetry', in effect, is the accolade to which all writings, in their highest flights of imagination, should aspire.

The *Oxford English Dictionary* gives this wide-ranging sense of the poetical as redundant, citing no examples after the seventeenth century. However, the idea that poetry is the highest literary activity survives to inform many more recent accounts of the nature of poetry, where the simple notion of poetry as metrical composition is rarely enough. For many poets and critics, poetic metre must be employed in a manner which speaks from the heart and the imagination. Thus Wordsworth declares in his 1800 'Preface' to the *Lyrical Ballads* that 'I have used the word "Poetry" … as opposed to the word Prose, as synonymous with metrical composition'. However, after acceding to the bald Johnsonian definition, Wordsworth goes on to insist that metrical composition must be used in a particular manner, a manner which epitomises imaginative activity. 'Poetry is the spontaneous overflow of powerful feelings', he declares, an idea later refined in even more elevated fashion in 1816: 'Poetry proceeds … from the soul of man, communicating its creative energies to the images of the external world'. In this and in several of the most notable conceptualisations of poetry which have been offered by significant English poet-critics, what we are actually dealing with is what a given poet or critic would *like* poetry to be rather than what it actually *is*. When we write of a poet's 'definition' of poetry – Wordsworth's 'emotion recollected in tranquillity' or Coleridge's notion of poetry as an art which 'brings the whole soul of man into activity' – what we are usually examining are idealist formulations, often made in some kind of poetical manifesto, rather than scholarly attempts to define poetry in a cool or dispassionate manner. Indeed, often these are prompted by an awareness that poetry as it is currently manifested is nothing like what the poetic critic is declaring it to be. Thus Wordsworth, faced with a residual fondness amongst the reading public for the Popean couplet and 'poetic diction', is simultaneously offering a call to arms and repudiating the inheritance of early eighteenth-century poetry. He is describing the best form of poetry, celebrating what poetry should be rather than describing what it is.

Wordsworth's expressive model of poetry with its emphasis on the emotional power of poetry, prompted a significant number of later, Victorian con-ceptualisations of poetry, the most concise formulation of which is Thomas Hardy's declaration that poetry is 'emotion put into measure', a definition which manages to combine in four words both the functional ('measure') and the idealist ('emotion'). John Ruskin's *Lectures on Art* (1870) poses our rhetorical question and answers thus: 'What is poetry? The suggestion, by the imagination, of noble grounds for the noble emotions.' It is in the face of such brazen idealism that modernist attacks on Romantic ideas of poetry were aimed, a fact best demonstrated in T. S. Eliot's (1888–1965) declaration that 'Poetry is not a turning loose of emotion, but an escape from emotion; it is not the expression of personality, but an escape from personality'. Just as Eliot is repudiating his immediate poetic inheritance, to a large extent the Romantic and post-Romantic assessments of poetry are themselves reactions against earlier, neoclassical notions of poetry. The Victorian poet-critic Matthew Arnold (1821–1888) testifies to this view: 'The difference between genuine poetry and the poetry of Dryden, Pope, and all their school, is briefly this … their poetry is composed in their wits, genuine poetry is conceived and composed in the soul.' In the face of this, and Coleridge's barb that 'To read Dryden, Pope &c, you need only count syllables', one should really let the accused speak for themselves and briefly encapsulate the neoclassical view of poetry, which pays rather less attention to the original and spontaneous creativity of the imagination and rather more to a sense of poetry as the well-wrought expression of commonly-held human truths. Pope's (1688–1744) *An Essay on Criticism* (1711) offers the finest summary of this view: 'True wit is nature to advantage dress'd / What oft was thought, but ne'er so well express'd'. Similarly, John Dryden writes in the *Essay on Dramatic Poesy* (1665) of a contemporary conviction that the great achievement of contemporary poetry was its capacity to 'mould our thoughts into easy and significant words; to retrench the superfluities of expression, and make our rhyme so properly a part of the verse, that it should never mislead the sense, but itself be led and governed by it'. However pragmatic Dryden's view, it should be noted that the Romantic poet's elevated sense of poetry has its antecedents in earlier English thought, as far back indeed, as Sidney's essay:

> Nature never set forth the earth in so rich tapestry as divers poets have done; neither with so pleasant rivers, fruitful trees, sweet-smelling flowers, nor whatsoever else may make the too much loved earth more lovely. Her world is brazen, the poets only deliver a golden.

I.2   THE KEY WORDS OF ENGLISH POETIC HISTORY

This section offers discursive definitions of the key words of poetical history, for, faced by a thousand years of written evidence of poetic activity in the British Isles, scholars distinguish periods which are labelled, from 'Old English' and 'medieval' poetry through to 'Romantic', 'modernist' and beyond. We use the term 'written evidence' because English poetry is actually much older than the millennium which has recently concluded. No one knows when the first vernacular (that is, native) poetry of the British Isles was composed and, given that it appeared in a pre-literate age, no one will ever know. When scholars write of the 'beginnings of English poetry' in the ninth and tenth centuries, they are referring to written poetry and, furthermore, to that small body of work which has had the good fortune to survive hundreds of years in manuscript form. Poetry in the sense of oral poetry, whether in the form of song, spiritual incantation or ballad, has a much longer history in these islands. The Roman conquerors of the first century BC certainly brought their own highly developed poetical culture with them, but indigenous poetry is older even than that. Almost all peoples, no matter how 'primitive' or undeveloped to the modern eye, have their poetic culture. In ancient Britain, poetry was doubtless used for the purposes of song, ritual, religious ceremony or in tribal history passed down and expanded from generation to generation. It is likely that ancient Celtic peoples in Britain privileged the figure of the bard, a personage who saluted the achievements of his people in poetry and it is also likely that key religious functionaries, whom we now label druids, also used poetry in their incantations. However, for obvious reasons, we lack documentary records of the poetic products of a pre-literate age. It is not until well after the settlement of much of Great Britain by Germanic tribes, principally in the sixth and seventh centuries, that we have evidence, in the form of the earliest surviving indigenous poetry, of the nature of poetry in pre-Conquest England.

The oldest surviving poems in the English tradition are Anglo-Germanic. Whilst the Anglo-Saxons were the dominant force in English culture – if one can call it that – for the three hundred years before the Norman Conquest of

1066, the vast majority of surviving manuscripts in Anglo-Saxon, or 'Old English' as it is commonly referred to today, date from the latter part of that dominance: *Beowulf*, *The Dream of the Rood*, *The Battle of Maldon* and the 'Advent Lyrics'. **Old English poetry** is exotic to the modern eye, its works rather like pearls from the deepest and most remote of oceans. It speaks of a world, social, martial and religious, highly alien to our own. Much Anglo-Saxon poetry develops themes originally sung of by the ancient German bards. This is not to say that these poems were originally oral compositions; though they share many of the mannerisms and narrative conventions of bardic poetry, they might rather be said to offer elaborate and highly wrought derivatives of that poetry. The surviving poetic products of the Anglo-Saxons are best characterised by epic forms and spiritual preoccupations. In perhaps the most notable Old English poem, *Beowulf*, with its remarkable mythological terrain of dragons and other grotesquerie, we see a striking fusion of Germanic folktale and Christian apologetics. Tales of derring-do and martial prowess, whether local (*The Battle of Maldon*) or other-worldly (*Beowulf*), are common. The epic sweep of these tales is complemented by the epical religious panoramas of the *Later Genesis* (a kind of Old English *Paradise Lost*) and the heroic dream vision of the *Dream of the Rood*, in which Christ's cross tells the story of the Crucifixion. And the Christian mysticism evident in these works is also manifested in the two most notable Old English 'elegies', *The Wanderer* and *The Seafarer*, in which the narrative voices interpret hardship and grief in the wider spiritual context of God's ultimately benign purposes.

The critical term for poetry composed in the Middle Ages, the period between the Norman Conquest and the late fifteenth century, is **medieval**. The invasion of 1066 was an event which drove Anglo-Saxon culture into oblivion, but it also imported French and wider European culture in a way which was eventually to transform English verse and inform the flowering of vernacular poetry in the fourteenth century, in the work of William Langland (c. 1330– c. 1386; the author of *Piers Plowman*), the anonymous 'Gawain-poet' and, most notably, that of Geoffrey Chaucer (c. 1343–1400). Linguistic colonisation followed the martial invasion and the English language changed irrevocably, and perhaps more rapidly than in any comparable period in its history, under the influence of French and other European languages. Anglo-Saxon developed into the language which we now label 'Middle English'. Similarly, cultural colonisation followed physical colonisation and English culture became more open to the impact of polished European culture than ever before. In particular, French culture had a seminal impact upon English civilisation and Francophile poetry became the norm. In particular, the French provided the key poetic form of the Middle Ages, the romance (if epic is the principal genre of Old English poetry, romance has that role in Middle English poetry). However, the influence was widespread; from the racy and bawdy fabliau, from the songs of the troubadours up to the refined versions of their work in the Breton lays, it permeated English culture, providing new conventional norms which informed vernacular poetry. The influence was also formal; most crucially in that the use of rhyme as the key sound-patterning of English poetry is also a French import and eventually replaced alliteration as the norm for vernacular verse.

As in Old English poetry, medieval poetry is a body of work which is unafraid to work within certain clearly defined conventions and sees genre as an opportunity rather than a constriction. Though there are a significant number of anonymous lyrics and ballads – often very beautiful and compelling – on secular and religious themes, most of the surviving poetry is narrative in form. Narrative verse, in its diversity of forms – the romance, the allegorical dream vision, the exemplum and the fabliau (see the Glossary below for definitions of these terms) – is without question the most significant kind of medieval poetry. Storytelling poetry, since the rise of the novel, has fallen into disuse; but it is the central technique of English medieval poetry from Chaucer's *Canterbury Tales* downward. It should be registered that there is no great premium here upon 'original' storytelling; Chaucer's brilliance as a narrative poet does not consist of inventiveness. Almost without exception, he is drawing upon pre-existing tales and in this he is entirely typical of his age, calling on a varied inheritance – native *and* European – of stories told and told again: from Greek and Roman mythology, from French culture (both folk-tale and 'sophisticated' poetry), from Italian Renaissance authors, from scripture and from tales told by preachers. Perhaps paradoxically, the achievement of the first great poet of the central English poetic tradition is based upon his skilful fusion of sources drawn from many languages, many cultures and many genres.

The **Renaissance** is a term applied to the supposed rebirth of literature and art which characterised European culture in the fifteenth and sixteenth centuries and which is generally seen as heralding the end of the Middle Ages. A wider, and perhaps more accurate, definition sees it as running from fourteenth-century Italy to the middle of the seventeenth century in England. Thus, according to this looser formulation, the Renaissance embraces literature as diverse as that of Boccaccio and Petrarch in Italy and, arguably, the post-Restoration work of John Milton (1608–1674) in England. 'Renaissance' is a word derived from the Latin *renascentia*, meaning rebirth, and the revival implied in the term is that of classical culture, which emerged from its previous status as, in large part, the province of clerics into a vibrant and formative influence upon artists and poets. Nonetheless, this is a 'neoclassical' phenomenon, characterised by vernacular literature rather than by the use of classical languages, with ancient culture providing the modern writer with the means to find a new voice of his own (and it is almost invariably 'his' own). The emergence of printing, the new, more humanistic view of man's role in the universe, the Reformation and counter-Reformation, the Copernican view of the cosmos; all of these are generally seen as characterising the Renaissance.

If we insist upon using the term – and despite the increasing popularity of the variant term 'early modern', it remains in place in many university English syllabuses and is ineluctable in most accounts of literary history – it should be registered that the Renaissance occurs much later in England than in continental Europe, Italy most particularly. The English Renaissance is generally dated as beginning at the point where the Tudor dynasty established itself, 1485. This is yet another literary historical convenience, however, as it is not until the reign of Henry VIII (1509–47) that a significant body of literary work emerges in the work of Sir Thomas Wyatt (c. 1503–1542) and Sir Thomas More (1478–1535). As a consequence, the English Renaissance is as much motivated by Italian Renaissance writings as it is by the classical culture which inspired the earlier cultural phenomenon. Italian works such as Castiglione's *The Book of the Courtier* and Machiavelli's *The Prince* have a great impact on English Renaissance political thought and philosophy. And in poetry, Ariosto, Boccaccio and, in particular, Petrarch inform English poetry perhaps as much as the classical authors Ovid or Virgil.

As far as English poetry is concerned, the Renaissance is commonly defined as the post-Chaucerian tradition from Wyatt, Sidney, Spenser, Shakespeare and Jonson through to Milton. Unlike the Italian Renaissance, which saw great achievement in the visual arts and political philosophy, the English Renaissance is principally a literary phenomenon. Most writers offering thumbnail sketches of the generic preoccupations of English Renaissance non-dramatic poetry stress its attention to epic forms (in Spenser and Milton most notably), to the pastoral (in Sidney, Jonson and others), the sonnet (in Sidney and Shakespeare) and also to the more miniaturist forms of the lyric (in poets too numerous to catalogue). Perhaps the supreme poetic products of the English Renaissance are dramatic: the late Elizabethan and early Jacobean verse drama of Shakespeare, Marlowe, Jonson and Beaumont and Fletcher. Furthermore, if the archetypical, defining characteristic of the English Renaissance is the new humanism, a stress upon human capacity and the importance of the potentialities of the individual as opposed to the collective, theocentric mindset which supposedly charac- terised the Middle Ages, then it is to cultural forms other than non-dramatic poetry that we must address ourselves: to the prose of More and Sir Francis Bacon, for instance, and to the verse dramas of Marlowe and Shakespeare (for the most notable humanistic poetry of the age is dramatic). It is not until the work of Milton that we encounter a great poet whose work is predominantly concerned with humanism, and even then in the hybrid form of Christian humanism.

The period between the Restoration of the monarchy in 1660 and the fall of the Bastille in 1789 is often referred to as the **neoclassical** period of English poetry, given the central importance of classical values and precedent to many of its leading figures, from Dryden, Pope and Swift through to Samuel Johnson. Since the revival of classical standards during the Renaissance, the main concern of English neoclassical thought had been the elaboration of a view of literature which appealed to Roman and Greek antiquity for its authority. The writing of poetry, and the criticism of poetry, is to be guided by the example of the ancients. As Pope writes in the *Essay on Criticism*, 'Learn hence for ancient rules a just esteem / To copy nature is to copy them'. As a consequence of this following of precedent, poets such as Pope and Dryden place no great emphasis on originality. Instead they tend to view the process of composition as being mimetic (like a mirror) and consequently stress the concept of imitation, especially of classical models. Here imitation is nothing to be ashamed of. Indeed, it is inevitable as, according to this neoclassical perspective, art is a reasoned and reasonable approximation of reality and the best art expresses eternal verities in a polished and agreeable manner. As Joseph Warton puts it, 'Wit and fine writing doth not consist so much in advancing things that are new, as in giving things that are known an agreeable turn'. The imitative neoclassical manner is also evident in the key generic forms of late seventeenth- and early eighteenth-century literature, with the major classical forms common: epic, tragedy, satire, ode, epistle, fable and eclogue. A key related concept is **Augustanism**, a term applied to English poetry from the Restoration of 1660 to the death of Pope in 1744 or, more narrowly, from the beginning of the reign of Queen Anne in 1702. The original Augustan age of the reign of the Roman Emperor Augustus (27 BC–AD 14) was the most notable period of Roman poetry in the work of Horace, Ovid and Virgil, and it seemed to some (led by the poet Goldsmith during the 1750s) that an analogy with this period could be made in the post-Restoration efflorescence of poetry in Dryden, Pope, Swift and others, who were writing against the background of a newly confident and expanding British Empire and who might be said to have brought the empire of letters to a highly polished state of refinement.

The 1790s are generally seen as marking the emergence of **Romanticism**, a literary form which in many ways repudiates the dominant poetical mode of the earlier eighteenth century. Literary critics have often called this a 'shift in sensibility' from neoclassical to 'Romantic' evident in the period between 1789 and 1830. That said, it should be registered that the term 'Romantic' is actually a posthumous one, being first applied by Victorian critics looking back at the literature of the first part of their century. Though the label 'Romantic' is not one which any of the 'Romantic' poets would have applied to themselves, conventional literary history sees two sets of Romantic poets, divided, roughly speaking, into the first generation (Wordsworth, Coleridge and Blake) and a second, younger generation (Byron, Shelley and Keats).

Defining Romanticism is not easy; as the critic E. B. Burgum writes, he 'who seeks to define Romanticism is entering a hazardous occupation which has claimed many victims'. Nonetheless, it is certainly a label that it is very difficult to do without. Furthermore, it is worth dallying over Romanticism in a study of poetry as this supposed change in poetic values in many ways still conditions the way in which the common reader thinks about poetry today. Take the notion of what makes a good poem; though few contemporary poets would agree with the idea, many people would see this as poetry which is 'self-expressive', 'original' or 'imaginative'. All of these concepts are high Romantic notions. And, though it might seem odd to us today, none of them was particularly important to neoclassical poetics. In Romantic literature, we see the clear emergence of a central emphasis upon the 'imaginative genius' of the poet. Though praising imaginative originality might seem an eminently natural thing to the modern eye, this expressive model of creation is rather remarkable in eighteenth-century thought. According to the neoclassical literary paradigm, the poet derives his raw material from the perception of the world around him. To the Romantic, however, more emphasis is placed on the work of art coming from within, on the internal being made external and upon the interchange between poetic selfhood and the external world. Instead of simply imitating the external world, poetry – for the Romantic – often comes about as the result of an impulse within the poet. And the key term for this impulse is the 'creative imagination'. In the Romantic period, the emphasis has shifted from the neoclassical priorities of learning, judgement and decorum to a Romantic stress on the poet's natural spontaneity and genius.

Politically, Romanticism is permeated to the core by the French Revolution and France and the British reaction to it. *Intellectually*, it takes issue with the rationalist emphasis evident in much enlightenment thought. There is something within the human individual for which empiricist thought fails to account. And the Romantics have various names for that other: the sublime, the imaginative, the visionary, the poetic. *Thematically*, there is a concentration on 'nature'; but on the elemental side of nature rather than the carefully landscaped nature evident in neoclassical imagery. Wordsworth, Coleridge and Shelley offer a vision of the wild and sublime power of the landscape and the centrality of humanity's relationship with nature. *Emotionally*, English Romanticism often expresses an extreme assertion of the self and of the value of individual experience. *Poetically*, Romanticism took issue with the theoretical concerns and poetic practices of the neoclassical tradition: Wordsworth's literary criticism berates what he sees as the moribund formalism and laboured decorativeness of the 'poetic diction' of eighteenth-century poetry.

Above all, perhaps, selfhood is the central preoccupation of Romantic poetry. After Wordsworth, the poetic consciousness moves to the heart of English poetics. Certainly Romanticism stresses individual experience and, in particular, the individual experience of the poet, who is often characterised as a seer, a figure in receipt of intuitive truth who has a sense, sometimes strongly, sometimes tentatively, of the infinite and the transcendental. Romantic poetry manifests a stress on the poetic subject, whether in moments of exhilaration and inspiration or in periods of doubt and anxiety, as in the Romantic crisis lyric – Coleridge's 'Dejection' or Wordsworth's 'Immortality Ode' – where the poet feels a sense of poetic and personal loss.

One turns from 'Romanticism' to the term **Victorian** with some relief, given that it is relatively straightforward of definition. Though it is necessary, once again, to register the hazards of setting precise boundaries to poetic eras, the Reform Act of 1832 is generally seen as marking the start of a new artistic epoch: the 'Victorian' age which extends until the eve of the First World War. Although this period is named after Queen Victoria, it does not follow her dates precisely (she was on the throne between 1837 and 1901). Though literary historians have argued that the Victorian period does not possess the same depth of poetic talent as the Romantic period and that the age is more notable for its novelists and prose writers than for its poetry, there are several towering figures active in the period (Tennyson, the Brownings, Hopkins, arguably Arnold and Swinburne). Nonetheless, perhaps the most archetypically Victorian writers – the Brontës, Carlyle, Dickens, Eliot and Ruskin – are notable for prose rather than poetry. Nonetheless, many of the preoccupations of the prose resound through the poetry: doubt and scepticism, the crisis in and revival of faith, the nostalgia for some lost golden medieval world, and many of the same literary registers, from unashamed didacticism or fervid emotionalism to 'art for art's sake' aestheticism. And moving from thematic preoccupations to formal developments, the Victorian period is notable for a remarkable surge of poetic innovation and experiment: the revival of long-neglected verse forms (the rondeau, ballade, triolet, villanelle), the remarkable flowering of the dramatic monologue in Browning, and, perhaps most notably, the metrical experiments of Tennyson, Swinburne and Hopkins (with the last's work seeming to point forward to the emergence of free verse, the characteristic poetic form of modernism).

Modernist, in its widest sense, is a catch-all label for the experimental work in the literary and fine arts which occurred in the early part of the twentieth century. In part its literary stirrings were prompted by a belief that Victorian poetry was little more than an exhausted vein of Romanticism. The critic Edmund Gosse, writing in 1900, argued that the Victorian period had seen 'the maintenance, without radical change of any kind, of the original Romantic system, now just one hundred years old … poetry in England is still what it became when Wordsworth and Coleridge remodelled it in 1797'. Such a state of affairs was hardly to last indefinitely. Indeed, the poetic backlash was extreme; the modernist repudiation of the past spreads rather wider than a straight-forward shaking off of a lingering Romanticism and might be seen as an attempt to cut off from the entire post-Renaissance tradition. Certainly some of its adherents saw it that way, Herbert Read famously declaring in 1933 that modernism is 'an abrupt break with all tradition … five centuries of European efforts openly abandoned'. Modernism spreads across a diversity of cultural forms, being manifested in fine art movements such as Cubism and Futurism, and the complex images and fragmentary forms of these movements are also evident in modernism's literary products, alongside a fascination with new intellectual developments: Freudianism and anthropological thought most notably. And the complex narrative experimentation of the central modernist novelists such as James Joyce, William Faulkner and Virginia Woolf are also echoed in a poetic willingness (as in Eliot's *The Waste Land*) to use complex multi-layered poetic techniques and employ collage-like poetic structures and fragmented narratives told from multiple points of view. However, as far as English poetry is concerned, its central act of rebellion is the renunciation of metrical poetry in favour of free verse (see the extended discussion in Chapter 4 below). Its talismanic figures are two American expatriates, Ezra Pound (1885–1972) and, most notably of all, T. S. Eliot. Underpinning the work of the most important modernist poet, Eliot, is a sense of cultural dislocation, both in the collapse of pre-modernist artistic values and traditions and in a sense of loss and isolation in the face of a modern world emerging from the chaos of the First World War to an uncertain future.

I.3   EXERCISES

1. In 1813, Lord Byron described poetry as 'the lava of the imagination whose eruption prevents an earthquake'.

(i) What do you think the metaphors 'lava of the imagination' and volcanic 'eruption' mean in this context?

(ii) What type of conceptualisation of poetry (mimetic, expressive and so on) is this?

(iii) To which other ideas of poetry addressed in this chapter is Byron's grandiloquent remark closest? How is his conceptualisation similar – and how is it different – from pre-nineteenth-century accounts of the nature of poetic composition?

(iv) Do you find this metaphor of creation convincing and/or appropriate?

(v) What other metaphors of poetic composition can you think of?

2. The critic Helen Vendler wrote in 1988 that 'the word "poetry" is often used to mean: how people construct an intelligibility out of the randomness they experience; how people choose what they love; how people integrate loss and gain [and] how they distort experience by wish and dream'.

(i) This is a very idealistic conception of poetry. Do you agree with all or any of it?

(ii) Is poetry really capable of imposing order on human experience, as this passage suggests?

(iii) Is poetry best understood in terms of its impact on human emotions?

3. 'If I read a book and it makes my whole body so cold no fire can ever warm me, I know that is poetry. If I feel physically as if the top of my head were taken off, I know that is poetry. These are the only ways I know about it. Is there any other way?' (Emily Dickinson).

(i) How does Dickinson characterise the emotional and physical effects of reading poetry? Why are her metaphors so extreme?

(ii) Have you ever experienced such a visceral (instinctive or physical) reaction to reading a poem?

(iii) As a rhetorical flourish, Dickinson's words are very powerful. However, surely, there are many 'other ways' of experiencing poetry. What might they be?

4. This is Edmund Spenser's opening appeal to the Muses, the classical personification of the arts, in his poem 'The Teares of the Muses' (1591):

> Rehearse to me, ye sacred Sisters nine,
> The Golden Brood of great Apollo's Wit,
> Those piteous Plaints and sorrowful sad Tine,
> Which late you poured forth as ye did sit
> Beside the Silver Springs of Helicone,
> Making your Musick of heart-breaking Mone.

(i) Why did classical and Renaissance poets characterise their inspiration as female?

(ii) Why did epic poets from Virgil to John Milton begin their major works with an address ('apostrophe') to the muse of poetry?

5. In Ted Hughes's famous poem 'The Thought Fox' (1957), the poet imagines himself at midnight, awaiting inspiration and staring at a 'blank page'. Suddenly, something happens:

> Through the window I see no star:
> Something more near
> Though deeper within darkness
> Is entering the loneliness.

He characterises this as a fox, and portrays the animal darting into his head in a metaphor which captures the moment of poetic inspiration:

> … with a sudden sharp hot stink of fox
> It enters the dark hole of the head.
> The window is starless still; the clock ticks,
> The page is printed.

(i) Why have poets so frequently identified inspiration as something external, whether metaphorised as a muse or, indeed, a fox?
(ii) What do you make of the poet's remarkable metaphor of his head as a 'dark hole'?

2

The shape of poetry

2.1 THE AESTHETICS OF PRINT

Poems are not merely things that we *read* but also things that we *see*. We are aware at a glance of whether a poem is written in a regular or irregular form, whether its lines are long or short, whether the verse is continuous or stanzaic, and so on. Moreover, all these facets of a poem may be entirely lost if one's only experience is of its being read aloud. This visual dimension of their work is something that poets have been conscious of for hundreds of years, and many have fashioned works that expressly aim to draw the reader's attention to their visuality. In this chapter, we will look at some of the ways in which poets have exploited the visual dimension, both in shape poems and in the poetic stanza itself.

We tend to think of poems in terms of their meanings or formal effects, but at the most elementary level, we experience a poem as an assemblage of characters, which are normally given clarity and relief by being reproduced on a white background. Of course, this may seem too obvious to need to be stated, but it is worth bearing in mind that poems have not always had such properties. Before the invention of print, poems were transmitted orally or through the written hand, so the conditions of aesthetic reception were very different; and it seems inevitable that in the future we will increasingly encounter poetry, as well as other types of writing, in the form of electronic text, read directly from the screen. To say that poetry has much to do with black characters on white paper is to state how it has come to be mediated by one particular technology: that of print.

The effect of the invention of print in the fifteenth century was, over a period of time, to create an unprecedented standardisation in the appearance of literary texts. Under the regime of print, each copy of a work will be identical, and moreover its visual appearance will be very similar to that of other printed works of the same kind. In contrast, in a culture where works can be reproduced only by being copied out longhand, neither of these conditions applies. The rise of print obviously impacted on all categories of texts: poetic and non-poetic. Yet, this having been accepted, it remains the case that the relation to the print medium of poetic and non-poetic texts is somewhat different. Poets, as a rule, exert a much greater degree of control over the visual appearance of their works than do prose writers. Indeed, one might even say that what actually *defines* a poem is that the terminal word in each line will have been fixed by the poet, thus allowing us to talk about a phenomenon rarely, if ever, invoked in connection with prose writings: the 'line-ending'. In prose works such as novels, the terminal word in each line is there by accident or, to be more exact, it derives from a decision of the print-setter (or compositor) rather than the author. The line-ending is thus the outstanding example (among some others discussed elsewhere in this chapter) of how poets exert control over the visual appearance of their works in ways that remain unavailable to, or at least rarely exploited by, prose writers.

2.2   PICTOGRAMS AND CONCRETE POEMS

One aspect of this phenomenon of visuality is the 'concrete' or 'shape' poem, where the words are arranged on the page in a way that mimics or reinforces the poem's meaning. A 'poem' of this sort is Lewis Carroll's (1832–1898) 'The Mouse's Tale', taken from *Alice's Adventures in Wonderland* (see page 25).

Obviously, the poem (in so far as we can call it one) works through a pun on 'tail'/'tale'. Alice seemingly does not know that 'tale' is another word for 'story', and so when the mouse delivers his 'long and sad tale', she forms it mentally into the shape of a physical 'tail'. 'The Mouse's Tale' qualifies to be spoken of as a poem on two grounds. In the first instance, it seems to have been conceived after a more regular fashion than the casual reader might think. It contains a discernible rhyme-scheme, and there is a distinct break after the word 'do', as if the poem should be understood as formed out of two stanzas. The rhyme words of the first stanza are 'mouse', 'house', 'you', 'denial', 'trial' and 'do'; and in the second: 'cur', 'Sir', 'breath', 'jury', 'fury' and 'death'. Clearly, Carroll has shuffled the poem's physical arrangement with the effect that most rhyme words fall in the interior, rather than at the end, of their respective lines, but the poem still adheres to an orthodox structure, though at a more submerged level. Even leaving aside the hidden rhyme scheme, however, we would argue that 'The Mouse's Tale' deserves to be called a poem simply on account of the fact that it contains 'line-endings', in that the terminal word of each line (rhyming

'Fury said to
a mouse, That
he met in the
house, "Let
us both go
to law: I
will prose-
cute *you* –
Come, I'll
take no de-
nial: We
must have
the trial;
For really
this morn-
ing I've
nothing
to do."
Said the
mouse to
the cur,
"Such a
trial, dear
sir, With
no jury
or judge,
would
be wast-
ing our
breath."
"I'll be
judge,
I'll be
jury,"
said
cun-
ning
old
Fury:
"I'll
try
the
whole
cause,
and
con-
demn
you to
death".'

or otherwise) has been set by the author. Indeed, Carroll has dictated to his publishers not just the spatial organisation of his poem but even the comparative size of the lettering to be used in individual lines. The poem works as a pictogram or concrete poem, in that its actual shape mimics an aspect of its subject-matter. A tale told by a mouse is reproduced in the form of a mouse's tail.

Carroll's poem, of course, is a sort of nonsense joke, but poets have also exploited the visual dimension of their poems in more serious-minded contexts. One such example is George Herbert's (1593–1633) religious poem 'Easter-wings':

Lord, who createdst man in wealth and store,
Though foolishly he lost the same,
Decaying more and more,
Till he became
Most poore:
With thee
O let me rise
As larks, harmoniously,
And sing this day thy victories:
Then shall the fall further the flight in me.

My tender age in sorrow did beginne:
And still with sicknesses and shame
Thou didst so punish sinne,
That I became
Most thinne.
With thee
Let me combine
And feel this day thy victorie:
For, if I imp my wing on thine,
Affliction shall advance the flight in me.

At Easter, Christians remember Christ's death and rising from the grave, these events being followed a few days later by his ascent into heaven. The traditional account of Christ's final days, in other words, is imbued with strong images of flight and ascent, and these bear an obvious relation to the title and theme of Herbert's 'Easter-wings'. At the same time, the idea of inward flight has been invoked by Christians as a way of describing the experience of faith, particularly the sensation of being infused by the Holy Spirit; and Herbert's poem also seems to allude to this. In the first stanza, the poem is expressly concerned with the spiritual history of mankind as a whole. Man was originally born into an earthly paradise but then 'foolishly he lost the same' and as a result became spiritually impoverished; however, as a result of Christ's sacrifice, mankind has been able to replenish itself with the prospect of everlasting life. In the stanza's final line, Herbert even seems to endorse the controversial theory of the 'felix culpa' ('happy blame'): this was the idea that the fall of mankind could be seen, in retrospect, as having been a good thing, since without it there would have been no reason for the merciful sacrifice of Christ to have occurred. The second stanza is altogether more personal, relating to feelings that Herbert, or the poem's narrator, has about his own spiritual deficiency. As the stanza progresses, however, this sense of inadequacy is tempered by a new-found buoyancy, as the narrator imagines Christ's resurrection ('this day thy victorie') and finds in it a stimulus towards his own spiritual renewal.

The first thing that you notice about the poem is how Herbert adjusts his line-lengths to mould the poem into a shape: that of two hour-glasses, one stood on top of the other. Moreover, the line-lengths are carefully measured to what is happening thematically. The first stanza begins on a note of buoyancy ('Lord, who createdst man in wealth and store'), then shrinks into pessimism in the middle and finally unfolds once more into optimism. As the poem strikes these different notes, the line-length is modified so as to mirror these wavering sentiments. So, for example, the moment of greatest spiritual despondency ('Most poore') coincides with the shortest line. The second stanza makes for a similar, though slightly less pure, version of the same phenomenon. The moment of greatest spiritual depletion is again marked by the stanza's thinnest line ('Most thinne'), before a movement towards renewed hope and optimism sees the lines once more broaden ebulliently across the page.

The poem above has been set down as it *appears* in the standard edition of Herbert's *Works* edited by F. E. Hutchinson, but exactly how Herbert intended it to look remains a contentious issue. All Herbert's poems were published posthumously, and in all the existing manuscript versions the lines are written in horizontal fashion as above. Yet when Herbert's friend, Nicholas Ferrar, oversaw the earliest publication of his work in 1633, the poem appeared on its side, with the lines running vertically. If you tilt the page so as to produce the same effect, you will see that the shape of the poem transmogrifies in this way from that of two hour-glasses to two sets of butterfly wings laid adjacent to each other: the same wings that are alluded to in the poem's title. Although dropping the poem on its side obviously makes it hard to read, not to do so means the reader misses out on a visual pun that Herbert probably considered as integral to the work.

There is a further small visual stratagem that again has to do with the relationship between how Herbert intended the poem to look and the form in which it has been transmitted down to posterity. One of the surviving manuscripts shows the poem written out in a single hand identified as belonging to Herbert himself. In line 8 of the manuscript, however, a second hand has changed the original phrase 'do by degree' to the single word 'harmoniouslie' (further adjusted to 'harmoniously' in the version above). Similarly, the final word of line 9, which originally stood as 'sacrifice', has been changed to 'victories'. These small changes, which as you can see have passed into the text of the standard edition, are almost certainly a corruption of what Herbert intended. For if you insert back into the poem the original readings 'do by degree' and 'sacrifice', what you may notice (though perhaps only if you are very perceptive) is that every line terminates with the letter 'e', a silent reinforcement of the poem's preoccupation with the Christian festival of 'Easter'. It should be stressed that the shape of the poem, either as two butterflies or as two hour-glasses, and the repeated terminal letter 'e' are available only to the gazing eye. This is to say that if you heard the poem being read out, you would be at a loss to notice these details, but also even to read through the poem in a sequential way is not necessarily to bring them to light. What the poem seems to ask you to do is to study it visually in the same way that you would pore over a painting.

2.3   VISIBLE BUT UNREADABLE

One way of describing the effect achieved by Herbert might be to say that the visual appearance of the poem *enacts* its meaning. Although such techniques of visual enactment are not uncommon in poetry, their appearance has always been subject to the fashions of verse-making prevalent at different times. There seems a marked absence of such effects, for example, in the eighteenth century, mainly because so much poetry during the period was written in regimented rhyming couplets, giving poets little scope for the sort of ambitious effect engineered by Herbert. In the early twentieth century, however, with the rise of 'free verse' (a technique of verse-composition that exempted itself from all formal rules), the exploitation of visual enactment became altogether more common. The poet who has probably been most tireless in fashioning effects along these lines is the American E. E. Cummings (1894–1962), one of whose poems is given below:

> l (a
> le
> af
> Fa
> ll
> s)
> one
> l
> iness

It is hard to know how to start discussing this poem, but we can perhaps begin by saying that it consists of nine lines, made up of two distinct syntactical units: the first being the single word 'loneliness', and the second, bracketed within the first, being the clause 'a leaf Falls'. It goes without saying that Cummings has carved up his poem so as to make the lines unusually short, but at the same time the line divisions are not arbitrary, but have clearly been drawn with a view to the realising of particular effects. Lines 3 and 4, af/Fa, for example, mark a chiasmus: that is, they mirror each other in a back-to-front way. Similarly, Cummings deliberately breaks up the enfolding word 'loneliness' in a way calculated to make us think how much loneliness, as both a word and concept, has to do with 'oneness' (as in lines 7 and 9).

Although the poem contains words, the meanings that we recover from it are more akin to those of a visual image than of a written text. For one thing, the poem is literally unreadable. In the case of Herbert, we remarked on how much would be lost if you just heard the poem being read aloud, but in the case of Cummings, it would be hard to imagine how the poem could possibly be read out. It is difficult enough, in normal circumstances, to cast the voice in such a way as to express punctuation (especially parentheses), but where a parenthesis falls inside a single word, this creates intractable problems. Similarly, if we only experienced the poem by hearing it read out, we would languish oblivious to the crucial visual pun in which the falling of the leaves is mimicked by the words themselves tumbling down the page. Moreover, to miss this insight is also to miss out on the important comparison drawn in the poem between autumn and loneliness, both being characterised by a sense of decay or despondency.

To say that the Cummings poem is unreadable is really to say that, in order to read it, you have to make certain choices in the absence of any authorial guidance as to which is the correct one. Should you try to disentwine the two syntactical units and read them sequentially, or allow them to remain in their existing scrambled relation? Should you try to convey the acute brevity of the lines, or instead give priority to the syntactical unit over the line unit? The ambiguities here are ones that poets have become increasingly interested in providing for their readers. The contemporary poets Peter Reading (b. 1946) and Tom Raworth (b. 1938), for example, have both written poems comprised of two or more columns of text, where the reader has to decide whether to read across the page or to scan down each column in turn. The effect of this technique seems to be twofold. In the first instance, it baffles our conventional sense that, in connection with the English language, reading is defined by a left to right sweeping of the eye down a field of text: in such poems reading becomes instead an optical free-fall down a column of text to be followed by a sudden jag upwards to the top of another column. Secondly, such poems break up the communality of reading: we can no longer blithely assume that we are reading such poems in the same way as all other readers, a circumstance that we normally take for granted.

As we write now, some poets are beginning to experiment with a new sort of non-readerly poem: the poem on hypertext. Hypertext is the name given to a particular way of manipulating text on screen, in which by clicking on a word or icon, we can be transferred instantly to another piece of text electronically linked to the one we have just left. This way of encountering text is not 'reading' as such, in the sense of an indeflectible sweeping of the eye; instead, it could be thought of as a sort of associative hopping. Hypertext allows readers to route themselves through texts in ways that are highly individualistic: in theory, you could chart a course through a text that might not previously have been taken by any other reader. Although the hypertext poem is something that will belong to the future, it still reinforces what poets recognised as long ago as Herbert: that a poem can exercise us visually in a way that is distinct from our merely *reading* it.

2.4   LAYOUT AND PUNCTUATION

One by-product of the widespread use of word processors is that it is now easier to empathise with poets in the range of decisions they have to make concerning the appearance of their works. For example, as we started composing this chapter, we clicked on an icon in order to centre our chapter title, and then brought down the 'Style' menu in order to put the title in *italics*. We then clicked on a further icon so that our main text should appear as both left- and right-aligned. Even before getting this far, we had determined both the size and style of our typeface, selecting these from a range of menu alternatives. All these details relate to what is generally called 'layout': how a text appears in terms of the size and style of the characters and the general organisation of the page. Of course, it might be thought that these details do not actually form part of a poem, for such incidentals are the business of the printer rather than the author. Yet we would argue the opposite, that these minutiae of visual appearance are an integral part of practically any published poem. As an example, we propose looking at a short section of a poem that very self-consciously exploits the devices of layout, T. S. Eliot's 'The Hollow Men':

> Between the idea
> And the reality
> Between the motion
> And the act
> Falls the Shadow
> > *For Thine is the Kingdom*
>
> Between the conception
> And the creation
> Between the emotion
> And the response
> Falls the Shadow
> > *Life is very long*

> Between the desire
> And the spasm
> Between the potency
> And the existence
> Between the essence
> And the descent
> Falls the Shadow
> > *For Thine is the Kingdom*
>
> For Thine is
> Life is
> For Thine is the
>
> *This is the way the world ends*
> *This is the way the world ends*
> *This is the way the world ends*
> *Not with a bang but a whimper.*

We do not want to produce an interpretation of this section of the poem so much as to suggest how Eliot uses details of layout to provide a framework in which the activity of interpretation can take place. He does this by differentiating between three distinct categories of text. In the first place, the passage contains a body of text in roman type, all of which is aligned against the left margin. Eliot further emphasises its left alignment by introducing a sort of anaphoric rhyme, or a rhyme scheme that is specific to the first word of each line as opposed to the terminal one. Thus the repeated words 'Between', 'And', 'Falls', 'For' and 'This' hammer out what is practically a rhyme scheme of their own. A second body of type is italicised and right-aligned, the three short lines belonging to this category being clearly distinguished from the roman type. The effect is to create an antiphonal relation between the two typefaces: the roman type seems to convey a distinct 'voice', this being answered by a second voice which emanates from the italics. Finally, at the bottom of the page, there is a third category of type, this time italicised and also left-aligned. As an attentive reader, we now need to decide whether this body of type can be associated with either of the two voices identified thus far, or whether it constitutes a third voice. This is not a question that we are going to attempt to resolve here; rather we want to emphasise that the very perception that such a dilemma exists is inseparable from the details of layout that Eliot has worked into the poem.

We want to finish this section by discussing another form of ordering – of a kind that once more impacts on issues of meaning – that we expect to find in a poem: punctuation. The point of addressing punctuation in a chapter expressly concerned with the visual dimension of poetry is that punctuation is specific to written rather than spoken language: it is something that we *see*. It would be considered as very peculiar if anybody spoke so fastidiously that you could detect the insertion into their speech of punctuation marks like hyphens, colons and semi-colons. Of course, it might be thought that punctuation marks, even in poems, are something that we can simply take for granted, but this is not always the case. Here, for example, is another (untitled) poem by E. E. Cummings:

O sweet spontaneous
earth how often have
the
doting

      fingers of
prurient philosophers pinched
and
poked

thee
, has the naughty thumb
of science prodded
thy

      beauty . how
often have religions taken
thee upon their scraggy knees
squeezing and

buffeting thee that thou mightest conceive
gods
      (but
true

to the incomparable
couch of death thy
rhythmic
lover

        thou answerest

them only with

        spring)

The message of the poem seems to be that the only law that animates the natural world is the great one of death and rebirth: each year dies in winter and is reborn in the spring, just as individual creatures die off and are replaced by their offspring. The nature of earthly life, in other words, is very simple, but humans, either scientists, philosophers or the religiously minded, are deter-mined to look for deeper meanings and underlying causes. If the meaning of the poem is not too elusive, its *form* is nonetheless curiously vexing. We enter most poems through the gateway of a title, but here Cummings (not unusually for him) disdains to provide us with one, and the poem, rather than ending in a noticeable climax, instead dribbles away in a long parenthesis, its ending being unmarked even by a full stop. The poem continually brings to our attention issues to do with its own articulation on the page. The lines are broken up with exaggerated verve, sometimes Cummings even driving a line-split between the components of an individual phrase (like 'doting / fingers'). Punctuation as a rule is a retroactive notation, in that we normally place a punctuation mark *after* the word or the sequence of words it is supposed to govern (think of question marks, full stops and so on). Here Cummings, however, begins one line with a comma and in line 13 allows a full stop to float free on the line, unattached to the syntactical units on either side. Moreover, the same line sees the start of the poem's second and final sentence, which Cummings introduces without the normal signalling of an initial capital.

It would be wrong to think that these unusual techniques of layout must stand in a close relation to the theme of Cummings' poem, for he uses much the same portfolio of devices in all his poems. Rather the poem challenges our suppositions about how poetry should be organised on the printed page, both in terms of how poetry-specific techniques (like lineation) are used, and how, in the language in general, words are marshalled together through the medium of punctuation. Of course, most poems do not challenge us in this way: Cummings is an exception to the rule. But his work does show how punctuation can be, for the poet who cares to make it so, a flexible resource rather than just a dull necessity.

2.5 THE POETIC STANZA AND STANZAIC FORM

It might justifiably be said that the sort of poetic visual effects we have discussed so far remain, on the whole, curious and rare. This is true enough, but we now want to turn to a poetic phenomenon that is common to a large amount of poetry in nearly all literary periods: the poetic stanza. Whilst the reader might want to argue that the stanza is not *really* a visual effect, certainly not of the kind we have discussed so far, it matters here because all stanzaic forms when ren-dered in print address themselves to the reading eye. Even people supposedly well informed about poetry (such as the authors of this book) would be hard put to give an accurate description of a poem's stanzaic form merely through hearing the work being read aloud. A poem's stanzaic form is most evident when it is encountered in its visual dimension.

Perhaps the most notable aspect of the visual organisation of poetry on the printed page is the division of many poems into groups of lines, or 'stanzas':

> She dwelt among the untrodden ways
>   Beside the springs of Dove,
> A Maid whom there were none to praise
>   And very few to love:
>
> A violet by a mossy stone
>   Half hidden from the eye!
> Fair as a star, when only one
>   Is shining in the sky.
>
> She lived unknown, and few could know
>   When Lucy ceased to be;
> But she is in her grave, and oh,
>   The difference to me! (Wordsworth)

A stanza is a subdivision or section of a poem, and a poem's stanzas generally share the same line-length, rhyme scheme and poetic metre. Pauses between stanzas are marked by a space line on the printed page. A poem divided into stanzas is thus referred to as 'stanzaic'. The term 'verse' is not infrequently used for stanza, especially with reference to the lyrics of pop songs or hymns, but should perhaps be avoided, given that a verse is more properly a single line of a poem. Some stanzaic verse consciously exploits the visual capacities of print for effect, as in Herbert's 'Easter-wings' and as in George Wither's (1588–1667) early seventeenth-century lyric '*Ah me*! Am I the Swaine?', where the poem's fourteen-line stanzas are set diamond-like on the page, mirroring the bejewelled and highly wrought emotional terrain of the lyric:

> *Ah me*!
> Am I the Swaine,
> That late from sorrow free,
> Did all the cares on earth disdaine?
> And still untoucht, as at some safer Games,
> Play'd with the burning coals of Love, & Beauties flames?
> Was't I, could dive, & sound each passion's secret depth at will;
> And, from those huge overwhelmings, rise, by help of Reason still?
> And am I now, oh heavens! for trying this in vaine,
> So sunke, that I shall never rise againe?
> Then let Dispaire, set Sorrows string,
> For *Strains* that dolefulst be,
> And I will sing,
> *Ah me*.

However, fourteen-line stanzas are rarities and such striking pictorial effect remains a conscious oddity. The ordinary poetic stanza rarely attends to its typographical placing quite as self-consciously.

A book which gave examples of all of the stanzaic forms used throughout English poetic history would be a very long one, and such a gargantuan project is outside the province of this particular volume. Consequently, our focus is upon the key stanzaic forms of English poetry. To this end, what follows is a survey of the various line-lengths used in the poetic stanza which pauses, where appropriate, to examine the most notable stanzaic forms (ballad stanza, *ottava rima*, the Spenserian and so on). We shall begin with the shortest stanzaic form, the **couplet**.

A couplet is a pair of linked verses which are generally of the same length and which are linked most particularly by rhyme. The most notable manifestations of the two-line couplet are found in continuous verse rather than in stanzaic poetry (see Chapter 4 below). However, the couplet has occasionally been used as a stanzaic form. For instance, the Victorian poet and artist D. G. Rossetti (1828–1882) uses stanzaic couplets in his poem 'The White Ship':

> But at midnight's stroke they cleared the bay,
> And the White Ship furrowed the water-way.
>
> The sails were set, and the oars kept tune
> To the double flight of the ship and the moon:
>
> Swifter and swifter the White Ship sped
> Till she flew as the spirit flies from the dead:
>
> As white as a lily glimmered she
> Like a ship's fair ghost upon the sea.

These broken couplets are not entirely convincing. Here the poem's form impedes its content, given that the breaks gently interrupt the drive of the story, surely something which is to be avoided in a narrative poem. In fact, these seem like quatrains (that is, the traditional standard four-line stanza) which have been severed for unnecessary effect and would read more convincingly if set as such:

> But at midnight's stroke they cleared the bay,
> And the White Ship furrowed the water-way.
> The sails were set, and the oars kept tune
> To the double flight of the ship and the moon:
>
> Swifter and swifter the White Ship sped
> Till she flew as the spirit flies from the dead:
> As white as a lily glimmered she
> Like a ship's fair ghost upon the sea.

Stanzaic couplets seem less contrived in their occasional use in medieval balladry, a cultural form where the conscious appearance of artlessness is rather more becoming:

> But, bonny boy, tell to me
> What is the customs o' your country.
>
> The customs o 't, my dame, he says,
> Will ill a gentle lady please.
>
> Seven king's daughters has our king wedded,
> An' seven king's daughters has our king bedded.
>
> But he's cutted the paps frae their breastbane
> An' sent them mourning hame again. ('Gil Brenton')

A **tercet** is three successive lines bound by rhyme. Three successive lines of the same length which rhyme together *aaa* are called 'triplets', and triplets have sometimes been used as a stanzaic form:

> Why dost Thou shade Thy lovely face? O why
> Does that eclipsing hand so long deny
> The sunshine of Thy soul-enlivening eye?
>
> Without that light, what light remains in me?
> Thou art my Life, my Way, my Light; in Thee
> I live, I move, and by Thy beams I see.
>
> Thou art my life; if Thou but turn away,
> My life's a thousand deaths: Thou art my Way;
> Without thee, Lord, I travel not, but stray. (Francis Quarles)

The most significant variant of the three-line stanza is the *terza rima*, which as its name (which means 'third rhyme') suggests is an Italian import. The *terza rima*, which derives from Dante's *The Divine Comedy*, uses tercets linked in a particular rhyme pattern: *aba bcb cdc* and so on, closed by a line which rhymes with the second line of the final tercet. In the preface to *The Prophecy of Dante*, that great user of Italianate forms, Lord Byron (1788–1824), declares that the 'measure adopted is the *terza rima* of Dante':

> Many are poets who have never penn'd
>   Their inspiration, and perchance the best:
>   They felt, and lov'd, and died, but would not lend
> Their thoughts to meaner beings; they compress'd
>   The god within them, and rejoin'd the stars

> Unlaurell'd upon earth, but far more bless'd
> Than those who are degraded by the jars,
>   Of passion, and their frailties link'd to fame,
>   Conquerors of high renown, but full of scars.

This is continuous verse, of course, but the form has been utilised in stanzaic poetry by several post-Romantic poets. However, its significance as a stanzaic form is principally a result of its adaptation in Shelley's (1792–1822) great 'Ode to the West Wind':

> O, wild West Wind, thou breath of Autumn's being
>   Thou from whose unseen presence the leaves dead
> Are driven like ghosts from an enchanter fleeing,
>
>   Yellow, and black, and pale, and hectic red,
> Pestilence-stricken multitudes! O thou
>   Who chariotest to their dark wintry bed
>
> The wingèd seeds, where they lie cold and low,
>   Each like a corpse within its grave, until
> Thine azure sister of the spring shall blow.

The tercet is also used in the highly wrought stanzaic form of the villanelle, a lyric which uses only two rhymes and consists of five three-lined stanzas (rhyming *aba*) and a final four-line quatrain. The first and third lines of the opening stanza are repeated alternately as a refrain in the succeeding stanzas and form a final couplet in the last stanza. The opening lines of Dylan Thomas's (1914–1953) 'Do not Go Gentle into that Good Night' illustrate the technique well:

> Do not go gentle into that good night,
> Old age should burn and rave at close of day;
> Rage, rage against the dying of the light.
>
> Though wise men at their end know dark is right,
> Because their words had forked no lightning they
> Do not go gentle into that good night.
>
> Good men, the last wave by, crying how bright
> Their frail deeds might have danced in a green bay,
> Rage, rage against the dying of the light.

Despite the significance of poetry such as this, tercets of whatever kind, stanzaic or continuous, are not common in English poetry. In their stanzaic form, they do not offer the range of possibility available in the four-line stanza; and in continuous verse they lack the pithy and epigrammatic potential of the couplet. In the couplet, we see a form which is most significant in continuous poetry, and tercets, however attractive they might be, are relatively rare. It is only in stanzas of four lines and more that the stanza really comes into its own. And it is in the most common and arguably the most important stanzaic form, the four-line quatrain, that we see the diversity of stanzaic poetry best illustrated.

A stanza of four lines is called a **quatrain**. Though the unseparated, rhymed four-line 'building blocks' of the first eight or twelve lines of sonnets are also referred to as quatrains, the stanzaic form is the most significant. Though unrhymed quatrains have very occasionally been used, the stanza generally exploits rhyme. The rhymed quatrain is the most common stanzaic form in English poetry and, indeed, in the poetry of many European cultures. It is the stanza of many hymns, of ballads, of popular songs, uniting both more popular cultural forms with the polished lyric of canonical English poetry. It has several forms. Occasionally a stanza of two couplets *aabb* has been used, giving an air of delicacy and simplicity, as, for example, in Robert Herrick's *Hesperides* (1648):

> Here a pretty Baby lies
> Sung asleep with Lullabies:
> Pray be silent, and not stirre
> Th' easie earth that covers her.

A quatrain rhymed *abba* has also been used in pastoral and other forms of lyric, by such poets as Ben Jonson (1572/3–1637) and his seventeenth-century contemporary Lord Herbert of Cherbury (1582–1648):

> When with a love none can express,
>   That mutually happy pair,
>   Melander and Celinda fair,
> The season with their loves did bless.

However, the most usual form of the quatrain has 'alternate' rhymes, invariably on the second and fourth lines of each stanza (as in the *abcb* and the *abab* forms) and often on the first and third as well (*abab*):

> And did those feet in ancient time
> Walk upon England's mountains green?
> And was the holy Lamb of God
> On England's pleasant pastures seen? (William Blake)

> How sweet the name of JESUS sounds
> In a believer's ear?
> It soothes his sorrows, heals his wounds,
> And drives away his fear. (John Newton)

The quatrain has great flexibility, allowing poets to achieve a variety of poetical effects. Thus in Lawrence Binyon's elegiac 'For the Fallen' (1914), long, sonorous and mournful lines are succeeded by a short concluding line. Here form echoes content, with end-stopped, stately and mournful lines giving way to the abrupt ending which neatly symbolises the truncated lives of the dead:

> They shall not grow old, as we that are left grow old;
> Age shall not weary them, nor the years condemn;
> At the going down of the sun, and in the morning,
> We will remember them.

The most significant of all quatrains, the stanza of all trades, is the 'ballad stanza' (or 'ballad metre'). The ballad stanza alternates four-stress lines ('tetrameters') with three-stress lines ('trimeters') rhymed *abab* or *abcb*. Critical opinion is divided as to whether or not the *abab* rhyme pattern is, strictly speaking, in the ballad metre, but we would admit it, along with the uncontentious *abcb* pattern. As the name suggests, 'ballad stanza' derives from the ancient folk ballad tradition. However, it has been pressed into service in a variety of different ways, whether offering fervent eulogies of the Almighty in hymnody (as in the example by Newton cited above), lamenting a lost mistress in the love lyric or in the Romantic period adaptations and imitations of medieval balladry (Coleridge's 'The Rime of the Ancient Mariner', Keats's 'La Belle Dame sans Merci'). From the martial or supernatural themes of late medieval ballads to the melancholic seventeenth-century love lyric, from the eighteenth-century comic poem to the introspective Romantic visionary poem and Victorian narrative poetry, ballad metre possesses a remarkably adaptable musicality:

> The king sits in Dumferling toune,
>   Drinking the bluid-red win:
> O quhar will I get guid sailor,
>   To sail this ship of mine?

> Up and spak an eldern knicht,
>   Sat at the kings richt kne:
> Sir Patrick Spence is the best sailor,
>   That sails upon the sea. (Anon., 'Sir Patrick Spence')

Gather ye rosebuds while ye may
  Old Time is still a flying:
And this same flower that smiles to day
  To morrow will be dying. (Herrick)

John Gilpin was a citizen
  Of credit and renown,
A train-band captain eke was he,
  Of famous London town. (Cowper)

Strange fits of passion have I known:
And I will dare to tell,
But in the Lover's ear alone,
What once to me befell. (Wordsworth)

Once more the gate behind me falls;
  Once more before my face
I see the moulder'd Abbey-walls,
  That stand within the chace. (Tennyson)

The most significant quatrain form outside of ballad stanza is the so-called 'heroic quatrain' or 'heroic stanza', a five-stress iambic quatrain rhymed *abab* which is sometimes referred to as the 'elegiac stanza' after its use in Thomas Gray's (1716–1761) famous 'Elegy Written in a Country Church-Yard':

The boast of heraldry, the pomp of pow'r,
And all that beauty, all that wealth e'er gave,
Awaits alike th' inevitable hour,
The paths of glory lead but to the grave.

A five-line stanza is called a **quintain**. The quintain, which is sometimes referred to as a 'quintet', is perhaps most notable as the poetic form of the limerick, but there are also a number of stanzaic variants. The simplest form of stanzaic quintain builds upon the ballad stanza with a third *b* rhyme giving a rather melancholic conclusion which resembles a poetic echo. It is demonstrated in Sir Robert Ayton's (1570–1638) lyric, 'When thou did thinke I did not love', where the use of a truncated final two-foot line adds to the mournful sense of loss and deprivation:

When thou did thinke I did not love
Then thou did dote on mee,
Now when thou finds that I doe prove
  As kinde as kinde can bee,
    Love dies in thee.

Shelley avoids the danger of redundancy in the final line of his *ababb* stanza in the 'Ode to a Skylark' by lengthening the last line and letting it bear the main thematic weight of each stanza:

> We look before and after,
>   And pine for what is not:
> Our sincerest laughter
>   With some pain is fraught;
> Our sweetest songs are those that tell of saddest thought.

The *ababa* form is also used occasionally, but not without an attendant danger of the final line seeming rather like an unnecessary embellishment. However, George Herbert's 'Employment' manages to avoid making the last line seem like an afterthought by using truncated second and fourth lines which build up to the resolution provided by the fifth line:

> But we are still too young or old;
>   The man is gone,
> Before we do our wares unfold;
>   So we freeze on,
> Until the grave increase our cold.

Though the word 'sestet' is most commonly applied to the second part of a Petrarchan sonnet, six-line stanzas are also known as **sestets**. Stanzaic sestets are found occasionally in lyric poetry, as in Shelley's 'A Summer-Evening Churchyard, Lechlade, Gloucestershire':

> The wind has swept from the wide atmosphere
> Each vapour that obscures the sunset's ray;
> And pallid evening twines its beaming hair
> In duskier braids around the languid eyes of day;
> Silence and twilight, unbeloved of men,
> Creep hand in hand from yon obscurest glen.

Here Shelley bolts on a couplet to the elegiac stanza and his poem is experimental rather than contributing to a vibrant stanzaic tradition. However, there are two notable sestet forms which are reasonably common and need to be discussed here. Both are adaptations of ballad metre: the '*rime couée*' and the 'Burns stanza'. The *rime couée* (French for 'tailed rhyme'), which is sometimes referred to as the 'romance stanza', involves a straightforward doubling of the four-stress lines of the ballad stanza, rhymed *aabaab* or *aabccb*. It is not uncommon in early English romances, hence its alternative name, but its most individual use is found in Christopher Smart's (1722–1771) extraordinary eighteenth-century poem *A Song to David*:

> Beauteous the moon full on the lawn;
> And beauteous, when the veil's withdrawn,
>   The virgin to her spouse:
> Beauteous the temple deck'd and fill'd,
> When to the heav'n of heav'ns they build
>   Their heart-directed vows.

Though the so-called Burns stanza is named after the great Scottish poet who used it so frequently, it is actually much older, having been used in medieval romance. It is a sestet rhymed *aaabab* with lines 1, 2, 3 and 5 four-stressed and lines 4 and 6 containing only two stresses. The most famous poem in the form is perhaps Burns's (1759–1796) address 'To a Mouse':

> But, Mousie, thou art no thy lane,
> In proving *foresight* may be vain;
> The best-laid schemes of *Mice* an' *Men*,
>   Gang oft a-gley,
> An' lea'e us nought but grief and pain,
>   For promis'd joy.

A stanza of seven lines is known as a **septet**. It should be acknowledged that its use in lyric poetry is insufficiently widespread to permit us to make generalisations about it. However, there is one particular form worth close attention, given that the earliest stanzaic invention of English canonical poetry is a septet: the Chaucerian 'rhyme royal' (or *Rime Royal*), a seven-line iambic pentameter which rhymes *ababbcc*. This is sometimes referred to, after its inventor, as the 'Chaucerian stanza'. It is used in Chaucer's *The Parliament of Fowles* and parts of the *Canterbury Tales*, but its most notable manifestation is in Chaucer's long narrative poem *Troilus and Criseyde*:

> Wher is myn owene lady, lief and deere?
> Wher is hire white breast? wher is it, where?
> Wher ben hire arms and hire eyen cleere,
> That yesternyght this tyme with me were?
> Now may I wepe allone many a teere,
> And graspe aboute I may, but in this place,
> Save a pilowe, I fynde naught t'embrace.

The stanza, with its initial expansive breadth which culminates in a resounding final couplet, is very well suited to Chaucer's narrative purposes. Chaucer's invention was taken up by his imitators and successors, by Dunbar, Henryson and Spenser most particularly, with a notable late sixteenth-century example in Shakespeare's *The Rape of Lucrece*. However, after that it is rare, and it is superseded in narrative poetry by the heroic couplet (another of Chaucer's innovations), blank verse and the Spenserian stanza (see below).

A stanza of eight lines is referred to as an **octet** or, more rarely, as an octave. By far the most important eight-line stanzaic form is the *ottava rima*. Like the rhyme royal, the *ottava rima* has an iambic pentameter base. Rhyming *abababcc*, it is an English adaptation of the Renaissance Italian metre of Luigi Pulci. It was pioneered in the 1810s by John Hookham Frere (1769–1846) and perfected by Lord Byron, and the great classic of the English manifestations of the stanza is Byron's *Don Juan*. Here the stanza is used to great effect in Byron's improvisational raillery and his use of bathetic (that is, intentionally and comically anticlimactic), multiple and ingenious rhymes. And whilst retaining the epigrammatic force of the couplet in the final two lines, the expansive nature of the *ottava rima* suits Byron's talent for humorous digression:

> 'Tis pity learned virgins ever wed
>   With persons of no sort of education,
> Or gentlemen, who, though well-born and -bred,
>   Grow tired of scientific conversation:
> I don't choose to say much upon this head,
>   I'm a plain man, and in a single station,
> But – Oh! ye lords of ladies intellectual,
> Inform us truly, have they not hen-peck'd you all?

We shall conclude with an example of the most significant nine-line stanza, the **Spenserian**. Though longer stanzas have been used (as in the Wither poem cited above), our focus here is upon the most common stanzaic forms, and space precludes attentions to rarer forms or conscious oddities. The 'Spenserian' is named after its inventor, the sixteenth-century poet Edmund Spenser:

> He durst not enter into th'open greene,
>   For dread of them unwares to be descreyde,
> For breaking of their daunce, if he were seene;
>   But in the covert of the wood did byde,
>   Beholding all, yet of them unespyde.
> There he did see, that pleased much his sight,
>   That even he him selfe his eyes envyde,
> An hundred naked maidens lilly white,
> All raunged in a ring, and dauncing in delight. (*The Faerie Queene*)

The Spenserian stanza is iambic, with the first eight lines in pentameters (five-stress lines) and the last line having the defining characteristic of a concluding longer line of six feet (an 'alexandrine'). The rhyme scheme is generally *ababbcbcc*. Though one must always be wary about generalising about a form which has been used a variety of different ways, James Beattie's description of the stanza has much truth to it. For Beattie, it enables the poet to give range, in turn, to the 'droll or pathetic, descriptive and sentimental, tender and satirical … I think it the most harmonious [stanza] that ever was contrived. It admits of more variety of pauses than either the couplet or the alternate rhyme [i.e. the ballad stanza]; and it concludes with a pomp and majesty of sound, which, in my ear, is wonderfully delightful'.

After Spenser, the stanza has a long afterlife in English poetical history, providing the metre for a number of significant longer narrative poems: James Thomson's *The Castle of Indolence*, Beattie's *The Minstrel*, Wordsworth's *Guilt and Sorrow*, Byron's *Childe Harold's Pilgrimage* and Shelley's *The Revolt of Islam*. Whilst Beattie and Thomson in particular exploit the languorous potential of the Spenserian, this is not to say that it cannot be used in an urgent and direct manner. And no one can imbue the stanza with more pace and vigour than Shelley, most notably in the *Revolt of Islam*. This is one of Pestilence's speeches:

> 'What seek'st thou here? The moonlight comes in flashes –
> The dew is rising dankly from the dell –
> 'Twill moisten her! and thou shalt see the gashes
> In my sweet boy, now full of worms – but tell
> First what thou seek'st. 'I seek for food.' ''Tis well,
> Thou shalt have food; Famine, my paramour
> Waits for us at the feast – cruel and fell
> Is famine, but he drives not from his door
> Those who these lips have kissed, alone. No more, no more!'

Elsewhere in his poem Shelley exploits the slow-moving cadence of the Spenserian to its fullest effect, but here he invests it with drive and urgency through multiple breaks in the line (textual 'gashes') which echo the powerful word in line 3, running the sense over the line-ends (thus diminishing the impact of the rhymes) and breaking the final alexandrine up, all of which culminates in the implacable power of the final exclamation. Shelley's work is testimony to the remarkable range and potential of the English poetic stanza.

2.6   EXERCISES

George Herbert, born in Wales in 1593, was a scholar, poet, and, late in his short life, a clergyman at Bemerton in Wiltshire. He seems to have written religious verse throughout his life, many of his poems dramatising, in Herbert's own words, the 'spiritual conflicts between God and my soul before I could subject my will to Jesus, my Master'. The poem beneath could be seen in this respect as representative of much of Herbert's writing. All of Herbert's poems were published posthumously and are based on manuscripts gifted by the poet as he was dying to his friend Nicholas Ferrar.

Denial

WHEN my devotions could not pierce
    Thy silent ears;
Then was my heart broken, as was my verse:
    My breast was full of fears
      And disorder:

    My bent thoughts, like a brittle bow,
      Did fly asunder:
Each took his way; some would to pleasures go,
    Some to the wars and thunder
      Of alarms.

    As good go any where, they say,
      As to benumb
Both knees and heart, in crying night and day,
    Come, come, my God, O come,
      But no hearing.

    O that thou shouldst give dust a tongue
      To cry to thee,
And then not hear it crying! all day long
    My heart was in my knee,
      But no hearing.

    Therefore my soul lay out of sight,
      Untuned, unstrung:
My feeble spirit, unable to look right,
    Like a nipped blossom, hung
      Discontented.

    O cheer and tune my heartless breast,
      Defer no time;
That so thy favors granting my request,
    They and my mind may chime,
      And mend my rime.

1. How would you describe Herbert's emotional and spiritual state as represented in the poem? Do you think this has altered by the end?

2. What do you think Herbert means by saying that his verse is 'broken'? Does the poem actually show his verse to be in this broken condition?

3. How would you describe the properties of the stanza used by Herbert in this poem?

4. Can you comment in particular on the rhyme scheme used in the poem? You will notice that the poem ends on the word 'rime'. In what way is the idea of 'rhyming' important to the poem's theme?

5. What do you think a poet gains in general from the adoption of a stanzaic form as complex and intricate as the one Herbert uses here?

6. Have a go at composing a short poem of your own that uses Herbert's stanza above as a model. How hard do you find this, and to what extent does the stanza itself determine the tone or even content of the poem?

3

The sound of poetry

3.1 POETIC SOUND EFFECTS: AN OVERVIEW

Poetry, as well as being something that we *see*, is also something that we *hear*. There remains even now a vibrant tradition of poetry being delivered orally or 'recited'; and even the silent reading of poetry, if properly performed, should allow the lines to register on the mind's ear. This chapter is concerned with poetic phonology, or with the way poets achieve effects through deploying linguistic sound. However, it might be useful as a preliminary to make a distinction between the kinds of sound that can be involved in poetry. In the first place, there is what is commonly called 'segmental sound', relating to the sounds of the letters and syllables as they exist in independent units. In the second, there are sounds that we can term 'suprasegmental', arising at a level above that of the individual syllables in the form of rhythm and metre. The second category of such effects will be discussed in the next chapter, while the first forms the subject-matter of the present one.

Because this chapter will be about sounds, it might be useful to make a cautionary statement about the relation between sounds and spelling. In English, as in other languages, no stable correlation exists between how a word is spelt and how it sounds. So, for example, non-native speakers of the language can easily be bemused by the range of different sounds that can be generated by a single sequence of letters such as 'ough'. In order to demonstrate this, you might like to think how you would pronounce each of the following words: 'bough', 'tough', 'cough', 'though', 'thought', 'through', 'lough' and 'hiccough'. What you will have noticed, of course, is that the same combination of letters is pronounced differently in each word, so that words like 'bough' and 'tough', in spite of their similar appearance, could never be used together to form a rhyme (or only of a very specialised kind). Because of this very inconsistent relation between spelling and pronunciation, linguists have designed a more complex notative system by which to represent the sounds of the language, called the phonetic alphabet. In this chapter, when we discuss a sound occurring in a poem, we sometimes use the precise phonetic symbol for it, placed within slash marks. This is in order to make clear that we are referring to a particular linguistic sound that might be produced in different words through different combinations of letters.

The technique of using words in a way that exploits their sound rather than merely their meaning is something with which we are all familiar from an early age in the form of tongue-twisters like 'Round and round the ragged rocks the ragged rascal ran'. Of course, the alliteration here does not serve any aesthetic purpose but simply teases the tongue's agility, but the effect is not in principle unlike forms of sound-patterning used by poets. A useful example of such patterning with which to begin is provided by the opening stanza of Samuel Taylor Coleridge's 'Kubla Khan':

> In Xanadu did Kubla Khan
> A stately pleasure-dome decree:
> Where Alph, the sacred river, ran
> Through caverns measureless to man
> Down to a sunless sea.

'Kubla Khan' has become a celebrated poem, partly because of its strange circumstances of composition. Coleridge claimed to have made it up during his sleep. Having awoken, he began transcribing the work, only to have to break off to deal with a visitor. When he returned to the labour of transcription, he found his mind had blanked, and this accounts for why the poem has survived only as a fragment. This claim that the poem formed itself spontaneously in the poet's unconscious, however, seems belied by the dense and complex way in which it organises sound. We can in fact identify and enumerate as many as six distinct sound patterns. (1) The stanza has the rhyme scheme *abaab*, which means that every line-ending rhymes with at least one other. (2) Each rhyme word alliterates with the word immediately preceding it, as 'Kubla Khan', 'dome decree', 'river, ran' and 'sunless sea', the one slight exception being line 4 where 'measureless' and 'man' are separated by the preposition 'to'. (3) The first line contains assonance, with the complete run of vowel sounds across the line, as expressed in phonetic terms, being /ɪ/æ/æ/uː/ɪ/uː/æ/æ/. You might note in particular that all the vowels in the place 'Xanadu' recur in the name 'Kubla Khan', except in an exactly reverse order. (4) Lines 1 and 2 are linked together by a pattern of consonance, involving the letter 'd', with the sound chiming of 'Xana<u>du</u> <u>did</u>' being picked up in the next line by '<u>dome</u> <u>d</u>ecree'. (5) In similar vein, a pattern of consonance on the letter 'r' unites lines 2 and 3. This is initiated by 'dec<u>r</u>ee', but then comes to a crescendo in the next line with 'sac<u>r</u>ed <u>r</u>iver <u>r</u>an'. (6) The word 'measureless' (line 4) makes links both forwards and backwards: its first two syllables rhyme internally with 'pleasure' in line 2, and its last syllable 'less' makes for a rhyme repetition with 'sunless' in line 5.

We may already have used some words here with which you are not familiar, so we propose to clarify the key terms used to describe sound-patterns in poetry. Definitions of these terms are subject to some variation, and what has mainly concerned us is to introduce definitions that will be used consistently throughout this book. The word 'alliteration' is used here to mean the commencement of adjacent or closely related words with the same sound or letter; so we can say that 'ragged rocks' alliterates on the letter 'r' and 'prize pig' on the letter 'p'. For our purpose, it does not matter whether the alliterating letters are vowels or consonants, only that they fall at the beginning of the words in which they occur. The term 'consonance', we take to mean the repetition between closely related words of any consonantal sounds. So 'ragged rocks' is an example of consonance as well as of alliteration; however, the phrase 'grea<u>t</u> heigh<u>t</u>' demonstrates consonance in its repetition of the final 't', though this repetition is not alliterative. The term 'assonance' we use to refer to the recurrence of the same vowel sound, especially in stressed syllables. The key thing to note here is that the repetition of sound may occur in spite of variability in spelling, so that the phrase 'A tr<u>ai</u>tor to the n<u>a</u>tion' shows assonance on the phonetic sound /eɪ/, though this sound is spelt differently in the two words.

The point of the 'Kubla Khan' excerpt above was to demonstrate the very sophisticated ways in which poets can orchestrate sound. Of course, not all poets avail themselves of sound-patterning in this way, but many have done in the past and many poets nowadays continue to use such techniques. This phonological dimension of poetry in fact is something that is often seen as distinguishing it from the rival media of prose fiction and drama. To explain why this should be the case, why poetry should have come to stand in an unusually significant relation to linguistic sound, involves harking back to some of the earliest poetry written in the British isles, by the Anglo-Saxons.

In nearly all cultures, the advent of poetry long pre-dates the emergence of theatre or the rise of imaginative kinds of prose writing. In fact, in a large number of cultures, poetry can be dated back to pre-literate times: that is, to times during which the sole significant form of communication between people was through word of mouth, since the skill of writing, and the techniques of reproducing written material (as through printing), were so little advanced. In England, a recoverable poetic culture, if only on a minute scale, dates to about the seventh century. This culture was predominantly oral: it consisted of poems being composed in the head, recited aloud to gathered audiences, memorised by listeners, and further revised and embellished, perhaps across a period of generations. A culture in which poetry is alive, but not in written form, inevitably places a weighty onus on the human memory: memory becomes the only means by which a composed work can gain a passage into posterity.

Anglo-Saxon poems, as those produced by similar societies, possess a built-in mnemonic device (or device to aid the memory): this is alliteration. Traditionally, Anglo-Saxon poets composed their verses not of lines but of half-lines, each half-line being separated from its fellow by a gap when the poems were actually written down. As an example of such an Anglo-Saxon poem made more available to the contemporary reader, we can look at the beginning of Ezra Pound's translation into modern English of 'The Seafarer':

> May I for my own self-song's truth reckon,
> Journey's jargon, how I in harsh days
> Hardship endured oft.
> Bitter breast-cares have I abided,
> Known on my keel many a care's hold,
> And dire sea-surge, and there I oft spent
> Narrow nightwatch nigh the ship's head
> While she tossed close to cliffs.

Pound has dispensed with the break between the two half-lines alluded to above, but in many of his lines one can detect a stop around the mid-line where there falls a break in the syntax or sense. However, what the poet *has* fastidiously preserved from the original, at least in many of the lines, is alliterative patterning. Moreover, this occurs in a highly formulaic way: two alliterating syllables occur in the first part of the line (conforming to the first half-line) and one occurs in the second. This pattern can be discerned, for example, in line 4 with 'Bitter breast-cares … abided'; in line 6 with 'sea-surge … spent'; and in line 7 with 'Narrow nightwatch nigh'.

The effect of the alliteration is to create a formal connection between the first and second halves of the line (or between the first half-line and second half-line as it would originally have been). In this sense, it gives a structural integrity to the poem and also, as all sound-patterns do, lends it a sort of musicality. Yet the sound-patterning overall serves a functional rather than a descriptive purpose. The regularity of the alliteration makes such poems much easier to commit to memory, since if you remember the alliterating letter in the first half-line, you will know that there must be a further word in the second half-line beginning with the same letter. While such a device hardly makes accurate recall inevitable, it still remains a fall-back mechanism if the poem can not be remembered on the strength of its sense alone. It would seem a bit ironic in this light that Coleridge's 'Kubla Khan', a poem that has a dense pattern of alliteration, has become such a celebrated instance of poetic amnesia. But this perhaps only reflects how the use of sound-patterning had by Coleridge's day long since ceased to serve a mnemonic function.

3.2 ONOMATOPOEIA

If sound effects no longer retain their original mnemonic function, are we to assume them to be purely ornamental? Or can sound have the auxiliary function of conveying or reinforcing a poem's meaning? Indeed, can the sounds of words, irrespective of what the words actually mean, convey some import to the reader? The general issue here is to do with onomatopoeia, meaning, as the *OED* defines it, 'the formation of a name or word by the imitation of the sound associated with the thing or action designated'. The English language contains innumerable such words as 'crackle', 'murmur' and 'hiss', and a particularly prolific category involves names of animals or animal sounds like 'cuckoo', 'woof' and 'miaow'. It should be noted that the association of a sound with a particular word (thought of as representing the sound) is always culture-specific. For example, many cultures have words of an onomatopoeic nature to describe animal sounds, but these tend to be very different from one language to another.

The point of an onomatopoeic word is that its sound is actually meaningful; and there are many poems that work in total, or in part, on onomatopoeic principles. To consider the extent to which the pure sounds of words, as distinct from what they explicitly say, might be meaningful, it might be useful to take as an example a poem in which the words are not actually saying anything (or anything immediately intelligible). What we are alluding to here is the rare genre of the 'sound poem', one of whose chief exponents is the experimental Scottish poet Edwin Morgan (1920–2010). Cited beneath is his 'The Loch Ness Monster's Song', a poem that Morgan used to perform but which he also released in printed form:

> Sssnnnwhufffffl?
> Hnwhuffl hhnnwfl hnfl hfl?
> Gdroblboblhobngbl gbl gl g g g g glbgl.
> Drublhaflablhaflubhafgabhaflhafl fl fl –
> gm grawwwww grf grawf awfgm graw gm.
> Hovoplodok-doplodovok-plovodokot-doplodokosh?
> Splgraw fok fok splgrafhatchgabrlgabrl fok splfok!
> Zgra kra gka fok!
> Grof grawff gahf?
> Gombl mbl bl –

blm plm,
blm plm,
blm plm,
blp.

What we want to propose is that the poem tells a story, and that this story is conveyed to the reader mainly through the effect of sound. We say 'mainly' because the poem offers us several clues to meaning that are not phonological. Among these, the most important is the title, without which the poem would inevitably remain opaque, except perhaps to an interpretive guess of miraculous proportions. A second clue derives from punctuation (again not phonological): lines 1, 2, 6, 7, 8 and 9 all terminate with expressive punctuation (question or exclamation marks), which strongly implies that these lines involve creaturely agency, since only creatures, in particular ones naturally endowed with or ascribed human properties, can express perplexity or issue exclamatory noises.

Given these useful clues, we propose the following reading of the poem. The opening two lines, with their preponderance of 'f's and 'l's, seem to mimic the snuffling that the monster might make as, having popped its head up above the surface, it tries to expel water from its nostrils. The question-marks at the end of both lines also suggest the interrogative air of the creature breaking the surface and searching its new environment. The next few lines seem to detail a shift of mood. Lines 3 and 4 represent noises of an undefined kind that the monster emits, but by line 5 these noises have turned to aggressive growling, indicated by a prevalence of 'gr' consonantal clusters. In the next three lines, the growling sound gives way to more violent, explosive sounds, as 'Splgraw fok fok'. The most likely scenario, perhaps, is that the monster has seen something by which it feels threatened and which causes it to bristle with aggression. This passage comes to a conclusion in line 8 with the phonological sequence 'Zgra kra gka fok!', before, the threat perhaps seen off, the monster's tone seems to soften as the consonant sounds modulate once more. Line 10, with its 'mbl' clusters, could be indicative of the animal's vociferations turning to mumbling, or they could register the sound made as it starts to withdraw its body under the water. In any event, the dash suggests a sudden breaking off of sound, perhaps as the monster's head dips under water so that its grumblings become inaudible; and the last four lines suggest bubbles rising to, and breaking on, the empty surface of the loch.

This interpretation may or may not conform to what the poet himself intended by the poem but, given the help the reader is afforded by the poem's title and punctuation, the hypothesis that what is narrated is the monster's ascent to the surface and subsequent descent down to the depths again probably will not seem outlandish or implausible. It would be true to say that our interpretation draws more on particular conventions for representing sound than on any absolute meanings that individual sounds possess. So, for example, our suggestion that the poem's first word 'Sssnnnwhufffffl' represents the clearing of the monster's nostrils is based on the fact that in English nasal sounds are conventionally represented by the 'fl' cluster, as notably in the onomato-poeic word 'snuffle'. Similarly, the sound of animal aggression is usually expressed by the 'gr' cluster as in 'growl', though whether this word, as the word 'snuffle', is an objective and accurate transcription of the sound it represents remains a moot point.

Edwin Morgan's 'The Loch Ness Monster's Song', as a pure sound-poem, is itself a beast almost as uncommon as the one it recounts. Most poems are constituted by words, as distinct from sounds, and whatever sound effects they contain operate in tandem with the meaning created by the words. One device that poets sometimes use is to pattern their sound effects in such a way that they reinforce, or enact in some way, the literal meaning of the poem. An exercise of this kind is Edgar Allan Poe's (1809–1849) sequence of poems entitled 'The Bells', of which the first runs as follows:

> The bells! – ah, the bells!
> The little silver bells!
> How fairy-like a melody there floats
>   From their throats –
>   From their merry little throats –
>   From the silver, tinkling throats
> Of the bells, bells, bells –
>   Of the bells!
>
> The bells! – ah, the bells!
> The heavy iron bells!
> How horrible a monody there floats
>   From their throats –
>   From their deep-toned throats –
>   From their melancholy throats!
>   How I shudder at the notes
> Of the bells, bells, bells –
>   Of the bells!

A story exists concerning the poem's invention. In May 1848, Poe paid a visit to a female friend Marie Louise Shew and encumbered her with complaints about his lack of poetic creativity, remarking in particular on some church bells in the vicinity that 'I so dislike the noise of bells tonight, I cannot write'. His hostess then, taking up a pen, wrote the first couple of lines of the first stanza above, after which Poe composed the remaining ones; and the second stanza was constructed in a similar way. The first stanza represents the pealing of a set of light bells. Distinct chimes seem to be represented by the very word 'bells', as it occurs at the beginning and end of the stanza, and by the words 'floats' and 'throats' occurring in the middle. The succession of chimes is rapid, and is captured in the prevalence of short vowel sounds, as in the second line 'The little silver bells'. The second stanza represents the tolling of a heavier set of bells, whose chimes resonate longer, to mimic which the poem itself adopts techniques of sound elongation. The middle section of the poem acquires an extra line and there is a noticeable lengthening of the vowel sounds: 'merry little throats', for example, changes to 'deep-toned' throats. One other effect contrived by the poem might also be mentioned, though this is not directly relevant to sound. If you squint your eyes, the poem takes on a bell-like shape on the page, as each stanza plumps outwards, especially on the right, as the eye follows it down.

Poe's 'The Bells' is a studied exercise in creating a relation between the sound orchestration of a poem and its subject-matter. Few poems attempt this feat so systematically as Poe's, for one reason because there are considerable limits on what sound-patterns can be used to imitate. It would be hard to see how something as abstract as a sound-pattern could represent love or death; and, in one sense, Poe has made the exercise easier for himself by having one sound-pattern imitate another one: the sound of words imitating the sound of bells. This section, however, should have demonstrated both that we can attribute meanings (if only in a limited way) to linguistic sounds; and that poets can use sound-patterning to mimic or reinforce some sorts of poetic meaning.

3.3   SOUND–PATTERNING

Both Morgan's and Poe's poems could be seen, if perhaps a little cruelly, as reducing phonological effects to the level of gimmickry, and we want now to take as an example a poem that uses sound effects in a vivid way, yet without unduly foregrounding them. The poem we have chosen is D. H. Lawrence's (1885–1930) 'Gloire de Dijon':

> When she rises in the morning
> I linger to watch her;
> She spreads the bath-cloth underneath the window
> And the sunbeams catch her
> Glistening white on the shoulders,
> While down her sides the mellow
> Golden shadow glows as
> She stoops to the sponge, and her swung breasts
> Sway like full-blown yellow
> Gloire de Dijon roses.

> She drips herself with water, and her shoulders
> Glisten as silver, they crumple up
> Like wet and falling roses, and I listen
> For the sluicing of their rain-dishevelled petals.
> In the window full of sunlight
> Concentrates her golden shadow
> Fold on fold, until it glows as
> Mellow as the glory roses.

The poem is composed of two stanzas, the first of which begins with two lines that act as a framing device for the rest of the poem: a man observes a woman washing herself underneath a window. Leaving aside this initial frame, the two stanzas each consist of eight lines, mirroring each other at a number of points (to which we will return). The poem contains a remarkably dense manipulation of sound, which can perhaps be unravelled into three distinct sequences of phonological repetition. The first pattern concerns the vowel sound /əʊ/ and is present in the following words:

Stanza 1: window, shoulders, mellow, golden, shadow, glows, yellow, roses
Stanza 2: shoulders, roses, window, golden, shadow, fold, fold, glows, mellow, roses

The second pattern relates to the use of sibilance; setting aside noun plurals and verbs terminating in 's', the words displaying sibilance are as follows:

Stanza 1: rises, spreads, sunbeams, Glistening, sides, stoops, sponge, swung, Sway, roses
Stanza 2: Glisten, silver, roses, listen, sluicing, sunlight, Concentrates, roses

A further pattern concentrates on the sound /l/ as it occurs in the following sequence of repetitions:

Stanza 1: linger, cloth, Glistening, shoulders, While, mellow, Golden, glows, like, full-blown, yellow, Gloire
Stanza 2: shoulders, Glisten, silver, crumple, Like, falling, listen, sluicing, dishevelled, petals, full, sunlight, golden, Fold, fold, until, glows, Mellow, glory

Lawrence has clearly puzzled over the formal organisation of the poem, carefully building in a system of symmetries. Leaving aside the frame, both stanzas open with pronoun verb combinations ('She spreads'; 'She drips herself') and both end with the symbolic word 'roses'. Moreover, despite the fact that Lawrence repeats each of the key phonological items, like 'shoulders', 'Golden shadow', 'glows' and so on, these repetitions all take place *across* the two stanzas rather than being confined to just one of them. All the repetitions thus work to bind the two stanzas more closely together.

The poem makes use of the time-honoured techniques of erotic stimulation, especially in the way it concentrates not so much on the woman's body itself but on its relation to what comes into contact with it: initially, sunbeams, then shadow, and finally the beadlets of water that glisten on her shoulders. In reinforcement of this soft eroticism, Lawrence uses sounds to create an effect almost of slow-motion as the tongue is forced to trip carefully over the thick sound clusters, like 'bath-cloth underneath', 'mellow / Golden shadow glows', and 'glows as / Mellow as the glory roses'. The central symbol evoked by the poem is that of the loved woman as a rose. So in the first stanza, the woman's breasts are described as swaying like Gloire de Dijon roses; in the second, the water coating her shoulders is described like sodden rose petals; and finally (in a perplexing image) her shadow is seen as enfolded on itself like a flower head. As we have suggested, this *symbolic* association of a woman with the beauty and purity of the rose is longstanding, but Lawrence tries to thicken this symbol into a physical likeness: her body is seen as if physically *analogous* to a rose. An appropriate way of describing the working of the poem might be assimilation: the symbol of the rose flower flows outward in physically reconstituting the rest of the poem, and the woman's body in particular, in its own image. And a similar effect happens with the poem's sound effects. As the rose image spreads out and envelops the woman's body, so the sound constituents of the phrase 'glory roses' (/l/, /əʊ/ and /s/) spread out and insinuate themselves into the sound texture of the poem as a whole.[1]

3.4   RHYME

To most people, a rhyme is a sound repetition occurring at the end of a line of poetry. Yet such a definition is in fact flawed since a rhyme word can just as easily occur in the body of a line. Accordingly, the best understanding of rhyme is probably that which sees it as the near-occurrence of two words which contain a repetition of the final vowel and all linguistic sounds subsequent to it. So, for example, the words 'rope' and 'hope' would rhyme if they occurred in reasonable proximity since they share the vowel sound /əʊ/ and have the same final consonant (note that the final letter 'e' is unsounded). Equally, 'rope' and 'soap' also make for rhymes as, in spite of the difference in spelling, they still share the same vowel sound /əʊ/ as well as the final consonant sound /p/. A rhyme, then, is a precise category of sound repetition, very similar in nature to other categories like consonance and assonance, generally, though not always, occurring at the end of the line.

When anybody sits down to compose a poem, the decision either to rhyme or not to rhyme remains one of the first that has to be made. At certain points in the past, this decision has been very vexed. In the seventeenth century, for

example, Milton ostentatiously dispensed with rhyme for his epic poem
Paradise Lost, calling it an invention of a 'barbarous age' and a 'modern bondage';
similarly, Dryden, who actually wrote many rhyming plays as well as poems,
could write equivocally about rhyme as 'At best a pleasing sound, and fair
barbarity'. The most obvious case against rhyme has always been its artificiality.
In everyday language usage, we place at our disposal many of the resources that
poets themselves habitually use: we employ words, idioms, figurative language,
even rhythms of speech. But no normal person in everyday conversation uses
rhyme. The existence of rhyme in a poem, or perhaps especially in a play, has
always been seen as potentially detracting from the 'suspension of disbelief', or
the ability of the reader or audience to respond to a work as if it were real. This
was a case that Dryden, in his own day, felt a need to answer; and his response
still retains its relevance to the question as it arises today. Dryden pointed out
with good reason that rhyme is not the only artificial element in poetry, and
indeed is no more artificial, for example, than poetic metre; and he also drew
a distinction between where rhymes are used smoothly and where their
occurrence is disruptive, in the sense that the poet has to introduce an unusual
word, or to throw his words into an unusual arrangement, in order to clinch the
rhyme.

Rhyme can be seen as one of those poetic effects of which, in a successful
poem, the reader should at the same time be both aware and not aware. Of
course, there are rhymes of a specialised nature whose success is entirely
dependent on attracting the reader's notice, but very often our sense that a
poem's rhymes are particularly prominent is indicative of a shortcoming of
technique. Even major poets can be more or less assured in the deployment of
rhymes: Keats, for example, is one famous poet who has sometimes been
accused of being a maladroit rhymer. One manifestation of poor rhyming
technique is where a poet is forced into using a rare word or one not strictly
suitable to the sense, but another is where the natural word order has to be
disturbed in order for the rhyme to be procured. An example of the latter
shortcoming occurs in probably the most famous hymnic version of Psalm 23,
which dates to the 1650 Scottish Psalter. Here is the first verse:

> The Lord's my shepherd, I'll not want;
>   He makes me down to lie
> In pastures green; he leadeth me
>   The quiet waters by.

In order for the two rhyming words 'lie' and 'by' to be manoeuvred into
position at the line-endings, the hymnist has to take severe liberties with what
we would see as the proper word order. So in line 2 the sense that 'He makes
me lie down' is twisted into 'He makes me down to lie'; and in line 4 the

proposition 'by' is clumsily relocated to the end of the line in order the clinch the rhyme.

It would be misleading, however, to imply that the only value of a rhyme is to be imperceptible, for (as we shall see) there are certain specialised sorts of rhyme that depend expressly on jolting the reader's attention. Moreover, even orthodox rhymes should register on the reader, even if only in ways that remain subliminal. All this is to beg the most fundamental question about rhyme: why *do* poets resort to this strange compositional technique? We propose four distinct answers in response to this question:

1. Rhyme, as well as other sorts of sound-patterning, acts as a sort of musical accompaniment to a poem. It is an effect that appeals to the mind's ear, as opposed to all the other elements that appeal to the intellect or to the emotions.
2. Rhyme provides an important organisational principle for the poetic stanza. After all, to a large extent, we define different stanzas in terms of their rhyming scheme: so we might say, for example, that the Spenserian stanza in *The Faerie Queene* has the structure *ababbcbcc*. Most stanzas can be seen in these terms, as a sequence of lines plaited together on the basis of rhyme.
3. The convention of rhyme represents an enactment in miniature of one of the most important satisfactions that literary works can offer us: that of arousing and fulfilling (or defeating) our expectations. The pleasure of anticipation is something we feel, though in a more languid way, in connection with the unfolding of plot and the development of character. Acting on a much smaller scale, the introduction of a new rhyme term gives us a pin-prick of anticipation as the mind's ear casts ahead for a word that will continue or clinch the rhyme.
4. Rhyme poses itself as a handicap or impediment that poets have to overcome before they can bring a poem to fruition. One pleasure that we derive from reading a rhyming work, especially one with a complex rhyme scheme, is watching the poet triumph over this self-instituted adversity. This sort of pleasure is analogous to that we receive from watching animated films. Often we feel that the makers of such films would make life easier for themselves if they used real actors rather than, say, plasticine models, but on the other hand the film's skill in triumphing over the obduracy of its materials is something from which the spectator derives pleasure.

As we have said, rhyme is a poetic element of which we should remain at the same time both aware and not aware. Anyone who reads through a rhyming poem without noting the fact that it rhymed would clearly be guilty of inattention; but it would be equally inappropriate to read the same poem in a way that pauses and deliberates over every rhyme word. In most (though not all poems) the correct middle-way is to register the rhyme, but not to have our attention unduly hooked by it.

3.5 THE 'ORTHODOX' RHYME

There is no such thing nowadays as an 'orthodox' or 'correct' rhyme, but for earlier literary cultures such terms did possess meaning. In the early eighteenth century, one literary work that was seen as something of a copybook of impeccable poetic technique (including in its use of rhyme) was Alexander Pope's translation of Homer's *Iliad*, which was published in instalments between 1715 and 1720. Although Pope was aware of early English translations, he still worked largely from the Greek, and so was acquainted with the fact that Homer's poem, in its original form, did not rhyme. Nonetheless, he decided to render the poem in rhyming form. Take, for example, the lines below:

> Now pleasing *Sleep* had seal'd each mortal Eye,
> Stretch'd in the Tents the *Grecian* Leaders lie,
> Th'Immortals slumber'd on their Thrones above;
> All, but the ever-wakeful Eyes of *Jove*.
> To honour *Thetis'* Son he bends his Care,
> And plunge the *Greeks* in all the Woes of War:
> Then bids an empty Phantome rise to sight,
> And thus commands the *Vision* of the Night.
> Fly hence, deluding *Dream!* and light as Air,
> To *Agamemnon's* ample Tent repair.
> Bid him in Arms draw forth th'embattel'd Train,
> Lead all his *Grecians* to the dusty Plain.

The lines occur at the beginning of Book II and are an example of heroic couplets: that is, the verse lines consist of ten syllables with the rhymes falling exclusively on adjacent lines. As we have suggested that these rhymes in their own time would have been considered 'orthodox', it might be useful to spell out in what this orthodoxy would have consisted. For one thing, all the rhymes occur on a single syllable placed at the end of the line: moreover, with the exception of 'above' and 'repair', the entire word instrumental in the rhyme is also itself monosyllabic. Additionally, the rhymes fall on words that carry the main brunt of the meaning. Of the twelve rhyme words, accordingly, nine are nouns and two are verbs – nouns and verbs being the most meaning-laden of all the parts of speech. There is a train of logic in the fact that Pope's poem rhymes on words that also carry the heaviest semantic burden, for rhyme naturally tends to attract stress to a word, and thus it would be inappropriate if the rhyme fell on a word that, on the grounds of sense alone, would not normally be stressed. In the passage quoted, the stress on the rhyme term is reinforced also by the punctuation. Every line terminates with a punctuation mark of some sort, thus creating a syntactical halt which reinforces the emphasis on the final rhyme word.

The signal features of Pope's lines, then, are that his rhymes fall exclusively at the end of the line; their crispness is ensured by their restriction to a single syllable; and in the way they are used, they express a harmonisation of sound stress and semantic stress. The principles of good practice followed here belong very much to their time, yet they also represent a general standard against which we can chart certain sorts of 'deviation'. These deviations concern the use by poets of internal rhyme, polysyllabic and feminine rhyme, and pararhyme.

3.6   SOME 'UNORTHODOX' RHYMES

Pope's lines are technically end-rhymes, where a word placed at the end of a line rhymes with a similar-sounding word at the end of another line. Yet in principle there is no reason why the sort of sound effect we classify as rhyme should not occur in connection with a word or words falling in the middle of the line. This effect is called 'internal rhyme' and a good example of it, as indeed of numerous other sorts of sound effect, comes in Edgar Allan Poe's 'The Raven'. Given beneath are the first three stanzas:

> Once upon a midnight dreary, while I pondered, weak and weary,
> Over many a quaint and curious volume of forgotten lore –
> While I nodded, nearly napping, suddenly there came a tapping,
> As of some one gently rapping, rapping at my chamber door –
> ''T is some visitor,' I muttered, 'tapping at my chamber door –
>   Only this and nothing more.'
>
> Ah, distinctly I remember it was in the bleak December;
> And each separate dying ember wrought its ghost upon the floor.
> Eagerly I wished the morrow; – vainly I had sought to borrow
> From my books surcease of sorrow – sorrow for the lost Lenore –
> For the rare and radiant maiden whom the angels name Lenore –
>   Nameless *here* for evermore.
>
> And the silken, sad, uncertain rustling of each purple curtain
> Thrilled me – filled me with fantastic terrors never felt before;
> So that now, to still the beating of my heart, I stood repeating
> ''T is some visitor entreating entrance at my chamber door –
> Some late visitor entreating entrance at my chamber door; –
>   This it is and nothing more.'

Like Poe's sequence of poems 'The Bells', this gives the impression of being a studied exercise in poetic phonology. The deployment of sound effects is, in fact, so dense that we have space here only to discuss stanzas one and three. Both stanzas rhyme *abcbbb*: in other words, in each stanza, all the rhymes are specific to a single sound. Additionally, one rhyme in each of the stanzas involves a straight repetition of a single word: so in the first stanza, for example, 'door' rhymes with 'door'. This technique of rhyming by repetition is an equivocal one: in one sense, such rhymes are the most pure kind achievable; in another, they are the most lacklustre. The first stanza also contains two distinct assonantal sequences in 'up<u>on</u>', '<u>p</u>ondered', '<u>vo</u>lume', 'forg<u>ott</u>en' and '<u>nod</u>ded'; and '<u>lore</u>', '<u>door</u>' and '<u>more</u>'. While another sound sequence links together the sound /k/ in 'wea<u>k</u>', '<u>q</u>uaint' and '<u>c</u>urious'. A more pronounced technique in the same stanza, however, occurs in lines 1 and 3. Each line contains one word that stands in a relation of alliteration and rhyme to two other words in the same line. So in line 1, 'weary' rhymes internally with 'dreary', while at the same time alliterating with 'weak'. Similarly, in line 3, 'napping' rhymes internally with 'tapping' while alliterating with 'nodded' and 'nearly'. The third stanza is constructed in much the same way, with a pronounced sound sequence on the sound /s/: '<u>s</u>ilken', '<u>s</u>ad', 'un<u>c</u>ertain', 'ru<u>s</u>tling', 'fanta<u>s</u>tic' and so on. Moreover, like stanza 1, it creates the same scenario in which certain words possess relations both of rhyme and alliteration with other words. So, in line 1, 'uncertain' rhymes with 'curtain', while entering into a relation of consonance with 'silken', 'sad' and 'rustling'. In line 2, 'filled' rhymes with 'thrilled' while alliterating with 'fantastic', 'felt' and 'before'. Line 3 contains a single internal rhyme of 'beating' with 'repeating', which is further consolidated by the occurrence of 'entreating' in the next line. Meanwhile, in both lines 4 and 5, 'entreating' nestles up against and alliterates with the word 'entrance'. The poem, as a whole, is a mesmerising confection of phonological effects, but these are not merely an accompanying acoustic to its meaning. The subject-matter of the poem is the uncanny, and Poe's technique is itself an exercise in uncanniness. 'The Raven' is packed with mysteriously coincidental repetitions of sound that thicken its doomish atmosphere.

Poe's poem, then, is notable chiefly for the way that rhyme is worked into its very tissue rather than each rhyme, in the more common way, being perched at the end of the line. But his rhymes also differ from Pope's by often consisting of more than a single syllable. So, in the first stanza, 'dreary' and 'weary' chime together, as do 'napping', 'tapping' and 'rapping'. These rhymes bear witness to two related, though technically distinct, phenomena. They are 'polysyllabic' and also 'feminine', these being the two categories of rhyme that we are going to address next.

There is a long tradition in English poetry, in which perhaps the most distinguished exponents have been Samuel Butler (1613–1680), Jonathan Swift and Lord Byron, of rhymes being used to comic effect. The comedy tends to lie either in the poet's creating a mock-impression of his own incompetence by using ostensibly inept rhymes, or in his demonstrating an ingenuity in thinking up rhyme terms that is stretched to the point of ridiculousness. In both cases, the rhymes produced tend to express their far-fetched nature by being polysyllabic. An example of such a technique comes at the very beginning of Samuel Butler's mock-romance poem *Hudibras* (1663), which satirises the events of the Civil War:

> WHEN *civil* Fury first grew high,
> And men fell out they knew not why;
> When hard words, *Jealousies* and *Fears*,
> Set Folks together by the ears,
> And made them fight, like mad or drunk,
> For Dame *Religion* as for Punk,
> Whose honesty they all durst swear for,
> Though not a man of them knew wherefore:
> When *Gospel-trumpeter*, surrounded
> With long-ear'd rout, to Battel sounded,
> And Pulpit, Drum Ecclesiastick,
> Was beat with fist, instead of a stick:
> Then did Sir *Knight* abandon dwelling,
> And out he rode a Colonelling.

Butler's poem is written in octosyllabic lines (that is, lines with eight syllables), a verse form that has a particular association with comic rhymes, mainly because the brevity of the lines makes the rhyme return all the more quickly and so gives it greater prominence. It is no coincidence, then, that Swift, another comic rhymester, also wrote habitually in octosyllabics. Butler starts out with conventional monosyllabic rhymes ('high' / 'why'; *Fears* / 'ears'; 'drunk' / 'Punk'). In line 7, however, he begins a series of more complex polysyllabic rhymes: 'swear for' / 'wherefore'; 'surrounded' / 'sounded'; 'Ecclesiastick' / 'a stick'; 'dwelling' / 'Colonelling'. The ingenuity here is very much like that shown by the waspish American wit Dorothy Parker when, over the dinner table, she was set the task of manufacturing a pun on the improbable word 'horticulture'. Quick as a flash (supposedly), she came up with the sentence: 'You can take a "horticulture" (whore to culture) but you can't make her think'. Not just does this parodic *bon mot* achieve a far-fetched pun on 'horticulture', but it also manages to allude to the aphorism that 'You can take a horse to water but you can't make it drink'. It's in a spirit of witty word-play very similar to this that Butler rhymes 'swear for' with 'wherefore', and 'Ecclesiastick' with 'a stick'. The last four couplets all rhyme on bi-syllables, but some also exhibit the unusual technique of a sound sequence contained in two words being made to rhyme with the same sequence contained in just one. 'Surrounded' / 'sounded' is also particularly complex, for as well as the rhyme on the last two syllables, the first syllable of the first rhyme word ('sur'), which does not actually form part of the rhyme, alliterates with the first syllable of 'sounded'.

Whenever a syllable becomes the vehicle for a rhyme, this fact necessarily makes it more pronounced; and one of the features of correct rhyming (as observed by poets like Pope) was that rhymes were allowed to fall only on syllables that, simply by virtue of the line's meaning, would carry a rhythmical stress. In fact, when we encounter a rhyme on a syllable that would not ordinarily be stressed, we can often feel quite thrown as to how it should be pronounced. The terminology adopted by critics in this area is regrettably sexist: rhymes falling on stressed syllables, and for that reason 'strong', are called 'masculine', whereas rhymes on unstressed syllables are termed 'feminine'. One particular category of feminine rhyme relates to the distinction between the stem of a word and its inflectional ending. If we take the word 'hope', for example, we can say that it consists simply of its own stem. However, the word 'hoped' consists of the stem 'hope' plus the inflection 'ed' (which in English indicates past tense), and the word 'hoping' consists of the same stem plus the inflection 'ing' (which indicates action of a continuous nature). In the same way, we can add to the word's stem to create words like 'hopeful' and 'hopeless' as well as 'hopefully' and 'hopelessly'. Regardless of whether the inflection consists of one or more than one syllable, it will not normally be stressed, the stress being placed instead on the word's stem. Rhymes made on inflections, then, represent a particularly specialised technique.

One feature of inflections is that they are highly uniform: the past tense of many verbs is formed by adding 'ed' to the stem; many adverbs are formed by adding 'ly' (as 'quickly'); and many adjectives can be converted into nouns by the simple addition of 'ness' (as 'happiness'). In other words, so long as a poet is prepared to rhyme on an inflection, the task of rhyming becomes much easier, with an almost endless range of options from which to choose. Such rhymes, then, are not in general seen as indicative of a high degree of poetic skill, yet there remain ways of applying them that can still seem subtle and imaginative. Let's take, for example, the first few lines of Gerard Manley Hopkins's (1844–1889) 'The Windhover':

> I caught this morning morning's minion, king-
>   dom of daylight's dauphin, dapple-dawn-drawn Falcon, in his riding
> Of the rolling level underneath him steady air, and striding
> High there, how he rung upon the rein of a wimpling wing
> In his ecstasy! then off, off forth on swing,
> As a skate's heel sweeps smooth on a bow-bend: the hurl and gliding
> Rebuffed the big wind. My heart in hiding
> Stirred for a bird, – the achieve of, the mastery of the thing!

Hopkins's poetic technique is notoriously idiosyncratic; and this poem is remarkable for its dense patterns of alliteration (as 'daylight's dauphin, dapple-dawn-drawn Falcon'), though these are not our primary concern here. The rhymes in the stanza, in spite of all falling on the syllable 'ing', belong to two distinct categories. The rhyme words 'king' (as in 'king-dom'), 'wing', 'swing' and 'thing' are all composed entirely of their own stems, and each of them is stressed. But at the end of the other lines, the rhyme falls on an inflection, as 'riding', 'striding', 'gliding' and 'hiding'. Notice, too, that the lines are of irregular length, and that Hopkins is happy to cut his lines to the convenience of the rhyme. So in line 1 he breaks the line in an unorthodox way around 'king-/dom' in order to extract a rhyme, not from the word's final syllable, but from its initial one. When Hopkins rhymes a stressed with an unstressed syllable, as 'king' with 'riding' or 'striding' with 'wing', something rather odd is occurring. In some sense, such rhymes are really 'eye rhymes': that is, they are more apparent to the eye than they are detectable to the ear. It is the sameness of spelling rather than the sameness of sound that clinches the rhyme.

What characterises the feminine rhyme, then, is our sense of such rhymes failing to chime properly or being in some way 'out of key'; and this effect occurs in even more pronounced form in connection with another rhyming type: the pararhyme. Pararhymes form a very specialised category of sound effects, and only a small number of major poets seem to have been drawn to them. Those who *have* used them extensively, however, include W. H. Auden, Dylan Thomas and also Wilfred Owen, as in his poem 'Strange Meeting':

> It seemed that out of battle I escaped,
> Down some profound dull tunnel, long since scooped
> Through granites which titanic wars had groined.
> Yet also there encumbered sleepers groaned,
> Too fast in thought or death to be bestirred.
> Then, as I probed them, one sprang up and stared
> With piteous recognition in fixed eyes,
> Lifting distressful hands as if to bless.
> And by his smile, I knew that sullen hall,
> By his dead smile I knew we stood in Hell.

Across a large body of war poems, Owen (1893–1918) unremittingly draws a portrait of a world shattered and out of joint; and here his rhymes, as if in sympathy, refuse to chime properly or to become full. In technical terms, pararhymes are formed by the sound sequence consonant–vowel–consonant, where the two consonant sounds are the same but the vowel sound different. Examples of pararhyming words might thus be 'hat' and 'hot' or 'raid' and 'road'. In Owen's poem, 'escaped' and 'scooped' are rhymed together, as are 'groined' and 'groaned'; indeed, all the rhymes (leaving aside the strange 'eyes' / 'bless' rhyme) share the same format of identical consonantal sounds separated by divergent vowel sounds. Such rhymes are probably best seen not as a muted or partial versions of full rhymes but as belonging to an opposite principle. Traditionally, rhymes establish a strong sense of sameness and uniformity at the line-ending, whereas the statement made by Owen's rhymes is one of divergence, things falling apart rather than coming together. In this sense, a pararhyme can act not as a partial rhyme but as a negation of the very principle of rhyme; and it is apt that Owen should use this in a poem condemning war as a negation of life.

3.7 SOME INDETERMINACIES OF RHYME

We naturally tend to think of rhyme as an absolute: we may not understand what a poem is saying, but we suppose that we can state categorically whether or not it rhymes. Moreover, we tend to associate rhyme with formality: the presence of rhyme in a poem will provide a principle of strictness and regularity regardless of what other effects the work contains. What we want to suggest here is that these assumptions (while perhaps true enough in general) should not be taken as applying to all rhyming poems. For one thing, whether or not a poem actually contains rhyme can on occasions be teasingly ambiguous. As an example of a poem where rhyme figures in this furtive way, we propose taking Dylan Thomas's 'The Force that through the Green Fuse Drives the Flower'. Here are the first two stanzas:

> The force that through the green fuse drives the flower
> Drives my green age; that blasts the roots of trees
> Is my destroyer.
> And I am dumb to tell the crooked rose
> My youth is bent by the same wintry fever.
>
> The force that drives the water through the rocks
> Drives my red blood; that dries the mouthing streams
> Turns mine to wax.
> And I am dumb to mouth unto my veins
> How at the mountain spring the same mouth sucks.

When we have presented this poem to students, our experience has been that they have found nothing to say about rhyme because they see the poem as being non-rhyming. Yet we think this is not merely wrong but the opposite of the case, since Thomas is in fact very resourceful in mobilising the line-ending. We interpret the first stanza as rhyming *ababa*, and the second *ababa*. The 'a' rhymes in the first stanza are all feminine, falling on 'flower', 'destroyer' and 'fever': the fact that they fall on non-stressed syllables indeed makes for one reason why the unvigilant reader can fail to notice them at all. But an even more vestigial rhyme comes with the placement of '<u>trees</u>' against '<u>rose</u>'. This might not strike you as a rhyme at all, but in fact it conforms to the category of the pararhyme (as defined above): 'rees' and 'rose' share the same initial consonant sounds separated by a different vowel sound. Thomas's second stanza admits an even more remote sort of rhyme, for which (as far as we are aware) there is no technical term. This links together the three words of identical-sounding ending: 'rocks', 'wax' and 'sucks'. These are not pararhymes (which require two shared consonant sounds) and should perhaps instead be seen as a form of consonance. Yet we normally think of consonance as an effect within a line rather than one that occupies the line-ending; and its position here means that it masquerades as a curious sort of half-rhyme.

Thomas's poem is a good example of how on occasions the rhyming or non-rhyming status of a poem can offer a puzzle, to be resolved only through a subjective act of interpretation. Moreover, just as whether the existence of a rhyme in a poem can be misty, so too can the related issue of whether a poem might be said to have a rhyme scheme. We generally assume that when rhyme occurs in a poem, it does so in an orderly and regular way. So if we take the Spenserian stanza in *The Faerie Queene*, we can say that its rhyme scheme is *ababbcbcc*: in other words, every line-ending rhymes with at least one other, and the rhymes are exclusive to just three different sounds. But, at a higher level, the regularity of the stanza guarantees the regularity of the whole poem, since the same rhyme scheme is duplicated throughout the thousands of stanzas out of which Spenser's massive poem is constructed. In recent times, poets have increasingly been attracted to what we shall call 'free rhyming', where a poem contains rhymes but where these are not integrated into any overarching rhyme scheme. A good example of a poem where rhyme occurs on this irregular basis is T. S. Eliot's *The Waste Land*. Beneath is a passage from the third part, 'The Fire-Sermon', which depicts a clumsy and passionless sexual liaison between a typist and her lover, the events being watched over (and participated in) by Tiresias, who assimilates all the male and female characters in the poem:

> I Tiresias, old man with wrinkled dugs
> Perceived the scene, and foretold the rest –
> I too awaited the expected guest.
> He, the young man carbuncular, arrives,
> A small house agent's clerk, with one bold stare,
> One of the low on whom assurance sits
> As a silk hat on a Bradford millionaire.
> The time is now propitious, as he guesses,
> The meal is ended, she is bored and tired,

> Endeavours to engage her in caresses
> Which still are unreproved, if undesired.
> Flushed and decided, he assaults at once;
> Exploring hands encounter no defence;
> His vanity requires no response,
> And makes a welcome of indifference.
> (And I Tiresias have foresuffered all
> Enacted on this same divan or bed;
> I who have sat by Thebes below the wall
> And walked among the lowest of the dead.)
> Bestows one final patronising kiss,
> And gropes his way, finding the stairs unlit …

If we were to express the rhyme 'scheme' of the passage, it would be as follows: *abbcdedfgfghihijkjkjklm*. A more illuminating way, however, of analysing how rhyme functions is by dividing the passage, on the basis of the placement of full stops, into its constituent grammatical units. The first three lines, looked at in this light, form one unit, consisting of a non-rhyming line followed by a couplet. The next four lines (from full stop to full stop) again constitute a distinct unit, in which the second and fourth lines rhyme while the others are non-rhyming. This verse-structure is called a quatrain, though the term is sometimes reserved for four-line verse-units in which *all* the lines rhyme. The next three units, in any event, do conform to this stricter definition, where the first line rhymes with the third and the second with the fourth. The section finally ends with two unrhyming lines ending on 'kiss' and 'unlit'. The passage, as a whole, is thus a mish-mash of different rhyming techniques. Some lines fail to rhyme altogether; there is one quatrain rhyming *abcb* and three others rhyming *abab*; and a rhyming couplet appears near the beginning. Whereas for earlier poets, rhyme was a device for importing structure and regularity into their verse, for Eliot it is a device to which he resorts more casually and opportunistically. Some parts of his poem rhyme in quite a strict way; others are entirely free of rhyming. The poem as a whole can be said to rhyme, but it would be misleading for anyone to claim that it actually had a rhyme *scheme*.

3.8   RHYME AND MEANING

We hope this chapter will have introduced you to some of the complexities of rhyme in poetry. In particular, it should have brought home that rhyme is not a single phenomenon but an umbrella term for several sorts of sound effect; moreover, the very detection of a rhyme, or of a larger scheme of rhymes into which it fits, can depend on an impression or an interpretation. We want to finish, however, by moving away from the mere cataloguing of different sorts of rhyme and discuss instead how rhyme can aggregate or express meaning in a piece of verse. Does rhyme have the flexibility, like some other sound effects we discussed earlier, to mimic or reinforce the content of a piece of writing? To consider this important issue, we propose taking a section from *Richard II* Act IV Scene i where Richard is on the verge of resigning his crown to the usurper, Henry Bolingbroke:

RICH.	To do what service am I sent for hither?	
YORK.	To do that office of thine own good will	
	Which tired majesty did make thee offer:	
	The resignation of thy state and crown	
	To Henry Bolingbroke.	180
RICH.	Give me the crown. Here, cousin, seize the crown.	
	Here, cousin,	
	On this side my hand, and on that side thine.	
	Now is this golden crown like a deep well	
	That owes two buckets, filling one another,	185
	The emptier ever dancing in the air,	
	The other down, unseen, and full of water.	
	That bucket down and full of tears am I,	
	Drinking my griefs, whilst you mount up on high.	
BOL.	I thought you had been willing to resign.	190
RICH.	My crown I am, but still my griefs are mine.	
	You may my glories and my state depose,	
	But not my griefs; still am I king of those.	
BOL.	Part of your cares you give me with your crown.	
RICH.	Your cares set up do not pluck my cares down.	195
	My care is loss of care, by old care done;	
	Your care is gain of care, by new care won.	
	The cares I give, I have, though given away,	
	They 'tend the crown, yet still with me they stay.	
BOL.	Are you contented to resign the crown?	200
RICH.	Ay, no; no, ay; for I must nothing be.	
	Therefore no 'no', for I resign to thee.	
	Now, mark me how I will undo myself.	
	I give this heavy weight from off my head ...	

The passage conveys vividly the great upheaval about to occur in the lives of the two men, in their relationship and in the kingdom at large: the king's subject is about to become king, and the king to be reduced to a mere subject. This exchanging of roles and identities is encapsulated in Shakespeare's prolific use of pronouns. Between lines 188 and 195, the run of pronouns is as follows: 'I', 'my', 'you', 'I', 'you', 'My', 'I', 'my', 'mine', 'You', 'my', 'my', 'my', 'I', 'your', 'you', 'me', 'your', 'Your', and 'my'. Twenty pronouns are introduced into a mere eight lines of verse, all of these either first- or second-person pronominal forms, as if at this moment, only two people materially exist in the world: Richard and Bolingbroke. Shakespeare is trying to capture a moment of absolute equilibrium in the transference of power, in which for a moment neither man can truly be said to be king or subject, in which the identities of both of them dissolve into indeterminacy. In visual terms, this is conveyed by the fact that from line 183 ('On this side my hand, and on that side thine'), the crown is held (literally) by both men at the same time, a stasis that lasts probably until line 204 when Richard finally concedes his resignation: 'I give this heavy weight from off my head'. What we want to argue here is that our sense of the two men's being locked together in this moment of constitutional *impasse* is expressed in formal terms through Shakespeare's use of rhyme. In the first part of the passage, there are a couple of (possibly inadvertent) feminine rhymes ('hither' with 'offer'; 'another' with 'water'), but the rhymes only become signal from line 188. Initially, Richard produces a couplet of his own (rhyming 'I' with 'high'), but Bolingbroke next begins a rhyme which he completes ('resign' with 'mine'). Richard then produces a rhyming couplet of his own before Bolingbroke initiates a rhyme which it is again Richard's prerogative to complete. So just as the men are united in terms of each (both literally and figuratively) having one hand on the crown, so they are bound together phonologically by the sharing of rhymes.

Yet it is not only that Richard and Bolingbroke rhyme together that is significant; for it is worth looking at the exact words that compose their rhymes. In the first instance, Bolingbroke's 'resign' (relinquishing possession) rhymes with Richard's 'mine' (asserting possession); in the second, Bolingbroke's 'crown' (a symbol of ascendancy) rhymes with Richard's 'down'. In fact, if one takes the full sequence of rhyme words from line 188 to 199, one can see that they summarise the entire drama of rise and fall, seizure and dispossession, unfolding before the audience: 'I', 'high', 'resign', 'mine', 'depose', 'those', 'crown', 'down', 'done', 'won', 'stay' and 'away'. In this sense, the rhymes provide a running commentary on, and summation of, the action being played out between the two characters. Rhyme, here, is not incidental or merely 'ornamental'; it is alive to the issues that are driving the play. Of course, in most works, rhymes are not used in a way that is so intimate with the action being described; but in the hands of a skilled rhymer, like other sound effects, they can be used to express the themes and issues of a literary work.

3.9 EXERCISES

Below is a poem by the current (2009–) British Poet Laureate, Carol Ann Duffy (b. 1955), who was born in a poor district of Glasgow but moved to England with her family when she was six. She began writing at an early age and has produced numerous poetry collections, plays and books for children. The poem below comes from her 1999 collection *The World's Wife*, which explores the lives of famous or notorious men through the perspective of women closely associated with them. The collection aims to recover the historically marginalised female point of view. The poem beneath concerns Sisyphus, the King of Corinth, who in Greek legend was punished for tricking the Gods by being compelled to spend his time in the underworld ceaselessly pushing a boulder up a steep hill. Excruciatingly for Sisyphus, the stone would always roll back down before reaching the top. The poem is particularly distinctive for its manipulation of various kinds of sound effect.

Mrs Sisyphus

That's him pushing the stone up a hill, the jerk.
I call it a stone – it's nearer the size of a kirk.
When he first started out, it just used to irk,
but now it incenses me, and him, the absolute berk.
I could do something vicious to him with a dirk.

Think of the perks, he says.
What use is a perk, I shriek,
when you haven't the time to pop open a cork
or go for so much as a walk in the park?
He's a dork.
Folk flock from miles around just to gawk.
They think it's a quirk,
a bit of a lark.
A load of old bollocks is nearer the mark.
He might as well bark
at the moon –
that feckin' stone's no sooner up
than it's rolling back
all the way down.
And what does he say?
Mustn't shirk –
keen as a hawk,
lean as a shark
Mustn't shirk!

1. Try to list the full range of sound effects, including orthodox and non-orthodox types of rhyme as well as different techniques of alliteration. What do you think the poem gains by these techniques? Think about what Duffy

is doing at the beginning and end of lines and also in the main body of her lines.

2. How would you gauge the tone of the poem? If you find it amusing, in what way is it so?

3. Experiment with writing a poem of your own which, like Duffy's, is structured throughout by the repetition of the same or similar sounds.

4. Try to write a poem in which one character, like Mrs Sisyphus, comments irreverently on the behaviour of another, or in which the main speaking voice belongs to someone who could be seen as marginal to the action.

NOTE

1. For a detailed discussion of the poem, see Anne Cluysenaar, *Introduction to Literary Stylistics* (London, 1976).

4

Metre and rhythm

Here are two words with the same meaning:'prosody' and 'metrics'. Both mean the study of the art of versification, in particular the analysis of metre, rhythm, rhyme and stanza. Rhyme and stanzaic form are discussed elsewhere in this book, so this chapter confines itself to the study of metre and rhythm, the sound–patterns evident in the aural reception of poetry. In fact, as far as poetry is concerned, rhythm and metre are difficult concepts to differentiate one from another, and many critics use them as synonymous or as easily interchangeable terms. This is not to deny that the two concepts are distinguishable in the overall literary context: 'metre' is a term which is confined to the study of poetry, whilst 'rhythm' is a looser concept, with a significance outwith the formal boundaries of verse. One can certainly analyse the rhythm of a poem, but one can also speak of the rhythm of a prose essay, of a piece of oratory, or, for that matter, of the 'rhythmical' sound made by a moving steam engine. Poetry is but a specialised form of language, and all language has rhythm; the difference is that poetry – free verse excepted – has a discernible rhythmic regularity. What sets poetry apart is the *consistency* of its patterning. Poets can – and do – deviate from their 'base metre' for poetic effect (as discussed below), but it is this regularity of sound effect which is one of the key distinctions between poetry and prose. It is helpful to think of metre as a subset of the larger concept of rhythm and, consequently, to consider formal rhythmical analysis of recurring poetic sound-patterning as indistinguishable from metrical analysis. Thus metre is a specific form of rhythm, and might best be defined as 'the measurable sound-pattern evident, in varying degrees of regularity, in a line of poetry'.

4.1 COMPLEXITIES IN THE STUDY OF METRE

We must preface our discussion of metre by acknowledging the fact that prosodological analysis is not generally seen as an activity likely to warm a student's heart. This is because the supposed 'rules' of prosody so often seem to be flaunted. Why, the student wonders, does the poet frequently deviate from the formal structure – or 'frame' – of the poem? Why does there often appear to be a syllable 'missing' – or an 'extra' syllable – at the end of a verse line? Why does a poem which manifests a regular pattern of stress occasionally deviate from it, say at the start of a given line? Why, in short, is the metrical regularity evident in one line so often absent from the next? These are good questions and we shall attempt to answer them all. In so doing, we hope to demonstrate that there is no real reason why metrical study should be seen as inordinately complicated. After one has mastered a few key terms and become familiar with the commonest metrical forms, the study of metre is actually far less daunting than it might appear at first sight.

One might reasonably ask *why* the analysis of metre is seen as such a challenging and complex discipline. The frequent variations from the base metre mentioned above are partially responsible; however, this impression is also attributable to the fact that metrical analysis seems rather over-generously stocked with imposing words drawn from classical languages. There are also historical and linguistic complexities attendant to the study of metre. The reader of pre-twentieth-century poetry has to be aware of the fact that the English language itself changes and that the pronunciation of individual words today is sometimes different from what it was in previous centuries (and radically different from what it was when the poet Chaucer was writing). Thus the conventional stress-pattern evident in the contemporary pronunciation of a given word may not be the same as it was, for instance, in the sixteenth century. In addition, sound-patterning is also to a certain extent dependent upon accent and habits of pronunciation which can vary amongst different kinds of readers. Not everyone pronounces every word in the same way and, mercifully, not every reader has the same accent. Similarly, poets themselves may have national or regional antecedents and ways of speaking which inform their metrical composition. An American or South African poet writing in English does not always work from the same pronunciatory base as an English person and nor does every English poet conform to a uniform standard; as the Yorkshire poet Tony Harrison (b. 1937) famously points out in his poem 'Them and [uz]', for the north-countryman Wordsworth 'matter' and 'water' were full rhymes. Furthermore, two people with a similar accent are perfectly capable of disagreeing over the due emphasis which should be placed upon individual words within a given line of poetry. The underlying problem here is that we expect to find metrical analysis, with its pseudo-scientific jargon, to be an exact science. And it's not. While it is unlikely that one can generate the same number of metrical accounts of a given line of poetry as the number of readings which critical ingenuity can provide for the meaning of a literary work, it is perfectly possible to generate two – and sometimes more – equally plausible metrical accounts of a line of verse. A contentious line from *Paradise Lost* will not be interpreted prosodologically from as wide a range of positions as, say, the debates over the significance of Satan in the poem; however, critics can, and do, quarrel over the way in which a particular line can be scanned. Prosodological analysis of metre, like so much else in literary criticism, is to a certain extent a matter of opinion. Metre gestures towards objective scientific analysis but remains an art with a significant degree of subjectivity within it.

4.2   THE KEY METRICAL UNITS

The core terms in the study of metre are **syllable**, **foot** and **stress**. A syllable is a word, or portion of a word, made by a single effort of the organs of speech. It either forms a word or is an element of a longer word; thus, in the previous sentence, 'a', 'is', 'word' are examples of single-syllable words (monosyllables), whilst the two-syllable words 'portion', 'single' and 'organs' are disyllabic and 'syllable' itself polysyllabic (that is, a word containing three or more syllables). A line of verse, like all other examples of language in use, subdivides into syllables. It can contain almost any practical number of syllables up to eighteen (though longer lines than this, though freakishly unusual, have been used). However, lines in English poetry most commonly consist of eight or ten syllables:

> O what can ail thee knight-at-arms, (Keats)

> I wandered lonely as a cloud (Wordsworth)

> And trust me not at all or all in all (Tennyson)

> Bitter constraint, erroneous and forlorn (Pope)

Whilst a syllable might be described as a naturally occurring physiological event, a 'foot' is a term constructed purely for the purposes of prosody (like language itself, metrics is a conventional system of description). Syllables gathered together in twos and threes form metrical units called 'feet'. A metrical foot pays no attention to the boundaries of words. It can contain two or even three words or, on the other hand, rather less than one. It is important to register at this point that it is the foot which is the basic measurement of English metrical analysis rather than the word or the syllable. Most feet contain two or three syllables which demonstrate particular patterns of emphasis or 'stress' (these patterns and the various kinds of feet are discussed below). The two-syllable feet (which are by far the most common in English verse) are 'disyllabic' and the three-syllable feet 'trisyllabic' (there are four-syllable feet, but these are so rare as not to concern us here). The first two lines here are made up of disyllabic feet, whilst the second two are made up of trisyllabic feet:

> The sound | must seem | an ech|o to | the sense (Pope)

> Deep in | the sha|dy sad|ness of | a vale (Keats)

> I am slain | by a fair | cruel maid (Shakespeare)

> O'er the vine-|cover'd hills | and gay reg|ions of France (Roscoe)

Feet gathered together in various numbers (but most commonly in groups of four or five) form 'lines' (the old-fashioned term 'verses' is still occasionally used).

Each individual foot, as well as containing a given number of syllables, has a characteristic and particular pattern of emphasis or 'stress' (these patterns are discussed in some detail below). Stress is, simply enough, the emphasis placed upon a given syllable in the reading of a line. Another way of thinking about stress is to think of the stressed syllables in a verse line as the place where the beat falls. You may find the term 'accent' used as synonymous with stress in some critical works; however, we use 'stress' as the more suggestive word and because the word 'accent' has overtones of the way in which people speak as well as the way in which they place emphasis in reading poetry. Some syllables in a verse line are sounded more forcefully than others; that is, some are 'stressed' and others 'unstressed' (again, the terms 'accented' and 'unaccented' are also used). In this, poetry follows the patterns of ordinary speech, of course. Take the word 'forcefully' itself; whether it is used in everyday conversation or in poetry, the first of the three syllables is sounded more emphatically than the second and third. Again, it is the regularity of stress-patterning and the poet's systematic arrangement of the conventional stresses already evident in the wider linguistic system which sets poetry apart from the more usual manifestations of the English language.

To illustrate stress-patterning, take these lines from Thomas Gray's 'Elegy Written in a Country Church-Yard'. Read them aloud and note where the stresses occur as you do so:

> On some fond breast the parting soul relies,
>   Some pious drops the closing eye requires;
> E'en from the tomb the voice of nature cries,
>   E'en in our Ashes live their wonted fires.

You will have noted as you read this quatrain that there is a discernible pattern, a certain regularity of stress in the stanza. The lines very often feature unstressed syllables followed by stressed syllables. Here are the same lines marked according to the stresses placed on each syllable. The technical term for this process of marking lines of verse according to the sound-pattern within them is 'graphic scansion' (in contradistinction to the scansion of rhyme scheme, into *abba* and so on, discussed above). You should note that divisions between feet are marked | and that each stressed syllable has the symbol ⁄ above it and each unstressed syllable the symbol ˣ:

On some | fond breast | the par|ting soul | relies,

Some pi|ous drops | the clos|ing eye | requires;

E'en from | the tomb | the voice | of na|ture cries,

E'en in | our Ash|es live | their won|ted fires.

The regular, but not unvarying, emphatic pattern of verse lines (in this case an 'iambic' pattern of an unstressed syllable followed by a stressed syllable) is known as the underlying 'frame' of the poem (though you might see it referred to as the 'base'). As we stated earlier, this regularity and recurrence is one of the key distinctions between poetry and prose. To illustrate the difference between poetic regularity of stress and that found in prose, it is useful to examine the emphatic stresses of a passage of prose (for it is perfectly possible, though rather pointless, to analyse prose in a similar fashion). Take Francis Bacon's fine meditation on mortality in his essay 'Of Death':

Men fear death, as children fear to go in the dark; and as that natural fear in children is increased with tales so is the other. Certainly, the contemplation of death, as the wages of sin, and passage to another world, is holy and religious; but the fear of it, as a tribute due unto nature, is weak.

Here too the music of the prose is largely dependent upon stress. However, it is clear that Bacon's prose lacks the regularity of beat evident in Gray's poetry. Free verse apart, poetry read aloud is characterised by recurring, patterned stress and conditions the ear to the anticipation of that recurrence. Hence the critical division between the regular 'metre' of poetry and the irregular 'cadence' of prose.

Methods of metrical analysis which pay sole attention to stress rather than syllable-counting are called 'accentual systems'. On the other hand, those prosodological systems which are primarily focused upon the number of syllables in the line (rather than the length of the line or the stresses within it) are known as 'syllabic' systems. As we have seen, modern English metrical analysis addresses both stress and syllable. It focuses upon the pattern – and variations from that pattern – of a verse line consisting of a standard number of stresses in a line of a standard number of syllables (with all syllables, whether stressed or unstressed, being counted). Hence English metrics is a mixture of the accentual and syllabic systems and is sometimes referred to as an 'accentual-syllabic' system.

The accentual-syllabic methodology is by no means the only possible way of addressing poetry. Indeed, English poets have not always paid as much attention to the number of syllables in the line as is evident in the post-Chaucerian tradition. The earliest English verse in Old English (and that in alliterative Middle English) is accentual, measured according to the number of stresses in lines where the overall number of syllables is immaterial. Other metrical systems, modern French prosody, for instance, are syllabic, primarily focused on syllabic counting. Furthermore, syllable counting and stress-patterning have little importance in the study of classical poetry, which is measured metrically according to the length of a given syllable (the 'quantitative' measure). Despite this, English metrists have nonetheless imported the terminology applied to Greek and Roman poetry. Thus 'iambic' when used of classical poetry means a short syllable followed by a long one, but when applied to English verse means an unstressed syllable followed by a stressed one. This importing of terms designed to address one body of poetry into a system focused upon another which proceeds on an entirely different basis is somewhat unsatisfactory. However, this discourse is still in common use and, as such, needs to be understood.

4.3 METRICAL REGULARITY AND VARIANCE

Lines which conform exactly to the stress-pattern of the frame and contain the 'correct' number of syllables are known as 'regular' lines. Thus, for example, Gray's 'For them no more the blazing hearth shall burn,' and Milton's 'Of that forbidden tree, whose mortal taste' are examples of regular iambic lines (that is, ten syllable lines with five two-syllable feet which invariably 'rise' to the beat on the second syllable). However, such uniformity of stress is actually the exception rather than the rule. Unfortunately for students wishing to write impressively on metre, who are forced to keep their metrical wits about them, but fortunately for the variety and music of English poetry, verse is rarely as regular as this. Though most poems have a discernible and conventional frame, the poet will feel free to deviate from it to give variation of sound-patterning and to suit the theme of a line (a process of metrical variation often referred to as 'modulation'). Poets do not complete a professional qualification in prosody before launching their careers and neither do they sit down to write with the notion of metrical consistency foremost in their minds. Even that brilliant metrical innovator Tennyson was accused by the poet Coleridge of launching his career with poetry composed purely by instinct (the usual phrase is 'by ear') rather than with poetry informed by an immersion in technicalities: 'The misfortune is, that he has begun to write verses without very well understanding what metre is'.

Thus a poet will generally have a particular frame in mind, but will deviate from it like a musician extemporising around a basic rhythmical beat. Returning to Gray's 'Elegy' illustrates this point. Even here, in a poem noted for its metrical regularity, the poet feels free to deviate from the frame:

> Perhaps in this neglected spot is laid
> Some heart once pregnant with celestial fire,
> Hands, that the rod of empire may have sway'd,
> Or wak'd to extasy the living lyre.

Read the third line aloud. Here the stress falls upon the first syllable of the first foot rather than the second syllable. The tongue naturally emphasises the word 'Hands' rather than the word which we might expect from the conventions of the metrical frame ('that'): 'Hánds, thãt the rod of empire may have sway'd'. Rendering the line regular murders its sense and challenges the tongue: 'Hañds, thát the rod of empire may have sway'd'. Gray's line is metrically irregular; he has inserted a falling foot at the start of his line (a 'trochee', see below). The metrical term for this modulatory device is 'substitution'. Technically speaking, Gray's verse demonstrates 'trochaic substitution in the iambic pentameter acatalectic'. We hope that by the end of this chapter you will be familiar enough with metrical terminology to understand what the words 'trochaic substitution in the iambic pentameter acatalectic' actually mean, but for now, setting technical language aside, the key fact to be recognised is that the poet has departed from the frame for poetic effect. The student who can recognise irregularity and, indeed, appreciate how common modulation is in English poetry, has made a giant step in metrical study. Armed with this knowledge, the reader of poetry who has mastered the basic concepts of metre will no longer be bemused to discover that most poems which have a given or recognisable metre contain lines which don't fit the frame. And why should they, all things

considered? Poems are not metronomes and most verse would sound mechanical if it was forced into absolute and monotonous regularity. Furthermore,
the most accomplished poets are not averse to metrical experimentation and it
is from a rhythmical semi-lawlessness that poetic innovation most often comes.

4.4 'MISSING' AND 'EXTRA' SYLLABLES

Apart from the substitution of a different foot into a verse line otherwise in a
standard metre, the most common metrical irregularity found in English poetry
is when a line appears to be too long or too short, say when a pentameter,
generally of ten syllables, includes lines of nine or eleven syllables. Inevitably,
there are Greek labels for such poetic devices. The line where the final foot
conforms to the prescribed number of syllables is 'acatalectic', whereas the
line where the last foot is short by a syllable is 'catalectic' (alternative and far
less tooth-breaking terms for acatalectic and catalectic are 'complete' and
'curtailed'). Oddly enough, these adjectives – unlike most others in the English
language – are used *after* the word which they describe. Thus one writes of the
'tetrameter catalectic' rather than the 'catalectic tetrameter'.

A line which lacks more than one syllable than that suggested by the frame
is 'brachycatalectic' and a line with an extra syllable 'hypercatalectic'. Thus, for
example, in the blank verse, ten-syllable unrhymed line, you will often see
deviation in number of syllables, most notably in hypercatalectic fashion:

> But peace to vain regrets! We see but darkly (Wordsworth)

> To be, or not to be, that is the question (Shakespeare)

Whilst the extra syllable is most common in the iambic line, the curtailed line
tends to be most common in trochaic verse. Shakespeare's octosyllabic poem
'The Phoenix and the Turtle' demonstrates the catalectic line in action:

> Reason, in itself confounded,
> Saw division grow together
> To themselves, yet either neither
> Simple were so well compounded
>
> That it cried 'How true a twain
> Seemeth this concordant one!
> Love hath reason, reason none,
> In what parts can so remain'.

Here every line in the first stanza is acatalectic, whilst each line in the second
is catalectic. Students confronted by lines which appear to have a syllable

missing have been known to scratch their heads at these 'defective feet'. In fact, the term itself is misleading, given that it implies that the likes of Shakespeare and Shelley are innumerate, misplacing syllables like amateurish car mechanics forgetting to bolt on a hub-cap. Truncating a foot is a matter of poetic choice rather than poetic incompetence.

4.5   FEET

We shall now concentrate on the key rhythmical terminology used in metrical analysis, beginning with the various kinds of foot. There are seven principal feet in English verse and we shall address each individually. In descending order of importance, these are the iamb, trochee, dactyl, anapaest, spondee, pyrrhic and amphibrach. The first four provide the basis for entire poems, whilst the last three are used only for modulatory substitution rather than to furnish the base metre of individual poems. There are other kinds of feet (cretic, ionic and so on) than the ones addressed below and, for reference purposes, the Glossary of poetical terms below includes the rarest ones. However, our focus in this chapter is on the most common types of foot.

As stated above, feet have two or three syllables; though some metricians have argued that there are such things as four-syllable feet, these are so rare that we need not address them here. Of the main feet, the iamb, trochee, spondee and pyrrhic are disyllabic and the amphibrach, anapaest and dactyl trisyllabic. Poems where the frame is disyllabic are said to be composed in 'double' (or 'duple') metre and those where the frame is trisyllabic in 'triple' metre. There are two kinds of duple metre: iambic metre and trochaic metre.

4.6   IAMBIC METRE

Until the turn to free verse in the first half of the twentieth century, iambic verse, in its various manifestations, was perhaps the most common and certainly the most significant metrical form in English poetry. An iambic foot (marked $^{x/}$ in graphic scansion) is in rising rhythm, consisting of an unstressed syllable followed by a stressed one, as in the words 'today' and 'compare'. This basic metrical unit (a single two-syllable foot in rising rhythm) is known as an 'iamb' or, less frequently, an 'iambus'. Lines which are predominantly written in iambs are consequently called 'iambics' and poems which are mainly written in iambic lines are thus 'iambic poems'. Here are some examples of regular iambic lines:

> Come live with me and be my love (Marlowe)
>
> Of that forbidden tree, whose mortal taste (Milton)
>
> Can man be free if woman be a slave? (Shelley)

Iambic verse, most notably in the ten-syllable, five-foot 'pentameter' line (which is often referred to as the 'heroic' line) is the metre of much of the most notable English verse. It is used in many of the principal stanzaic forms discussed above: the rhyme royal, *ottava rima* and, the final line apart, the Spenserian. Rhyme royal is a stanza made up of seven lines of iambic pentameter, as in Shakespeare's *The Rape of Lucrece*:

> But she hath lost a dearer thing than life,
> And he hath won what he would lose again.
> This forcèd league doth force a further strife,
> This momentary joy breeds months of pain;
> This hot desire converts to cold disdain.
>   Pure chastity is rifled of her store,
>   And lust, the thief, far poorer than before.

The eight-line *ottava rima* also has an iambic pentameter base. The great master of the English manifestations of the stanza is Lord Byron:

> 'Tis known, at least it should be, that throughout
>   All countries of the Catholic persuasion,
> Some weeks before Shrove Tuesday comes about,
>   The people take their fill of recreation,
> And buy repentance, ere they grow devout,
>   However high their rank, or low their station,
> With fiddling, feasting, dancing, masquing,
> And other things which may be had for asking. (*Beppo*)

The Spenserian, as seen in James Thomson's *The Castle of Indolence* (1748) consists of eight lines of iambic pentameter followed by a six-foot iambic (an 'alexandrine').

> A pleasing land of drowsyhed it was:
> Of dreams that wave before the half-shut eye;
> And of gay castles in the clouds that pass,
> For ever flushing round a summer sky:
> There eke the soft delights, that witchingly
> Instil a wanton sweetness through the breast,
> And the calm pleasures always hovered nigh;
> But whate'er smacked of noyance, or unrest,
> Was far far off expelled from this delicious nest.

The importance of the heroic line to key stanzaic forms notwithstanding, the two most important iambic pentameter metres are the heroic couplet and blank verse. Heroic couplets are rhymed iambic pentameters, and are generally continuously printed rather than set in stanzaic form. They are perhaps used to greatest effect by Alexander Pope:

> What dire offence from amorous causes springs,
> What mighty contests rise from trivial things, (*The Rape of the Lock*)

> Know then thyself, presume not God to scan,
> The proper study of mankind is man. (*An Essay on Criticism*)

Readers of Pope's extended poems in couplets will be aware that a Popean line rarely runs on ('overflows') to the next without pausing, a pause signalled by punctuation of various kinds. This tendency is known as 'end-stopping':

> Hope humbly then; with trembling pinions soar;
> Wait the great teacher death, and God adore.
> What future bliss, he gives not thee to know,
> But gives that hope to be thy blessing now,
> Hope springs eternal in the human breast;
> Man never *is*, but always *to be* blest:
> The soul, uneasy and confined from home,
> Rests and expatiates in a life to come. (*An Essay on Man*)

Here there is uniform end-stopping in each line. Furthermore, at the end of the second line of each couplet both syntax and sense reach an even clearer end-stopped pause than at the end of the first line. The couplets are thus said to be 'closed'; indeed, each couplet would also still retain sense and vigour after being abstracted and quoted separately. Pope's couplets use 'separation', that is, they resemble self-contained units; this gives the verse an epigrammatic force entirely appropriate to the sententious subject–matter of his poem.

The above notwithstanding, end-stopped lines do not provide the only pauses in a line of verse. Another key metrical device is the break within a line, or 'caesura', which the *Oxford English Dictionary* defines thus: 'In English prosody: A pause or breathing-place about the middle of a metrical line, generally indicated by a pause in the sense'. In graphic scansion, the caesura is marked thus: ‖ . In the Popean couplet, the caesura is often found at the end of the second foot. These are the concluding lines of Pope's *Messiah*:

> The seas shall waste, the skies in smoke decay,
> Rocks fall to dust, and mountains melt away;
> But fix'd his word, his saving power remains; –
> Thy realm for ever lasts, thy own Messiah reigns.

The verse here is uniformly end-stopped, but also contains caesuras in each line. In the first three heroic lines, they are in the standard position at the end of the second foot. However, in the concluding line, Pope has substituted a twelve-syllable, six-beat alexandrine line for the usual pentameter and thus places the break later in the (longer) line.You will also have noted the trochaic substitution at the start of the second line; Pope, who was not infrequently attacked by Romantic period poets as a monotonous versifier, is actually a highly resourceful user of modulation. And even when he is working purely within the formal discipline of the regular couplet, Pope achieves a variety of effect within its constraints, managing to make it appear as unforced and natural in conversational verse and acidulous satire as it seems in his meditative or critical writing.

Blank verse – continuous heroics which are unrhymed – is, if anything, even more important in canonical English verse. It is the line of Shakespeare's verse drama, of Wordsworth's *The Prelude* and of Milton's *Paradise Lost*:

> The world was all before them, where to choose
> Their place of rest, with Providence their guide;
> They hand in hand with wandering steps and slow
> Through Eden took their solitary way. (Milton)

Unlike the post-Popean couplet which, even in its less separated forms in the work of the likes of Samuel Johnson, tends to self-containment, blank verse is more expansive and allows poets to build long argument (whether sustained or digressive). And blank verse is commonly seen as echoing the patterns of rhetorical speech, making it an appropriate vehicle for verse drama, as in the blank verse used in Shakespeare's plays. Most importantly of all, because it admits of almost every kind of modulatory deviation from the frame and permits a smoother overrunning of lines than the couplet, poets see in unrhymed heroics an unparalleled metrical flexibility. For example, here are the first of lines of the poem generally seen as the masterpiece of English non-dramatic blank verse, Milton's *Paradise Lost*:

> Of man's first disobedience, and the fruit
> Of that forbidden tree, whose mortal taste
> Brought death into the world, and all our woe,
> With loss of Eden, till one greater man
> Restore us, and regain the blissful seat,
> Sing heavenly muse, that on the secret top
> Of Oreb, or of Sinai, didst inspire
> That shepherd, who first taught the chosen seed,
> In the beginning how the heavens and the earth
> Rose out of chaos; or if Sion hill
> Delight thee more, and Siloa's brook that flowed
> Fast by the oracle of God; I thence

> Invoke thy aid to my adventurous song,
> That with no middle flight intends to soar
> Above the Aonian mount, while it pursues
> Things unattempted yet in prose or rhyme.

Here the invigorating flexibility of blank verse is well illustrated. The entirely regular second line is actually the exception rather than the rule and the base metre simply provides the skeletal framework for the sinewy flesh of Milton's poetry. The poet feels free to deviate from the frame whenever the sense of his lines dictates and to offer musical variation from the potential dreariness of unmodulated poetry. There are fewer end-stopped lines than overflowing lines; from the first line onwards Milton frequently employs overrunning verse. Furthermore, his breaks are often much later in the line than in the Popean caesura, delayed until after the seventh syllable in line 1 and after the eighth in line 12 (given that the caesura is defining as falling in the middle of a line, the words 'break' or 'pause' are more appropriate in the metrical analysis of blank verse). Nor is the breaking uniformly limited to one internal pause per line: line 7 offers an example of the characteristically Miltonic two-break line and line 14 has no pause of any kind. Line 15 is hyperbrachic and there are several examples of inversions of rhythm, or 'trochaic substitution' to use the technical term (as in lines 6, 10, 14 and 16). And though the precise details need not concern us here, these lines also contain examples of the occasional modulatory feet (the spondee and pyrrhic) discussed below.

As noted in the previous paragraph, our extract from Milton's poem contains several examples of overrunning. In general, pithy heroic couplets have a higher percentage of end-stopped lines than is found in unrhymed heroics. Poets using blank verse not infrequently let the sense of one line overrun into the next:

> These, as they change, Almighty Father! these
> Are but the varied God. The rolling year
> Is full of thee. (Thomson)

>   that serene and blessed mood,
> In which the affections gently lead us on,
> Until, the breath of this corporeal frame
> And even the motion of our human blood
> Almost suspended, we are laid asleep
> In body, and become a living soul: (Wordsworth)

> Why do I know ye? why have I seen ye? why
> Is my eternal essence thus distraught
> To see and to behold these horrors new?
> Saturn is fallen, am I too to fall? (Keats)

This process, where poetic argument runs over the line end or sequence of line-endings without pause or punctuation is called 'enjambement'. The frequency of overrunning in blank verse notwithstanding, it must be pointed out that even in the most regular rhymed heroics, end-stopping is not invariable. Even Pope, the unquestioned master of the closed couplet, uses the device on occasion. Take this couplet from *An Essay on Criticism*:

> 'Tis with our judgments as our watches, none
> Go just alike, yet each believes his own.

Here the break in the line is in the middle of the final foot (remarkably late for Pope) and the line runs over, though still, it should be noted, to a closed resolution in the second line. Overrunning is not frequent, however, in Pope's work. Indeed, the poet's central importance in the history of the couplet has led to a sense that closed paired lines are the norm. However, this is a generalisation which needs to be heavily qualified. The heroic couplet need not have the regularity evident in the work of Pope. Though it is perhaps the most important verse form of the Augustan period of English poetry, it dates from well before the late seventeenth century. And poets using the couplet before Pope (Chaucer, Donne, Marvell) and after (Keats) have often used a more open couplet. John Donne's (1572–1631) brilliantly varied handling of the couplet in his 'Satire iii' is a good example of the relaxed and loose rhymed heroic:

> Know thy foes: The foule Devill (whom thou
> Strivest to please,) for hate, not love, would allow
> Thee faine, his whole Realme to be quit; and as
> The worlds all parts wither away and passe,
> So the worlds selfe thy other lov'd foe, is
> In her decrepit wayne, and thou loving this,
> Doth love a withered and worn strumpet; last
> Flesh (it selfes death) and joyes which flesh can taste,
> Thou lovest; and thy faire goodly soule, which doth
> Give this flesh power to taste joy, thou dost loath.

Here the first line of each couplet invariably overruns. Indeed, in the first couplet the second line itself is enjambed. The rhymes seem less important to the sense of the poem than in closed couplets, because the characteristically late breaks ensure that the rhymed words are less emphasised by the reader's tongue. Furthermore, rhyming a nine-syllable line with one of eleven syllables (as in the first couplet) does not engender a smooth flowing couplet in the manner of Pope. Donne also feels free to scatter pauses throughout the line rather than relying on the caesura, with breaks occurring as early as after the second syllable and as late as after the ninth. And the majority of lines here are either curtailed or extended in terms of their syllable count rather than being regular decasyllables.

Enjambement is found in almost all kinds of metrical verse. Paradoxically, it might usefully be illustrated by an example of badly handled overrunning. The poet William McGonagall (1825 or 1830–1902), noted since the nineteenth century for his lamentable style, has a poem, 'To Mr James Scrymgeour, Dundee', which contains one of the ugliest examples of the device in the history of British poetry:

> He is a man of noble principles,
>   As far as I can think,
> And the noblest principle he has got
>   Is, he abhors the demon drink.

Leaving aside the second line, which adds nothing to the poem except set up the *b* rhyme, and the stale cliché of the 'demon drink' in the last line, this stanza is metrically faulty. The break is far too early in the fourth line after the enjambement, focusing unwarranted stress upon the initial monosyllable and leaving the reader to contend with a jarring spondee ('is / he'), a spondee which is also ungrammatical in a way that suggests simple ignorance rather than poetic licence.

On occasions, an enjambed line possesses a 'weak ending', that is where a usually unstressed monosyllabic word inhabits the place normally reserved for a stressed syllable in an iambic verse line. Weak endings tend to be auxiliary verbs ('shall' and 'will' for instance), prepositions or conjunctions. To illustrate this device, here is a passage from one of the most notable speeches in Shakespeare's *The Tempest*:

> These our actors,
> As I foretold you, were all spirits, and
> Are melted into air, into thin air;
> And like the baseless fabric of this vision,
> The cloud-capped towers, the great gorgeous palaces,
> The solemn temples, the great globe itself,
> Yea, all which it inherit, shall dissolve.

The second line here has a weak ending. Furthermore, the final foot is both broken and is comprised of two unstressed syllables (a 'pyrrhic', see below), which serves to strengthen the impact of the ensuing line. One other point needs to be made here: line 5 offers an example of a related technique, the 'feminine ending', which in blank verse involves the hypercatalectic addition of an extra syllable which is unstressed (this is not to be confused with 'feminine rhyme', the rhyme on a disyllable which consists of a stressed followed by an unstressed syllable). Whereas a weak ending positions an unstressed syllable at the end of a line of ten syllables, the feminine ending places it at the end of a line of eleven syllables.

Though the heroic line is the most important iambic metre, poets have not infrequently worked in other iambic line lengths, most notably in 'tetrameters' (that is, four-foot lines). The most important verse form here is the iambic tetrameter in stanzaic quatrains:

> Come live with me and be my love,
> And we will all the pleasures prove,
> That hills and valleys, dales and fields,
> And all the craggy mountains yields. (Marlowe)

> When I survey the wondrous Cross
> On which the Prince of Glory died,
> My richest gain I count but loss,
> And pour contempt on all my pride. (Watts)

The first poem has the *aabb* rhyme not uncommon in love lyrics; the second uses the cross-rhyming more usual in lyrics with a more weighty subject-matter (both stanzaic forms are discussed above). Though frequently used in stanzaic verse, tetrameters have also not infrequently been used for sustained continuous iambic composition, notably by Jonathan Swift (1667–1745) and Samuel Butler:

> The Sun had long since in the Lap
> Of *Thetis*, taken out his *Nap,*
> And like a *Lobster* boyl'd, the *Morn*
> From *black* to *red* began to turn.
> When *Hudibras*, whom thoughts and aching
> 'Twixt sleeping kept all night, and waking,
> Began to rouse his drousie eyes,
> And from his Couch prepar'd to rise. (Butler, *Hudibras*)

> For poetry he's past his prime,
> He takes an hour to find a rhyme;
> His fire is out, his wit decayed,
> His fancy sunk, his muse a jade.
> I'd have him throw away his pen,
> But there's no talking to some men. (Swift, 'Verses on the Death
> of Doctor Swift')

Butler, indeed, bequeathed the name of his poem to his metre: 'Hudibrastics' – that is, comic verse in sustained octosyllabic couplets with ingenious comic feminine rhymes (as in 'aching' and 'waking' in the extract above). However, though it suits the burlesque methodology of Butler, octosyllabic verse is not easily pressed into the service of meditative or sublime writing, lacking as it does the stately flow of heroics. Even Milton occasionally struggles to subdue the celerity of the metre in his 'Il Penseroso' ('But hail, thou Goddess sage and holy, / Hail divinest melancholy') and perhaps it is little wonder that his preface to *Paradise Lost* endorses the unrhymed heroic line, glances at the 'bondage of rhyming' and endorses 'fit quantity of syllables' (the fit quantity being ten, of course).

4.7   TROCHAIC METRE

The other duple metre is the trochaic, the exact opposite of iambic, a falling rhythm where a stressed syllable is followed by an unstressed one. The basic metrical unit is the single trochaic foot, the trochee ($^{/x}$). This foot, as discussed above, is often used in substitution in iambic verse. However, it can also form the basis for entire poems in 'trochaic verse' (often simply referred to as 'trochaics'). If we might be allowed to indulge in blithe generalisation, trochaic verse, which leads off with a stressed syllable, is an attention-grabbing metre (compare the forceful trochaics with which a famous under-shaven caveman is announced: 'Flintstones, meet the Flintstones'). Certainly it is often used in rousing patriotic verse and stirring hymns:

> Land of hope and glory, Mother of the Free,
> How shall we extol thee, who are born of thee? (A. C. Benson)

> Onward, Christian soldiers!
>   Marching as to war,
> With the Cross of Jesus
>   Going on before. (S. Baring-Gould)

This passage from Shelley's *Prometheus Unbound* exploits the vigour of trochaic metre well:

> *Second Fury.*
> From wide-cities, famine-wasted;
>   *Third Fury.*
> Groans half-heard, and blood untasted;
>   *Fourth Fury.*
> Kingly conclaves stern and cold,
> Where blood with gold is bought and sold;

> *Fifth Fury.*
> From the furnace, white and hot
> In which –
> *A Fury.*
> Speak not; whisper not:

The metre here, like the atmosphere, is presumably influenced by the scenes featuring the witches in *Macbeth* which also use trochaics ('Double, double, toil and trouble'). Shelley's verse has an incantatory power and force which complements his lurid and violent rhetoric. The poet uses complete tetrameters in the first couplet and, making his form suit his content, employs curtailed ones thereafter as the pace quickens. One other device of importance in the passage is found in the fourth line, which offers an example of 'anacrusis': the insertion, for the sake of the sense, of a syllable at the beginning of a line before the formal metre resumes.

> Where blood with gold is bought and sold;

To examine the conventional use of trochaics in English non-dramatic verse, one might look at Mary Robinson's 'Stanzas. Written between Dover and Calais, in July, 1792':

> / x / x / x / x
> Bounding | billow | cease thy | motion;
> / x / x / x /
> Bear me | not so | sweetly | o'er!
> / x / x / x / x
> Cease thy | roaring, | foamy | Ocean!
> / x / x / x /
> I will | tempt thy | rage no | more.

Here the tempestuous nature of the scene is evoked in swift-moving trochaics. A poem about the bounding waves and roaring ocean uses, appropriately enough, the energetic momentum of trochaics. Robinson uses a complete final foot in the first line; the metrical falling to an unstressed final syllable momentarily suggesting the slowing down which is the subject of the half-line. Trochaics such as these, which are lacking in modulatory substitution, have a jaunty rhythm which is appropriate to stanzaic poetry but can weary the ear in sustained and continuous composition. Take the eighteenth-century poet John Dyer's locodescriptive poem 'Grongar Hill' where the breathless momentum of the unbroken trochaic tetrameter couplet militates against the picturesque solitude of the subject being described:

> Grongar Hill invites my song,
> Draw the landscape bright and strong;

> Grongar in whose mossy cells
> Sweetly-musing quiet dwells;
> Grongar, in whose silent shade,
> For the modest Muses made,
> So oft, I have the evening still,
> At the fountain of a rill,
> Sate upon a flowery bed,
> With my hand beneath my head;
> And strayed my eyes o'er Towy's flood,
> Over mead, and over wood,
> From house to house, from hill to hill,
> 'Till contemplation had her fill.

Compare this with Dyer's contemporary Thomas Parnell's 'The Hymn to Contentment', which is also in octosyllabic couplets, but uses iambic rather than trochaic tetrameters. The calmer metre of Parnell's poem better suits its meditative substance:

> The silent heart, which grief assails,
> Treads soft and lonesome o'er the vales,
> Sees daisies open, rivers run,
> And seeks, as I have vainly done,
> Amusing thought; but learns to know
> That solitude's the nurse of woe.

And further compare Dyer's work with Pope's 'Eloisa to Abelard', a poem which deals with similar issues and is also contemporaneous with 'Grongar Hill'. This is also in couplets, but this time in heroics:

> In these deep solitudes and awful cells,
> Where heav'nly-pensive contemplation dwells,
> And ever-musing melancholy reigns;

Pope's five-beat iambic line possesses a stately expansiveness when compared to the hurtling four-beat trochaic verses of Dyer. Many would doubtless argue, and with good reason, that another key difference between the two versifiers is, of course, that Pope is a much better poet than Dyer. However, an important part of poetic quality is making one's form suit one's content; if Pope is the superior poet, then one key reason is that he ensures that his metre is well chosen and complements his subject-matter. The sing-song of sustained trochaics renders Dyer's attempt at sublimity a metrical failure. Perhaps a sense of this motivated Milton in his 'L'Allegro' to use the upbeat trochaic appropriate to his theme of 'the happy man', but also to modulate by mixing his metre with occasional iambics:

Haste thee, Nymph, and bring with thee
Jest and youthful Jollity,
Quips and Cranks, and wanton Wiles
Nods and Becks and wreathèd Smiles,
Such as hang on Hebe's cheek,
And love to live in dimple sleek;
Sport that wrinkled Care derides,
And laughter holding both his sides.

The light-footed trochaic predominates, but the pace is slowed down by the insertion of iambics in lines 6 and 8. This device, which goes beyond the substitution of an individual foot, of using entire lines in a metre other than that of the frame is known as 'mixed metre'. Most often, as in the Milton passage, it is an occasional device of variation. However, whole poems have sometimes been composed in mixed metre (see the example quoted in section 4.9 below).

By far the most common trochaic line is the trochaic tetrameter, the four-foot line in falling rhythm. However, it is important to register here that poets working in this metre very often drop the final unstressed syllable of the line (as in the majority of the lines in the Dyer passage and as in the Robinson stanza, where complete and curtailed lines alternate). Here the catalectic line comes into its own, almost to the point where it becomes the norm. This is somewhat confusing to the reader of poetry who expects to see orthodoxy in the frame. Take Blake's (1757–1827) famous 'The Tyger', which is in trochaic tetrameters though it possesses several iambic lines:

/ x / x / x /
Tyger, | tyger, | burning | bright

/ x / x / x /
In the | forests | of the | night

/ x / x / x /
What immortal hand or eye

x / x / x / x /
Could frame thy fearful symmetry?

Only the fourth line is complete; the other lines in the stanza are curtailed and end on the fourth stressed syllable. This truncation is very frequent in the trochaic tetrameter, almost to the point where many poems written in this metre resemble seven-syllable 'heptasyllabics'. This fact, added to the frequent use of trochaic substitution at the start of iambic lines (which themselves end in a stressed syllable), does not make the identification of trochaic metre easy. However, if one bears in mind our point about the tendency to use catalectic final feet in trochaic metre, then the picture begins to clarify.

Generalising about particular metrical forms is not without its attendant hazards. Against every attempt to make overarching statements about the qualities of a given metre, many examples of lines which contradict such assertions might be found. However, we would dare the assertion that the heroic line, especially in regular and unbroken form, generally possesses a stately and unhurried quality which is not usually evident in the trochaic line, which has a sprightly and more urgent manner, most notably in its commonest form of the tetrameter line. To illustrate the differences in the measures, here are some lines from the poet Gray's remarkable ode 'The Progress of Poesy', which is actually a fine, though veiled, piece of literary criticism. Here the 'Loves', or Cupids, dance and disport themselves before the arrival of Queen Cytherea, the goddess of love:

> With antic Sports, and blue-eyed Pleasures,
> Frisking light in frolic measures;
> Now pursuing, now retreating,
> Now in circling troops they meet:
> To brisk notes in cadence beating,
> Glance their many-twinkling feet.
> Slow melting strains their Queen's approach declare;
> Where'er she turns the Graces homage pay,
> With arms sublime, that float upon the air,
> In gliding state she wins her easy way;

This is mythological description, but it is just as much an account of the qualities which Gray sees in the most common English metres: lines 1–6 describing the trochaic and lines 7–10 the iambic. Here the poet makes the form of his poem mirror its content. The first six lines are in trochaic tetrameter; Gray begins in complete lines and moves on to use resounding curtailed ones for the final rhyme (in lines 4 and 6). Trochaic metre, like the joys of the Cupids, is light, brisk and frolicsome. However, when the arrival of the Queen is imminent, then Gray switches to iambic metre; the measured, stately progress of the Queen is described in a suitable metre. For Gray, the slow, melting strains of iambic verse are best utilised in the description of 'sublimity', and of the profound and momentous aspects of life.

4.8   DACTYLIC METRE

A dactyl is a foot where a stressed syllable is followed, like an engine pulling two coaches, by two unstressed ones ($/^{xx}$), as in the words 'actually' and 'negative'. The first line of a famous nursery rhyme offers an example of the regular dactylic line: 'Pát a cáke, pát a cáke, báker's mán'. Poetry where the dactylic foot predominates is referred to, logically enough, as 'dactylic verse' or simply as 'dactyls'. Whilst dactylic verse (measured, of course, in quantitative terms of syllabic length rather than stress-patterning) was widespread in classical Greek and Roman poetry, notably in epic, it is not common in English poetry. It has been used in poetical lyrics, nonetheless, generally in heavily curtailed lines:

> From the low palace of old father Ocean,
>   Come we in pity your cares to deplore;
> Sea-racing dolphins are trained for our motion,
>   Moony tides swelling to roll us ashore. (Dryden)

However, as far as non-lyrical polite poetry is concerned, before the nineeenth century the dactylic foot is chiefly an occasional device of substitution:

> Shadowy | sets off the face of things; in vain. (*Paradise Lost*)

Like the other falling metre, the trochaic, dactylic verse can assume a bounding, almost military aspect, as in that resourceful metrician Tennyson's (1809–1892) 'The Charge of the Light Brigade'. Here complete dactyls alternate with curtailed ones in lines 4 and 9:

> Cannon to right of them
> Cannon to left of them
> Cannon in front of them
>   Volleyed and thundered
> Stormed at with shot and shell,
> Boldly they rode and well,
> Into the jaws of death
> Into the mouth of hell,
>   Rode the six hundred.

On occasions, dactylics are used for more melancholic or elegiac subject-matter, as in Thomas Hood's (1799–1845) poem about a female suicide, 'The Bridge of Sighs':

> One more unfortunate,
> Weary of breath,
> Rashly importunate,
> Gone to her death!
>
> Take her up tenderly,
> Lift her with care;
> Fashioned so slenderly,
> Young and so fair!

You will notice that lines 1 and 3 and lines 5 and 7 use triple rhymes and that the curtailed feet in lines 2, 4, 6 and 8 use single rhyme; the common use of the curtailed foot in dactylic verse testifies to the difficulties posed by the metre's appetite for triple rhyme. And even though Hood manages to subdue the boisterousness of the metre, it is clear why most poets have consistently preferred the wider possibilities offered to them in the duple metres.

4.9 ANAPAESTIC METRE

An anapaest is a metrical foot which consists of three syllables, with two unstressed syllables followed by a stressed one (xx/), as in the word 'intercede'. Though by no means as common as rhythmic inversion in duple metre, the foot is an occasional device in substitution:

>   x x /
> Alone | on a wide, | wide sea (Coleridge, 'The Rime of the Ancient Mariner')

Or it can be used as a mixed metre:

> I closed my lids, and kept them close,
> And the balls like pulses beat;

>   x   x   /   x   x /   x   x /   x   x /
> For the sky | and the sea, | and the sea | and the sky
> And the dead were at my feet. ('The Rime of the Ancient Mariner')

In the first stanza of Feste's mixed metre dirge from *Twelfth Night*, dactylic lines alternate with anapaestic ones:

> Come away, come away, Death,
> And in sad cypress let me be laid;
> Fly away, fly away, breath;
> I am slain by a fair cruel maid.

A poem where the foot predominates is an 'anapaestic verse', or, slightly confusingly, simply 'anapaests'. Like poems where the dactyl provides the frame, anapaestic verse is not common. The opening of Thomas Moore's (1779–1852) 'We may roam through this world' offers a rare example of regular anapaestic verse:

>   x   x   /   x   x   /   x x /   x x /
> We may roam | through this world, | like a child | at a feast,
>   x   x /   x x /   x   x   /   x x /
> Who but sips | of a sweet, | and then flies | to the rest;

Anapaestic verse is more commonly heavily modulated, notably by trochaic substitution and curtailment, as in perhaps the most well-known example of the metre in the English poetical canon, Robert Browning's (1812–1889) 'How they brought the good news from Ghent to Aix':

> I sprang to the stirrup, and Joris and he;
> I galloped, Dirck galloped, we galloped all three;
>
> / /   x   x /   x x /   x   x /
> 'God speed!' | cried the watch, | as the gate | bolts undrew
>
> /   x   x x /   x x /   x x   /
> 'Speed!' ech | oed the wall | to us gall | oping through;

Unlike dactylics, which have a heavy force, this rising trisyllabic metre is generally used to manufacture a speedy manner. This is certainly the case in the Browning poem. The somewhat breathless pace of the metre has been used most extensively in Horatian social satire by the likes of Moore, Christopher Anstey and N. T. H. Bayly, where its breezy lightness suits the poetry's tone. Anstey's *New Bath Guide* (1766) is typical and equally characteristic of sustained anapaestic poetry in that it is peppered with substitutions in the first foot of the line (for instance, two-stress 'spondees' (see immediately below) in lines 3 and 4 and a trochee in line 5) whilst being generally regular thereafter:

> Of all the gay Places the World can afford,
> By Gentle and Simple for Pastime ador'd,
> Fine Balls, and fine Concerts, fine Buildings, and Springs,
> Fine Walks, and fine Views, and a Thousand fine Things,
> Not to mention the sweet Situation and Air,
> What Place, my dear Mother, with *Bath* can compare?

4.10   OCCASIONAL FEET

Three other kinds of foot need to be discussed here: the spondee, pyrrhic and amphibrach. These do not form the basis of whole poems but are used occasionally within poems in the conventional metres. The **spondee** is another two-syllable foot. It consists of two stressed syllables together ($^{//}$). There is no such thing as 'spondaic verse'; a complete poem in spondees, perish the thought, would best be described as the literary equivalent of a round of machine-gun fire. Even a complete pentameter line of spondees is almost unheard of (apart from the Victorian poet Sydney Dobell's notorious 'Ah! Ah! Ah! Ah! Ah! Ah! Ah! Ah! Ah! Ah!'). Instead, the spondee is used to give rhythmic variation to iambic and trochaic verse. The spondee is seen to good effect in such lines as Pope's '"Shut, shut the door, good John!" fatigu'd I said,' the opening line of his 'Epistle to Dr. Arbuthnot', where the two spondees begin the poem in suitably emphatic and attention-grabbing style. Similarly, Shakespeare gives King Lear, in his rage, consecutive spondees:

> and when I have stole upon
> These son-in-laws, then kill, kill, kill, kill, kill, kill!

In Marlowe's *Doctor Faustus*, the doom-laden line 'Now hast thou but one bare hour to live' begins with a trochee and has a spondee in the third foot which is followed by a truncated stressed fourth foot, thus delivering an even more dramatic series of stresses which suggest the tolling of the soul's midnight: 'but one bare hour'. Similarly, 'The Rime of the Ancient Mariner' uses a monosyllabic broken spondee to emphasise the plight and isolation of the seafarer: 'Alone, alone, | all, all | alone'.

The **pyrrhic** foot might be described as the spondee's less self-confident alter ego. It is the direct opposite of the spondee and consists of two unstressed syllables (^{xx}). Again, it is a device of variation and is used only as a substitute foot in poems which employ one of the metrical frames. It is not used and probably could not be used as a frame or base for an entire poem. To illustrate the foot in use, this is one of the most notable lines Milton's *Samson Agonistes*:

$$\text{Eyeless | in Ga|za at | the mill | with slaves.}$$

Here Milton begins his heroic with a trochee, but also modulates with the substitution of a pyrrhic in the third foot. The **amphibrach** ($^{x/x}$) is a trisyllabic foot where the stress falls in the middle of the foot, as in the word 'important'. It is another modulatory foot. The most common place for the amphibrach is as the last foot of a blank verse line. Many hypermetrical feet are, strictly speaking, examples of amphibrachic substitution. Returning to the examples quoted above in our discussion of the 'extra' syllable demonstrates this fact:

> But peace to vain regrets! We see | but darkly (Wordsworth)

> To be, or not to be, that is | the question (Shakespeare)

Moving to a more recent example taken from popular culture, perhaps the most notable summer pop hit of the 1990s was Supergrass's 'Alright', a song which opens in regular anapaestic fashion and exploits the carefree possibilities of that metre:

> We are young, | we run free,
> We got teeth, | nice and clean,
> See our friends, | see the sights,
> Feel alright.

Though the fact may not have been at the forefront of the band's minds as they composed the song, what we have here is a fine example of generally regular anapaestics with, of course, amphibrachic substitution in the final foot. There is also an example of the 'cretic' foot (or 'amphimacer'), the unstressed syllable between two stressed syllables, in the words 'nice and clean'.

4.11   METRICAL VERSE LINES

This section addresses the most common metrical lines used in English poetry. As noted above, it is the foot which provides the basic building block in English metrics and the names given to verse lines reflect the quantity of feet in the line rather than the number of syllables. Thus a ten-syllable, five-foot line is called a 'pentameter' rather than a 'decasyllable' or some such. And thus an eight-syllable line in duple meter can be described as 'octosyllabic', but is best referred to as a 'tetrameter'. In theory, of course, a line of metrical verse could be of any length, but almost all practical lines contain between one and eight feet. Here we will examine the range of verse lines – from the anorexic single-foot monometer to the portly eight-foot octameter – with the exception of the most common lines, the five-foot pentameter and the four-foot tetrameter, which are discussed above in our examination of iambic and trochaic metre.

The Long John Silver of verse lines is the **monometer** which contains only one foot. We need not tarry over the monometer; the popular preference amongst poets as amongst the population at large – roguish pirates apart – is for more than one foot. There are occasional examples of entire poems written in monometers, but these are freakishly unusual and often give the sense that the poet is simply trying to exercise his or her wit on a rather unusual poetic challenge. Robert Herrick's (1591–1674) 'Thus I pass by' is perhaps the most well-known example:

> Thus I
> Pass by,
> And die
> As one
> Unknown
> And gone.
> I'd made
> A shade,
> And laid,
> I' th' grave;
> There have
> My cave,

> Where tell
> I dwell
> Farewell.

Rather than being the basis of entire poems, monometers are almost invariably used for occasional effect in poems written in more expansive verse lines. A poet might utilise a monometer as a refrain or to serve his or her thematic purpose. Take another of Herrick's poems, 'To Daffodils':

> We have short time to stay, as you,
>   We have as short a spring;
> As quick a growth to meet decay,
>   As you, or anything.
>   We die,
>   As your hours do, and dry
>   Away,
>   Like to the summer's rain;
> Or as the pearls of morning's dew
>   Ne'er to be found again.

Herrick's theme of mutability and the transience of existence is well complemented by the monometers in the fifth and seventh lines. His subject – the brevity of human life – is formally echoed by the use of the shortest metrical line.

The two-foot metrical line is called the **dimeter**. Like the monometer, the dimeter is most commonly found as an intermittent device used for metrical variance or dramatic effect in a poem which is otherwise composed in longer lines. Again, the most purposeful examples see the line serving to drive along the argument of the poem. In Thomas Randolph's (1605–1635) 'An Ode to Mr. Anthony Stafford to hasten him into the Country', the hastening is done in succinct dimeter lines and that which the poet wishes to escape described in longer lines:

> Come spurre away,
> I have no patience for a longer stay;
> But must go downe,
> And leave the chargeable noise of this great Towne.

Later in the poem, the lines again shorten, formally to echo the argument:

> Then worthy *Stafford* say
> How shall we spend the day,
>   With what delights,
>   Shorten the nights?

Dimeters are similarly used in stanzaic poetry: Felicia Hemans' (1793–1835) 'Music of Yesterday' is composed in combination quatrains of, successively, four-, three-, four- and two-feet lines:

> The chord, the harp's full chord is hushed,
>   The voice hath died away,
> Whence music, like sweet waters, gushed.
>   But yesterday.
>
> Th' awakening note, the breeze-like swell,
>   The full o'ersweeping tone,
> The sounds that sighed 'Farewell, farewell'!
>   Are gone – all gone!

Here the use of the shorter dimeter lines at the conclusion of each stanza reinforces the poem's theme of absence and lost beauty.

Though the dimeter is most usually a device of metrical variance, whole poems have sometimes been predominantly composed in the line. As with monometer verse, one often has a sense that these are formal poetic exercises, examples of poets exercising their wit and ingenuity. However, on occasions the metre seems entirely appropriate to the sense of the poem:

> Hear me, O God!
> A broken part,
> Is my best part:
> Use still thy rod,
> That I may prove
> Therein, thy love.

Ben Jonson's 'A Hymn to God the Father' ably utilises the curt dimeter line to convey the urgency of his plea to the almighty, an urgency reinforced, it might be added, by the use of a forceful opening spondee. On the other hand, Blake's dimeter lyric 'The Fly' uses simple monosyllables and overrunning lines to convey an air of delicacy and simplicity:

> Am not I
> A fly like thee?
> Or art not thou
> A man like me?
>
> For I dance
> And drink and sing:
> Till some blind hand
> Shall brush my wing.

Such adept handling eradicates the sense sometimes evident in the dimeter of a more expansive form struggling to get out. Here the metrical butterfly is not confined to its cocoon.

A **trimeter** is a three-foot verse line. As with the even shorter measures, there is still a danger here of the verse looking cramped or confined. However, in the hands of a resourceful metrist such as Swinburne (1837–1909), this danger can be overcome. These are the first three stanzas of the poet's 'Christmas Antiphones':

> Thou whose birth on earth
>   Angels sang to men,
> While thy stars made mirth,
> Saviour at thy birth,
>   This day born again;
>
> As this night was bright
>   With thy cradle-ray,
> Very light of light,
> Turn the wild world's night
>   To thy perfect day.
>
> God whose feet made sweet
>   Those wild ways they trod,
> From thy fragrant feet
> Staining field and street
>   With the blood of God.

And so it goes on in metrical triumph, for over sixty stanzas. Swinburne has set himself a difficult challenge: quite apart from the confines of the unvaried trimeter (which is made even shorter by the poem's almost unvarying use of the trochaic catalectic line), he uses three *a* rhymes in each short stanza, allied to internal rhymes in each opening line. But despite these self-imposed restrictions, Swinburne rises to the challenge, managing to make concision unconstrictive.

The four- and five-foot lines, the tetrameter and pentameter are discussed above, so the next line which we need to address here is the **hexameter**, the metrical verse of six feet. The most significant hexameter line is the iambic hexameter, which is generally referred to as an 'alexandrine'. The most extensive use of alexandrines in a sustained manner is found in Michael Drayton's early seventeenth-century work *Polyolbion*:

> When *Phoebus* lifts his head out of the Winters wave,
> No sooner doth the Earth her flowerie bosome brave,

> At such time as the yeere brings on the pleasant Spring,
> But Hunts–up to the Morne the feath'red *Sylvans* sing.

Here there is an internal break after the sixth syllable of each line, as in the overwhelming majority of Drayton's verses, and the poem could be set as trimeters with the first line overflowing without any loss of sense or damage to the music of the verse:

> When *Phoebus* lifts his head
> Out of the Winters wave,
> No sooner doth the Earth
> Her flowerie bosome brave,
> At such time as the yeere
> Brings on the pleasant Spring,
> But Hunts–up to the Morne
> The feath'red *Sylvans* sing.

Throughout hundreds of lines, Drayton rarely deviates from this practice; the alexandrine permits of little metrical variation when compared with iambic pentameter and it is small wonder that the latter became the line of choice for poets writing expansive meditative poetry, whether in blank verse or heroic couplets. After Drayton, the alexandrine does not often provide the basic line in whole poems and is most commonly used for variance, most notably in the last line of the Spenserian stanza (discussed above):

> Love, fame, ambition, avarice – 'tis the same,
> Each idle – and all ill – and none the worst –
> For all are meteors with a different name,
> And death the sable smoke where vanishes the flame. (Byron)

Pope's famous jest in *An Essay on Criticism,* in which form mirrors content harmoniously, is not without critical insight: 'A needless Alexandrine ends the song / That like a wounded snake, drags its slow length along'.

Trochaic hexameters are most uncommon, and, on the evidence of those which are to be found, perhaps understandably so. The poet Browning, who is normally an adept handler of trochaics, offers a six-foot falling line in his 'Before', a poem which seems metrically unnatural and lacklustre:

> Better sin the whole sin, sure that God observes;
> Then go his life out! Life will try his nerves,
> When the sky, which noticed all, makes no disclosure,
> And the earth keeps up her terrible composure.

Hexameters in triple metre are slightly more common in Victorian poetry, but still occasionally have the air of the metrical laboratory about them. For instance, Arthur Hugh Clough (1819–1861) struggles bravely to make the dactylic hexameter with extensive modulation an appropriate vehicle for conversational poetry, but perishes in the attempt:

> Dear Eustatio, I write that you may write me an answer,
> Or at least to put us again *en rapport* with each other,
> Rome disappoints me much, – St. Peter's perhaps, in especial;
> Only the Arch of Titus and view from the Lateran please me:
> This, however, perhaps, is the weather, which truly is horrid.

Here we are in the realms of conscious idiosyncrasy, experimentation which does not manage to appear spontaneous or natural, and it is not a pretty sight. Nonetheless, Clough's contemporary Swinburne shows what can be done in six-foot triple metre, managing to make his anapaestic hexameter lines in 'Hesperia' suit his purpose of creating a languid atmosphere of corruption. This is part of his description of Our Lady of Pain:

> With the thirst and the hunger of lust though her beautiful lips be so bitter,
> With the cold foul foam of the snakes they soften and redden and smile;
> And her fierce mouth sweetens, her eyes wax wide and her eyelashes glitter,
> And she laughs with a savour of blood in her face, and a savour of guile.

A metrical verse line which contains seven feet is known as a **heptameter**. As heptameters are almost invariably iambic or trochaic, they are sometimes referred to as 'fourteeners' on account of the standard number of syllables in the line. The heptameter is also occasionally referred to as a 'septenary'. Seven-stress lines are most commonly iambic, as in George Chapman's translation of Homer:

> And such a stormy day shall come (in mind and soul I know)
> When sacred Troy shall shed her towers, for tears of overthrow.

Chapman's early seventeenth-century *Iliad* is almost the last gasp of the long poem in heptameters; fourteeners are much commoner in that period of English literature before blank verse and the heroic couplet became the principal verse forms for sustained composition, as for instance in St Robert Southwell's remarkable 'The Burning Babe', first published shortly after the poet's death in 1595:

> As I in hoarie Winters night stood shiuering in the snow,
> Surpris'd I was with sudden heat, which made my heart to glow;
> And lifting vp a fearfull eye, to view what fire was neere,
> A pretie Babe all burning bright did in the ayre appeare;

In more recent centuries, the heptameter has become something of a conscious oddity or occasional metre, particularly in the nineteenth-century poetry of Macaulay, Swinburne and, perhaps most notably, Tennyson:

> I hate the dreadful hollow behind the little wood,
> Its lips in the field above are dabbled with blood-red heath,
> The red-ribb'd ledges drip with a silent horror of blood,
> And Echo there, whatever is ask'd her, answers 'Death'. ('Maud')

One other notable manifestation of the fourteener is in the so-called 'poulter's measure' pioneered by Thomas Wyatt and borrowed by the Earl of Surrey (c. 1517–1547), a rather prosaic and plodding metre, where iambic hexameter lines alternate with iambic heptameters, and one which is often hard to manage without the verse falling into clumsiness:

My love and lord, alas, in whom consists my wealth,
> Hath fortune sent to pass the seas in hazard of his health,
That I was wont for to embrace, contented mind's,
> Is now amid the foaming floods at pleasure of the winds. (Surrey, 'Lady
> > Surrey's Lament for her Absent Lord')

The leviathan metrical line comprising of eight feet is called an **octameter**. Again, these are comparative rarities, elephantine creations which often might easily be divided into tetrameters and set on the page as such. The most proficient exponent of the line is Tennyson, most notably in his 'Locksley Hall', composed in separated trochaic octameter couplets:

> Comrades, leave me here a little, while as yet 'tis early morn:
> Leave me here, and when you want me, sound upon the bugle-horn.

> 'Tis the place, and all around it, as of old, the curlews call,
> Dreary gleams about the moorland flying over Locksley Hall;

> Locksley Hall, that in the distance overlooks the sandy tracts,
> And the hollow ocean-ridges roaring into cataracts.

Well handled as these octameters are, the tongue naturally suggests pauses in the exact centre of each line, giving the appearance of cobbled-together tetrameters rather than an organically produced and flexible line. Only occasionally does Tennyson manage to make his lines avoid this tendency and make the octameter seem the only possible way of setting the verses:

> Yet it shall be: thou shalt lower to his level day by day,
> What is fine within thee growing coarse to sympathize with clay.

Tennyson's efforts notwithstanding, the most famous poem – perhaps notorious is the better word – extensively to use octameters is Poe's 'The Raven'. This
is the first stanza:

> Once upon a midnight dreary, while I pondered, weak and weary,
> Over many a quaint and curious volume of forgotten lore;
> While I nodded, nearly napping, suddenly there came a tapping,
> As of someone gently rapping, rapping at my chamber door.

The metre suits the sense in that the claustrophobic world-weariness of the
poem is described in near-interminable lines. Bringing in the terminology we
have addressed in this chapter and in previous ones, what can we say about these
lines? The lines see stressed syllables followed by unstressed syllables; that is,
the frame is trochaic: 'Once upon a midnight dreary, while I pondered, weak
and weary'. The lines each have eight feet; thus the stanza is composed of
octameters. The first three lines have sixteen syllables and the last fifteen; in
other words the first three lines are acatalectic and the final line catalectic. The
stanza contains four lines; that is, it is a quatrain, which rhymes *abcb* and the
second and fourth lines contain internal rhymes. In metrical terms, then, the
first quatrain of Poe's 'The Raven' is in trochaic octameter acatalectic with a
final line which employs trochaic octameter catalectic. We conclude this section
by commenting that if you are now capable of understanding the previous
sentence, then our purpose in this chapter has been achieved.

4.12   FREE VERSE

With that, we put metrical verse behind us. And so have many contemporary
poets. According to your poetic point of view, metre is either a welcome
structural discipline or a cumbersome straitjacket. Many poets in the twentieth
century were of the second opinion and employed 'free verse' (some critics
prefer the term 'nonmetrical verse', whilst others use the original French term
'*vers libre*'). This is poetry where the traditional rules of metrics, and in particular
the conventions of rhyme and metre, do not apply. We are not talking here
about variation or modulation from a metrical frame so much as a disregard for
prosodological convention.

   Given that the *raison d'être* of free verse is the repudiation of metrical fetters,
any attempt to offer a clear taxonomy of free verse is perhaps doomed to failure.
As a consequence, it is easier to characterise free verse with reference to what
it does *not* do rather than what it does. Free verse, the rebellious offspring of
conventional metre, does not conform to a regular or recurring poetic metre.
It also varies, if it uses it at all, its use of rhyme and nor does it feel obliged to

conform to a particular line-length. Though many twentieth-century poets have occasionally, and sometimes not so occasionally, worked with traditional metrical forms, the century's poetry is perhaps best characterised by free verse. In particular, it is the characteristic poetic form of high early twentieth-century modernism, the formal equivalent of the thematic repudiation of the tenets of Romantic and Victorian poetry. The modernist poets Ezra Pound and T. S. Eliot utilise free verse in much of their most significant work:

> If there were water
> And no rock
> If there were rock
> And also water
> A spring
> A pool among the rock
> If there were the sound of water only
> Not the cicada
> And dry grass singing
> But sound of water over a rock
> Where the hermit-thrush sings in the pine trees
> Drip drop drip drop drop drop drop
> But there is no water (Eliot, *The Waste Land*)

Here rhythmic effect depends upon other things than metre: upon repetition of central words ('rock' and 'water'), upon variety of lineation, upon density of emphasis throughout, and upon an incantatory force in the language. Line-length is determined with an eye to theme rather than metrical convention: short and condensed in its plainer language, elongated in its gestures towards poeticality ('Where the hermit-thrush sings in the pine trees'). There is occasional seeming metricality, as in line 7's approximating to a recognisable trochaic verse, but each line is fashioned in terms of length and rhythm to serve its theme rather than working with and deviating from a metrical base for variety of effect in the manner of conventional verse.

Given that free verse defies easy definition and is characterised by an unwillingness to conform to a metrical frame, then we as critics are rather left to our own devices in analysing rhythmical and linear patterns in free verse. Rather than recognising a metrical frame and examining a poet's occasional deviations from it, in nonmetrical verse each poem must be analysed on its own merits, an intellectually bracing if often challenging necessity. Take, for example, the American poet William Carlos Williams's (1883–1963) poem 'Death', which begins thus:

He's dead

the dog won't have to
sleep on his potatoes
any more to keep them from freezing

he's dead
the old bastard –
He's a bastard because

there's nothing legitimate in him any
                                        more
                                        he's dead

He's sick dead
                                        he's

a godforsaken curio
without
any breath in it

He's nothing at all
                                        he's dead

American poets, and in particular the expatriates Eliot and Pound, have been crucial in the development of free verse in English, and Williams explicitly argued that his poetry was shaped by the patterns of American speech, repudiating the key metrical device of the iamb in a way which stresses this fact. The iambic frame, which critics have argued was an approximate reflection of English speech patterns, could not reflect the rhythms of the American idiom: 'The iamb is not the normal measure of American speech. The foot has to be expanded or contracted in terms of actual speech … reflect[ing] the flux of modern life'. Accordingly, Williams skews his rhythms in a manner intended to suggests the raw materials of demotic speech patterns. With its hesitations, pauses and repetitions, 'Death' gestures towards the way in which ordinary people speak (or, perhaps more accurately, towards Williams's own under-standing of how they speak). And though this is nonmetrical verse, there is nothing haphazard about it; each line and break within Williams's poem is carefully placed to serve the poem's theme. Consequently, what *is* traditional here is the poetic desire to weld form to content, to ensure that structure complements a poem's argument.

In the main, 'Death' is denuded of figurative language, a tendency which actually heightens the effect of the one metaphor, the 'godforsaken curio'. Such a plain style is appropriate to Williams's attempt to capture the hesitations and prosaic nature of everyday talk about a dead person. And yet his unadorned sentiments themselves have a figurative power: the dog not sleeping on the dead man's potatoes might be true as a statement of fact, but it is also a metaphor which addresses the man's pitifully meagre emotional life. Variation of lineation rather than conformity to an expected number of feet is consciously chosen, leaving line-length a crucial factor in the analysis. A single syllable is used where appropriate; similarly, as many as eight are used where the sense demands it. And the short lines permit ambiguities, as in the monosyllabic line 'he's' which suggests that the dead man is capable of being described in terms of what he *is* as well as what he *was* – an effect which would evaporate if the lines were set 'he's a godforsaken curio without any breath in it'. Similarly, in granting an individual line to the word 'more', there is a suggestion that there is more to say about the dead man, a resonance that the alternative single line 'there's nothing legitimate in him any more' would not offer. The words speak of extinction but the lineation suggests something ongoing.

Repetition is the rhythmic crutch which often replaces metre in free verse. And it is here evident in the repeated use of the words 'he's dead', which resonate throughout the poem in a manner very close to the ancient poetical device of anaphora. The phrase is the heaviest of spondees, and possesses an air of closure which is reinforced by the space lines which often follow the word 'dead'. Nonetheless, throughout the poem, these words actually prompt meditation, being eventually followed by further description of the dead man. Ultimately the space lines give the sense of the speaking voice collecting his thoughts before launching into further description of the dead man. The poem seems to stop, only to start again, and a poem about death sees a constant rebirth of voice. Williams's poem attains the status, in the final analysis, of an elegy, an elegy denuded of highly-wrought rhetoric, but an elegy just the same. Williams's sparse free verse both experiments in nonmetrical rhetoric and ultimately affiliates itself to conventional poetic genre.

In conclusion, we would point out that if the early twentieth-century exponents of nonmetrical verse were poetic rebels, then their successors are working in a context where it is now something of an orthodoxy. Given the post-Romantic tendency for poets habitually to engage in Oedipal strife with their immediate predecessors, it would not be surprising if there was a return to some kind of metrical verse in the not so distant future. If free verse was the dominant poetic form for English poetry for much of the twentieth century, it remains to be seen what verse forms will best characterise the twenty-first.

4.13 EXERCISES

Scan the following extracts for their stress patterns. Use the symbol 'x' to indicate an unstressed syllable and 'ᐟ' to indicate a stressed syllable, as per this line by John Donne:

ᐟ x ᐟ x ᐟ x ᐟ
Go and catch a falling star

What do you think is the base metre of each extract? [The Donne line is trochaic.] What kind of line is used in each case (in terms of trimeter (3 stresses), tetrameter (4 stresses), pentameter (5 stresses), and so on? [The Donne line is a tetrameter.]

Haste thee nymph, and bring with thee

Jest and youthful jollity,

Quips and Cranks, and wanton wiles,

Nods and becks, and wreathed smiles.
– (John Milton, 'L'Allegro')

The western sun now shot a feeble ray,

And faintly scatter'd the remains of day:

Ev'ning approach'd; but oh what hosts of foes

Were never to behold that ev'ning close!
– (Joseph Addison, 'The Campaign, A Poem')

If e'er thy breath with freedom glow'd,

And spurned a tyrant's chain,

Let not thy strong oppressive force

A free-born mouse detain.
– (Anna Barbauld, 'The Mouse's Petition')

The Assyrian came down like the wolf on the fold,

And his cohorts were gleaming in purple and gold;

And the sheen of their spears was like stars on the sea,

When the blue wave rolls nightly on deep Galilee.
– (Lord Byron, 'The Destruction of Sennacherib')

Just for a handful of silver he left us

Just for a ribbon to stick in his coat

Found the one gift of which fortune bereft us,

Lost all the others she lets us devote.
– (Robert Browning, 'The Lost Leader')

The boy stood on the burning deck

Whence all but he had fled;

The flame that lit the battle's wreck

Shone round him o'er the dead.
– (Felicia Hemans, 'Casabianca')

When the castle's rich chambers were haunted and dreary,

The poor little hovel was still and secure;

And no robber e'er enter'd, nor goblin nor fairy,

For the splendours of pride had no charms to allure.
– (Mary Robinson, 'The Poor, Singing Dame')

I sang of leaves, of leaves of gold, and leaves of gold there grew:

Of wind I sang, a wind there came and in the branches blew.

Beyond the Sun, beyond the Moon, the foam was on the Sea,

And by the strand of Ilmarin there grew a golden Tree.
– (J. R. R. Tolkien, 'Song of Eldamar')

It was noon, and on flowers that languish'd around

In silence repos'd the voluptuous bee;

Every leaf was at rest, and I heard not a sound

But the woodpecker tapping the hollow beech-tree.
– (Thomas Moore, 'Ballad Stanzas')

Woman much miss'd, how you call to me, call to me,

Saying that now you are not as you were.
– (Thomas Hardy, 'The Voice')

Teach me half the gladness

That thy brain must know,

Such harmonious madness

From my lips would flow.
– (P. B. Shelley, 'To a Skylark')

Answers to these exercises can be found at pp. 227–31.

5

Comparisons and associations

5.1 LITERAL V. FIGURATIVE

This chapter is devoted to the way that poets make, and always have made, use of figurative or non-literal utterances. A figurative expression occurs where we use, or perhaps interpret, words to mean something other than what they literally say. A 'star', for example, is according to the dictionary 'a celestial body appearing as a luminous point in the night sky', but when we refer to a film or pop celebrity as a 'star', we understand the word in an expansive, metaphoric way: film celebrities are 'stars' in so far as they enjoy a high level of cultural visibility, much as stars stand out luminously against a black sky. What makes the association figurative is that film celebrities, like all human beings, are not literally like distant suns; they only become so if we exercise our imaginations to make a connection. Similarly, a comparison that seems plausible on a literal level, without the aid of the imagination, as for example saying that a mule is like a horse, does not count as figurative.

The *effect* of figurative language, either in poetry or prose, is to create what linguists call deviation or foregrounding. When we read or listen, our attention is never uniform but tends to fix on linguistic elements that in some way stand out. These elements may be repetitions of phraseology, or inversions of normal syntax, or figurative usages, where the words resist being constructed in a literal way. The experience of being pulled up short by some unexpected deviation is something we perhaps most associate with 'hard' or complex poetry, and a prevalence of figurative expressions is probably the most common cause of our sometimes finding poems difficult to understand. As an example of how sharply deviant figurative language in poetry can be, and of how easily it can baffle the reader, we can take the ending of Dylan Thomas's 'Fern Hill'. The poem portrays the narrator growing up on a farm, delighting in his surroundings and oblivious to the encroachments of adulthood. The last stanza runs as follows:

> Nothing I cared, in the lamb white days, that time would take me
> Up to the swallow thronged loft by the shadow of my hand,
>   In the moon that is always rising,
>   Nor that riding to sleep
>   I should hear him fly with the high fields
> And wake to the farm forever fled from the childless land.
> Oh as I was young and easy in the mercy of his means,
>   Time held me green and dying
>   Though I sang in my chains like the sea.

What interests us here are the final two lines with their numerous swerves from literalness. To put matters abruptly, the boy, as he is depicted in the poem, is not 'green and dying', nor is he 'held' by Time or revealed singing in his chains: moreover, even if he did sing in his chains, this does not, on immediate reflection, make him 'like the sea'. To disentangle the literal sense of these lines from their figurative expressions calls for a tortured process of teasing out. The boy is 'green' because he is like the new shoots of a plant, which tend to be more vividly green; he is 'dying' and 'held' (or 'chained') by Time because he is subject to ageing and death like all other natural phenomena; and he 'sings' because singing can be taken as representing a more general quality of high-spirited exuberance. The sea, in its turn, 'sings' because it generates noise; and it can be thought of as being in chains because it consists of movement and stasis, generating waves and billows while the water never actually goes anywhere. This phenomenon can be likened to a man struggling against chains but without ever breaking free from them. Thomas's lines, in their imaginative compression, are a bravura performance; however, at the same time, you might note that a reader who was not well versed in the conventions of figurative usage would be utterly at a loss about what is going on in them.

5.2   METAPHOR AND SIMILE

As we have said, figurative language occurs where words are used in such a way that they don't make some sense unless we depart from their strict dictionary definitions. All types of figurative language seem to incorporate a principle of 'transference' in that properties that are attached to one object are 'carried over' and applied to another. So we can say, for example, that at the end of Thomas's 'Fern Hill', the relation between captor and captive is carried over as a way of explaining how all natural things are subject to the passage of time. Similarly, when we refer to film celebrities as 'stars', we are transferring on to them two properties of literal stars as they appear in the night firmament: that they are highly visible but also exist at a huge remove from the people looking at them. This idea of transference between distinct objects is at the heart of *all* forms of figurative language, but how the transference occurs can vary. In metaphor, the transference takes place on the basis of the two objects being similar to each other: in other words, to say 'Brad Pitt is a star' is really to say that 'Brad Pitt's public visibility is *like* a star shining brightly in the night sky'. Similarly, when W. B. Yeats (1865–1939) writes in 'Sailing to Byzantium' that

> An aged man is but a paltry thing,
> A tattered coat upon a stick,

he is really noting that a wizened, shrunken old man is *like* 'A tattered coat upon a stick'. But just as important as that metaphors *imply* a likeness or similarity is that this is never explicitly stated, and instead a metaphor presents itself as a statement of identity: 'An aged man *is* ...'. Where a metaphor comes clean about the principle of likeness on which it is based, normally by the presence of the word 'like' or a variant like 'as', this is called a simile: we might say a 'metaphor' is a metaphor that conceals its status as such, whereas a simile is a metaphor that owns up to being one.

Although metaphor and simile should be seen as distinct types of figurative expression, poets will often ring the changes between them in a single poem. Wordsworth, for example, begins a famous poem by using the simile 'I wandered lonely *as* a cloud' but then breaks into metaphor as he spots 'a crowd, / A host, of golden daffodils' which are 'dancing in the breeze'. A more modern poem that interweaves simile and metaphor is Stephen Spender's (1909–1995) 'The Pylons':

> The secret of these hills was stone, and cottages
> Of that stone made,
> And crumbling roads
> That turned on sudden hidden villages.
>
> Now over these small hills, they have built the concrete
> That trails black wire;
> Pylons, those pillars
> Bare like nude giant girls that have no secret.
>
> The valley with its gilt and evening look
> And the green chestnut
> Of customary root,
> Are mocked dry like the parched bed of a brook.

> But far above and far as sight endures
> Like whips of anger
> With lightning's danger
> There runs the quick perspective of the future.
>
> This dwarfs our emerald country by its trek
> So tall with prophecy:
> Dreaming of cities
> Where often clouds shall lean their swan-white neck.

Spender's poem is about how electricity pylons, which in the poem are starkly literal but also symbolic of the onward march of progress, have desecrated the landscape of the valley. In the first two stanzas a prominent idea is that of secrecy, the word 'secret' falling almost at the start of the poem and then as the terminal word of the second stanza. When Spender writes that 'The secret of these hills was stone', he intends a double meaning: both 'secret' as 'essence' (as you might say that 'the secret of playing tennis is good hand–eye coordination') but also in the more literal sense of a secreted or hidden thing: stone, in this sense, is a secret because, lying beneath the ground, it is concealed from view. The idea of secrecy is continued in stanza 2 by the image of the pylons which Spender sees as huge sluttish girls ('that have no secret'), with dark hair flaring outwards ('trails black wire') exposing themselves with legs spread wide. The last two stanzas introduce a further important idea. This is the notion that the pylons are a presentiment of the future: as the observer follows the pylon trail as it extinguishes itself in the far distance, he sees this as an emblem of futurity itself. Moreover, what these pylons prophesy is the extinction of the country-side as it gets progressively taken over by urban dwelling ('Dreaming of cities').

Spender's poem is vividly figurative, mixing both similes and metaphors. Stanzas 2, 3 and 4 are given a kind of unity by each having a prominent simile. In stanza 2, the pylons are 'like nude, giant girls'; in stanza 3, the valley and the green chestnut 'Are mocked dry like the parched bed of a brook'; and in 4, in what is really a double simile (where one metaphor builds upon another), 'the quick perspective of the future' (meaning the sense of the future that we get from contemplating the nearly endless line of pylons) is 'Like whips of anger / With lightning's danger'. These similes are meant to be obtrusive but the poem is also laden with more covert metaphoric formulations. In line 1, the 'stone' is not literally the 'secret' of the hills, for it only 'lies underground' like a secret; the valley (line 12) is not literally 'mocked' by the pylons, nor indeed literally 'mocked dry'; the pylons are not actually 'tall with prophecy', nor do they really dream of cities 'Where often clouds shall lean their swan-white neck'. 'The Pylons' is a good example, then, of how a poet intent on writing a poem of a figurative nature has clearly thought hard about how he will formulate this figurative material, eventually hitting on a mixture of overt and covert figures: that is, similes and metaphors.

5.3   METONYMY AND SYNECDOCHE

It sometimes gets forgotten that there exist types of figurative expression, involving the principle of transference outlined above, that do not conform to either metaphor or simile. Two such figurative kinds are metonymy and synecdoche, metonymy being where transference occurs between objects that are closely associated without being entirely similar, and synecdoche where the process takes place between whole and part, or part and whole. These forms of transference are probably no less common in everyday language than metaphor or simile, but we are apt to be less conscious of them. If, for example, we want to make a cup of tea, we need to 'boil the kettle' – but, of course, we do not *literally* 'boil the kettle' but rather boil the water inside the kettle. Although it might seem pedantic to make the point, a transference is occurring here between the water and the kettle itself, the kettle being spoken of as if it were the water. As a transference, this is similar to what we have seen taking place in metaphors and similes, except that the basis on which it happens is not likeness but association, owing in this instance to the physical proximity between the containing kettle and the contained water. There are numerous idioms in English in which a particular object is used to stand in for an institution, activity or event and where the transfer from one to the other works on metonymic lines. For example, in Britain we have a welfare state that is supposed to protect us from 'the cradle to the grave', though, to deal in literal terms, hardly any child is nowadays put to sleep in a 'cradle' and many people are cremated rather than buried. The phrase is accordingly a slightly antiquated way of saying 'from birth until death'. The transference here is similar to that by which we might say that the 'pen is mightier than the sword', where 'pen' and 'sword' equate metonymically with 'propaganda' and 'armed force'. In a similar vein, James Shirley's (1596–1666) poem 'The Glories of our Blood and State' predicts that

> Sceptre and Crown,
> Must tumble down,
> And in the dust be equal made
> With the poor crooked sithe and spade.

Here 'Sceptre', 'Crown', 'sithe' (scythe) and 'spade' are all metonyms: crown and sceptre, objects that are associated with monarchy, are used to refer to the king; and the scythe and spade by the same process represent the country poor.

In synecdoche, the substitution involved concerns the relation of part to whole and vice versa, so that you might say that 'the company hired twenty new hands' where 'hands' really means 'employees', or the people of whom the 'hands' form a part. Similarly, in westerns the cowboy or bounty hunter is often referred to as a 'hired gun', where 'gun' refers to the person who is carrying the gun. Figurative expressions of one kind or another abound in nearly all sorts of language, but it is worth also noting that different types of usage often occur in close vicinity or are enfolded one inside another. If we take, for example, an expression like 'he's hit the bottle again', we can identify a metonymy ('bottle' standing for alcoholic beverages in general) and a metaphor (the verb 'hitting' being used in a loose way to express any compulsive form of behaviour). The movement between the two sorts of figurative language is fluid and seamless.

Although instances of metonymy and synecdoche can be found in innumerable poems, it would be wrong to give them the same status in poetry as metaphor and simile. The ability to make apt and vivacious comparisons between diverse objects is something that we tend to see as a vital part of a poet's kit-bag of skills. It is hard, on the other hand, to cite entire poems, rather than mere stray lines, in which the use of metonymy or synecdoche is constitutive of the overall effect. However, one area where metonymic devices come especially into their own is eroticism, and in particular the way in which in erotic writing sexual excitement is displaced from the body itself on to the clothing that adorns it. A skilful exponent of this erotic technique is the seventeenth-century poet Robert Herrick, and what follows are the first six lines of his poem 'Julia's Petticoat':

> The Azure Robe, I did behold,
> As ayrie as the leaves of gold;
> Which erring here, and wandring there,
> Pleas'd with transgression ev'ry where:
> Sometimes 'two'd pant, and sigh, and heave,
> As if to stir it scarce had leave.

By 'erring', 'wandring' and 'transgression', Herrick means that the petticoat in places rides up or drifts apart, revealing glimpses of Julia's delectable flesh. In line 5, however, he describes the petticoat in rather different terms ''two'd pant, and sigh, and heave'. Clearly, this is figurative, and the petticoat, rather than being spoken of as alternately cloaking and revealing the woman's body is here being figured *as* a body: after all, only a body can 'pant, and sigh, and heave'. The transference taking place here is metonymic: Julia's clothes are described in bodily terms not because her clothes are actually *like* her body but because body and clothing exist in physical proximity.

We want to finish this section by looking at a poem unusual for being structured throughout around the two figurative types of metaphor and metonymy, George Herbert's 'Mortification':

How soon doth man decay!
When clothes are taken from a chest of sweets
To swaddle infants, whose young breath
Scarce knows the way;
Those clouts are little winding sheets,
Which do consigne and send them unto death.

When boyes go first to bed,
They step into their voluntarie graves.
Sleep bindes them fast; onely their breath
Makes them not dead:
Successive nights, like rolling waves,
Convey them quickly, who are bound for death.

When youth is frank and free,
And calls for musick, while his veins do swell,
All day exchanging mirth and breath
In companie;
That musick summons to the knell,
Which shall befriend him at the houre of death.

When man grows staid and wise,
Getting a house and home, where he may move
Within the circle of his breath,
Schooling his eyes;
That dumbe inclosure maketh love
Unto the coffin, that attends his death.

When age grows low and weak,
Marking his grave, and thawing ev'ry yeare,
Till all do melt, and drown his breath
When he would speak;
A chair or litter shows the biere,
Which shall convey him to the house of death.

Man, ere he is aware,
Hath put together a solemnitie,
And drest his herse, while he has breath
As yet to spare:
Yet Lord, instruct us so to die,
That all these dyings may be life in death.

In Christian religion, mortification means the deliberate suppression of our
bodily passions and appetites, one way of achieving this being for the Christian
to make himself reflect constantly on the approaching certainty of death.

Herbert's poem is an exercise along these lines: it encourages us to appreciate how all the phases of our lives are characterised by events that can be seen as mirroring and foreshadowing the inevitable fact of death. The phases of life that the poem concentrates on are five (conforming to the first five stanzas), and each phase is represented by a particular happening with which this era of life is metonymically associated. So here infancy is represented by the baby being wrapped in swaddling clothes; the older years of childhood are figured by beginning to sleep in your own bed; the teenage years (as we would call them) are represented by 'musick' and 'mirth'; adulthood is represented by owning a dwelling; and old age is symbolised by loss of mobility causing the individual to be carried in a 'chair or litter'. Each event, in other words, summarises a whole phase of life associated with it.

To say so much is really to describe how the poem is laid out along one particular axis, but a further axis is provided by its use of metaphor. All of the discrete happenings that are taken as symbolising larger phases of life are also seen as providing a symbolic anticipation of death. Being swaddled as an infant is likened to being wrapped in a winding sheet; sleeping in your own bed is like being in the grave; enjoying music in our youth should make reverberate in our ears the sound of our own death-knell; being encircled by a house and home can remind us of the solitary confinement of the coffin; and being carried in a chair because of infirmity prefigures being carried in a bier 'to the house of death'. The summary that the poem comes to in its final stanza is that 'Man, ere he is aware / Hath put together a solemnitie', meaning that a person's years on earth can be seen as adding up to nothing more than a lifelong funeral ceremony. When we discussed the first 'axis' of the poem, we said that the events of the poem charted metonymically the whole growing up and ageing process. Along the poem's second axis, however, the same events are linked metaphorically to the single terminating event of death. The combination of these two axes makes the poem.

5.4   TENOR, VEHICLE AND GROUND

Metaphors and similes involve, as we have set out above, a transference of properties from one object to another on the grounds of similarity between the two objects. On practically all occasions where they occur, we can derive an additional distinction between the thing the figurative expression is about (which we can call the 'tenor') and the object with which this is compared as a means of drawing out its meaning (which we can call the 'vehicle'). So if we take two well-known opening lines from poems by Burns and Wordsworth respectively,

(a)   O my Luve's like a red, red rose

(b)   I wandered lonely as a cloud,

we can say that in (a) the tenor is Burns's lover who is compared with a rose (the vehicle), and in (b) the tenor is constituted by the speaker's lonely wandering which is seen as analogous to the movement of a cloud (the vehicle). Having introduced these two terms, we can now add a third: the 'ground'. This can be taken to mean the basis on which the comparison is made. In other words, the question a metaphor poses is 'in regard of what ground is the tenor like the vehicle?' If we apply this question to Burns's line, we can say that the lover is like a red rose because she is beautiful and fragrant and perhaps because she possesses red lips and rouged cheeks, a ruddiness of complexion being taken in the eighteenth century (though not so much in our own day) as a sign of female facial beauty. Of course, someone might suggest the ground of the simile to be that Burns's lady had a prickly character, or was troubled with greenfly, but such a person would probably be missing the point.

Even if all metaphors and similes contain the elements of tenor, vehicle and ground, this does not make it the case that all the three elements will be explicit every time a metaphor occurs. So in the case of 'O my Luve's like a red, red rose', we are given the tenor and vehicle but are left to deduce the ground on which the comparison is an apt one. But often a poet will give us tenor, vehicle and ground at the same time, as for example in the opening two lines of Seamus Heaney's (b. 1939) poem 'Digging':

> Between my finger and my thumb
> The squat pen rests; snug as a gun.

Here the comparison made is between the pen and gun (tenor and vehicle) but Heaney also lets us in on the precise ground of the comparison. Pens and guns might be thought similar, in an abstract way, in that they can both be used to promote political causes, but here Heaney is interested more immediately in a sort of physical cosiness: 'snug as a gun'. Both yield easily to the hand of those holding them, and it becomes clear that in this respect they are related to a third tool that figures importantly later on in the poem, the spade: 'the old man could handle a spade'.

Another variation occurs where a poet presents us with the tenor and ground of a comparison but not the metaphoric vehicle, or the object with which the tenor is being compared. Take these lines from the beginning of T. S. Eliot's 'The Love Song of J. Alfred Prufrock':

> The yellow fog that rubs its back upon the window-panes,
> The yellow smoke that rubs its muzzle on the window-panes,
> Licked its tongue into the corners of the evening,
> Lingered upon the pools that stand in drains,
> Let fall upon its back the soot that falls from chimneys,
> Slipped by the terrace, made a sudden leap,
> And seeing that it was a soft October night,
> Curled once about the house, and fell asleep.

These lines allude to a phenomenon that has now all but disappeared, that of the dense fog or 'pea-souper' which because of high pollution levels was common in British cities before the Second World War. These fogs were opaque, sodden and practically tangible. The literal scene that Eliot describes consists of the suffocating fog, a rather seedy and dirty urbanism consisting of terraced houses, chimneys spewing out soot and 'pools that stand in drains', and a late evening setting. The urban, night-time scenario, and Eliot's suggestion that the fog is like a soft animate thing, induces an extended metaphor in which the fog is likened to a cat that 'rubs its back', 'rubs its muzzle', 'Licked its tongue' and so on. But although Eliot uses feline expressions, he nowhere introduces the word 'cat'. The poem merely asserts that the fog is like some other object and tells you what the points of the comparison are: you as the reader have to deduce the object's identity. But another curious feature of the passage is that the cat seems to flicker between literal and figurative status. In the first two lines quoted, it is clear that the cat (or the thing that 'rubs its back') is not intended as literal but simply tells you more about the nature of the fog. But in the next few lines the fog seems to get left behind, and the cat vehicle is developed to such an extent that some readers end up supposing that the cat is actually literal. Only when you come to the final image of the cat curling around the house, which only an elephantine cat could possibly do, is the reader given irresistible confirmation of the cat's figurative status.

For a final example of the complex ways in which tenor, vehicle and ground can be manipulated in a densely metaphoric poem, we propose looking at Craig Raine's (b. 1944) vogue poem of the 1970s, 'A Martian Sends a Postcard Home':

> Caxtons are mechanical birds with many wings
> and some are treasured for their markings –
>
> they cause the eyes to melt
> or the body to shriek without pain.
>
> I have never seen one fly, but
> sometimes they perch on the hand.

Mist is when the sky is tired of flight
and rests its soft machine on ground:

then the world is dim and bookish
like engravings under tissue paper.

Rain is when the earth is television.
It has the property of making colours darker.

Model T is a room with the lock inside –
a key is turned to free the world

for movement, so quick there is a film
to watch for anything missed.

But time is tied to the wrist
or kept in a box, ticking with impatience.

In homes, a haunted apparatus sleeps,
that snores when you pick it up.

If the ghost cries, they carry it
to their lips and soothe it to sleep

with sounds. And yet, they wake it up
deliberately, by tickling with a finger.

Only the young are allowed to suffer
openly. Adults go to a punishment room

with water but nothing to eat.
They lock the door and suffer the noises

alone. No one is exempt
and everyone's pain has a different smell.

At night, when all the colours die,
they hide in pairs

and read about themselves –
in colour, with their eyelids shut.

It might be appropriate to begin by glossing the poem's meaning. Raine imagines a Martian visiting earth and trying to make sense of all the earthly phenomena he encounters. Unfortunately, his inexperience of his new planet means that, while making a series of fairly intelligent guesses about various human things and practices, he unerringly misconstrues the world around him. The first three stanzas are about books, objects that we hold in the hand, that sometimes contain illustrations and that have the power to make us laugh or cry. Stanzas 4 and 5 pursue a comparison between the obscurity of vision caused by mist and the effect of looking at engravings through protective tissue paper. In stanza 6, rain is compared to television, possibly because we normally look out at rain through windows and a window is like a television screen, but perhaps rather more because the pictures on television sets of the 1970s were often crossed with flickering lines which looked like streaks of rain. In stanzas 7 and 8, the Martian tries to describe taking a car journey but he confuses himself into thinking that the car remains stationary while the outside world moves quickly backwards, its backward rush being caught, as it were, on the 'film' of its rear-view mirror. The next four stanzas describe in oblique ways two appliances: in the first instance, a watch ('time is tied to the wrist') and then a phone. Stanzas 13 to 16 describe the experience of going to the toilet, the solitariness of this act convincing the Martian that some ritual punishment is being undergone. Finally, in the concluding two stanzas, the Martian relates the human activities of sleeping and dreaming. Throughout the poem, then, the Martian describes things about him exactly as he sees them: he is a literalist; but the way that Raine expresses his continual misunderstanding is through a skilful exploitation of figurative techniques.

The poem deliberately poses itself as a conundrum; at every turn some piece of information is held back, or a veiled expression is used in place of a more candid one, so that we are required to make a succession of interpretive leaps. In the first two lines, for example, we are told that

> Caxtons are mechanical birds with many wings
> and some are treasured for their markings –

We understand a comparison to be occurring; we understand the vehicle ('mechanical birds'); and we understand the ground of the comparison (that the mechanical birds and the thing to which they are being compared have 'wings' and sometimes valuable markings). However, Raine deliberately withholds the metaphor's tenor, or the literal thing about which the comparison is being made, by veiling it under the obscure word 'caxton'. The erudite reader may know, or be able to fathom out, that 'caxton' means a 'book', the word deriving from William Caxton, the inventor of the printing press; most readers, though, are likely to be left at a loss. In the first instance, then, the poem provides us with the vehicle and ground of the metaphor from which we have to extrapolate the tenor, but if we move on to stanza 6 the technique is quite different. Here the tenor is announced as 'rain' and this is likened to television, with the reader being left with the dilemma of teasing out in what way or ways this comparison holds true: as we have said above, one ground of the comparison could be, for instance, that looking at a television set is like looking through a window, as when it rains we are generally inside looking outwards through a screen of glass.

So far, the two metaphoric techniques we have noted have involved *one* term of the tenor–vehicle–ground notation being suppressed so as to create an interpretive gap which the reader has to fill, but in stanzas 10–12 Raine ratchets up the device by suppressing *two* of these terms. In our experience, most people interpret the 'haunted apparatus' of stanza 10 as a baby, which is an intelligent response but also an incorrect one. Raine is actually talking about a phone, which he elsewhere refers to as a 'ghost', an object that like a baby is often picked up and 'tickled' (or dialled) by adults. The Martian thinks it 'ghost-like' because it is undecidedly both alive and dead: although it mostly rests passively, on occasions it comes noisily to life, and speaks to, and receives speech from, humans. Raine skilfully constructs his implied comparison between phones and babies but does so without once mentioning either 'phone' or 'baby'. The upshot is that for many readers an interpretive short-circuiting occurs, and they interpret the appliance *as a* baby rather than as a phone being spoken of in baby-like terms. We can express the whole matter in a more technical way. The poem supplies us with the ground of a comparison (sleeping, snoring, crying and being tickled), and the reader is left either to flounder or to work out the metaphoric tenor and vehicle that will make sense of the ground. The fact that this can be done at all, even if not unerringly, says a lot for people's acquired skills in responding to figurative language.

5.5   CONCEITS AND EXTENDED SIMILES

A conceit is a particular type of metaphor: conceits tend to involve comparison of entities that, at first sight at least, are very dissimilar, and perhaps comically so; they tend to take into account not one but several discrete points of similarity between the compared objects; and they often exude a self-consciousness of their own ingenuity or virtuosity. The difference between a conceit and an ordinary metaphor is not one of category but one of degree: a metaphor that is complex and sustained, that involves a tenor and vehicle that seem sharply divergent, and that tends a little towards exhibitionism turns into a conceit. Conceits have become associated in particular with a seventeenth-century 'school' of poets called the 'metaphysicals', but conceits or extended metaphors can be found in poems of all periods. We can begin by taking as a first example some lines from Matthew Arnold's poem 'Dover Beach' (1867):

The Sea of Faith
Was once, too, at the full, and round earth's shore
Lay like the folds of a bright girdle furl'd.
But now I only hear
Its melancholy, long, withdrawing roar,
Retreating, to the breath
Of the night-wind, down the vast edges drear
And naked shingles of the world.

'Dover Beach' is a bleak poem, much beset by anxieties about the traumatic condition of human life and about the capacity of religious faith to offer support and consolation. Arnold imagines human life as a shoreline lapped by a 'Sea of Faith'; but rather than the tide alternately ebbing and flowing, the 'tide' of faith is now in full retreat from the 'naked shingles of the world'. The metaphor of the sea works on different levels: human life is imagined as sea-bound and therefore characterised by a depressing island-like solitariness; religious faith, like the sea, bounds the entire human world; and religious faith is everywhere seen to be in decline like a tide slowly but unceasingly going out.

The 'Sea of Faith' metaphor is developed across eight lines and involves several points of correspondence between tenor and vehicle; on the other hand, it doesn't exhibit a self-consciousness of its own figurative virtuosity as we tend to associate with conceits. Moreover, although the whole poem is set seemingly on a clifftop, the figure of the 'Sea of Faith' occupies only a discrete part of the overall poem. For a poem whose very totality is taken up with the working through of a conceit, we might turn instead to Andrew Marvell's (1621–1678) 'On a Drop of Dew':

See how the orient dew,
Shed from the bosom of the morn
    Into the blowing roses,
Yet careless of its mansion new,
For the clear region where 'twas born
    Round in itself incloses:
    And in its little globe's extent,
Frames as it can its native element.
    How it the purple flow'r does slight,
        Scarce touching where it lies,
    But gazing back upon the skies,
        Shines with a mournful light,
            Like its own tear,
Because so long divided from the sphere.
    Restless it rolls and unsecure,
        Trembling lest it grow impure,
    Till the warm sun pity its pain,

And to the skies exhale it back again.
    So the soul, that drop, that ray
Of the clear fountain of eternal day,
Could it within the human flow'r be seen,
    Remembering still its former height,
    Shuns the sweet leaves and blossoms green,
    And recollecting its own light,
Does, in its pure and circling thoughts, express
The greater heaven in an heaven less.
    In how coy a figure wound,
    Every way it turns away:
    So the world excluding round,
    Yet receiving in the day,
    Dark beneath, but brought above,
    Here disdaining, there in love.
    How loose and easy hence to go,
    How girt and ready to ascend,
    Moving but on a point below,
    It all about does upward bend.
Such did the manna's sacred dew distill,
White and entire, though congealed and chill,
Congealed on earth: but does, dissolving, run
Into the glories of th'almighty sun.

The poem consists of a comparison between a drop of dew as it has formed in a rose head and the human soul as it occupies the body. The first eighteen lines are devoted to the dew drop; the second eighteen to the soul; and the final four round off the poem. It might be as well to approach the poem first by simply paraphrasing what it has to say. The poet imagines a dew drop that has formed overnight in a rose flower; he notices how it is rounded and self-enclosed like a bead, and how it seems to form a little world unto itself, separated off from the flower in which it has taken up residence; he also notices how it reflects the light of the sky as if pining to return there, indeed almost as if shedding the tear-drop of itself in regret for not being there; and finally he narrates how, as the sun rises in the sky, the water drop evaporates into the air again. The poet now moves to the human soul and reflects that, could we but see one, we would appreciate how it too constitutes a self-enclosed world, residing in the human body but, at the same time, imagining and yearning for a return to the heavenly realm from where it came. Like the drop giving itself gladly to its own evaporation, the soul is 'loose and easy hence to go'.

What characterises Marvell's poem? For one thing, we sense an unusual degree of equality between tenor and vehicle, to the point where it would be hard to stipulate firmly which is which. In most metaphors, the relation between tenor and vehicle is skewed and uneven: the vehicle gets introduced only to afford us some insight about the tenor, and once that insight has been realised, it becomes, as it were, disposable. But Marvell is scrupulous in lavishing exactly the same number of lines on the dew drop as on the soul, so the poem impresses us as managing to speak about the soul in terms of the dew drop and about the dew drop in terms of the soul. But another important aspect of the poem relates to the linkage between the two key images, especially the use of the conjunction 'so' in line 19. If we were to speak somewhat flatly, we might say that the poem asserts that 'a soul is like a dew drop'; but it would be more precise to express the poem's meaning in causal terms: '*because* a dew drop has certain properties, a human soul must be ordered along the same lines'.

Marvell's poem practises what is called 'reasoning by analogy': it arrives at the proposition that the soul has particular properties through assuming it exists in a relation of analogy to another entity which boasts the same ones. Of course, the logic is flimsy (why after all should it be assumed that a dew drop and a soul will bear close similarity?), but even so the mere use of metaphor to support a line of argument might surprise us, given that metaphor has often been seen as an intrinsically decorative technique which, by dint of being 'imaginative', tends also to be non-rational. In poems of earlier periods, however, especially the seventeenth century, conceits were often deployed to clinch arguments and demonstrate logical positions. For a further, and particularly good, example of this, we can look briefly at the beginning of John Dryden's poem *Religio Laici* ('A Layman's Faith'):

> DIM, as the borrow'd beams of Moon and Stars
> To *lonely, weary, wandring* Travellers,
> Is *Reason* to the *Soul*: And as on high,
> Those rowling Fires *discover* but the Sky
> Not light us *here*; So *Reason*'s glimmering Ray
> Was lent, not to *assure* our *doubtfull* way,
> But *guide* us upward to a *better Day*.
> And as those nightly Tapers disappear
> When Day's bright Lord ascends our Hemisphere;
> So pale grows *Reason* at *Religions* sight;
> So *dyes*, and so *dissolves* in *Supernatural Light*.

The first ten lines of the poem make for an eloquent statement of a form of Christian belief called theism: that is the belief that we can apprehend the existence of God only through his *revealing* himself (in Christ, in the Bible, in our own lives) rather than, as some people in Dryden's day believed, through using our rational faculties to produce reasons why God *must* exist. Dryden advocates an attitude to God characterised by a simplicity of faith, and which resists any attempt to rationalise God's existence and actions. Again as a way of getting to grips with the poem, it might be best to offer a summary paraphrase.

The poem begins with the image of some travellers wandering lost and aimless, trying unsuccessfully to find their way by the faint beams of the moon and stars. This image he associates with the relation between the soul and the reason: the light of reason, too, is distant and weak, unable to point the way for the erring soul. Similarly, just as when the lights of the night sky are consumed by the greater light of the rising sun, so the flickering lamp of reason will be dissolved into the vastness of '*Supernatural Light*'. In other words, our minds cannot deduce for us that God exists; only the overwhelming force of God's revelation to us can demonstrate that.

Just as in Marvell's 'On a Drop of Dew', except perhaps more so, the purpose of the conceit is to sustain an argument. Once more the fact of causation is indicated through the conjunction 'so', which occurs in lines 5, 10 and 11. The meaning of the lines might be rendered as follows: 'Just as the stars prove too dim to direct "*wandring* Travellers"', so too is the light of reason too dim to guide the human soul'. The poem lures you into the chain of its reasoning: once we accept the initial analogy, we find ourselves swept along indeflectibly to a set of conclusions about the relation between reason and the soul and about the proper practice of religious faith. The only way to duck out of these conclusions is to refuse at the outset to comply with the analogy being proposed. The multifaceted nature of Dryden's metaphor, its participation in a process of argument, and its knowing virtuosity have taken us a long way from some of the simple comparisons, like Wordsworth's 'I wandered lonely as a cloud', which we encountered earlier in the chapter. And this might usefully caution us that figurative language is a very broad church.

5.6 DEAD AND DYING METAPHORS

It is hard to sum up what makes for a good metaphor. Craig Raine's early poetry is full of crisp metaphors that draw surprising but also convincing comparisons between different things. In the poem which we discussed earlier, a phone is likened to a baby; and in other poems that Raine published alongside 'A Martian', he describes dead dandelions as 'bald as drumsticks', some dead trout as 'aristocrats with monocles', and an open packet of cigarettes as a 'miniature organ' (that is, the individual cigarettes are stacked like organ pipes). As we encounter these comparisons, we feel a sudden jolt of recognition at their aptness, but also a sense of their being hard won, or won in the face of an overriding implausibility and unlikelihood. Raine convinces us that we *do* behave towards phones somewhat as we treat babies, but at the same time we know that this analogy is secured against the backdrop of a myriad ways in which phones and babies are entirely dissimilar.

Yet this recognition of a principle of analogy between otherwise dissimilar things does not account for all metaphors. For example, Keats (1795–1821) uses some very rich figurative language to describe a Grecian urn:

> Thou still unravished bride of quietness,
> Thou foster-child of silence and slow time.

The lines are beautifully evocative, but they do not cause in us that jolt of recognition we talked about above. Nobody would respond to them by saying, 'Yes, I can see, even though I'd never noticed it before, that a Grecian urn really is like an "unravished bride of quietness"'. Rather the lines create a sort of aura of figurative association that, while rich and challenging, does not necessarily prompt in us a fresh perception about the relation between things in the world.

Yet to speak in such terms about metaphors being successful or unsuccessful perhaps fails to do full justice to how *useful* metaphors can be to us in a whole range of different contexts. Moreover, metaphors should not be seen as a kind of stylistic bolt-on, as a way merely of embellishing a pre-decided thought or idea, for metaphors can have a deeper role in actually shaping the way in which we think about the world that we inhabit. Indeed, metaphors may not just determine how we frame individual ideas but also how we accommodate them in larger systems of concepts. The philosophers of language George Lakoff and Mark Johnson describe metaphors that serve this function as 'orientational', since most have to do with positioning in space.[1] To draw upon an example given by them, we might say that how we think about sickness and health is governed by a perception that healthiness always tends 'upwards' whereas sickness and death always tend 'downwards'. This elementary principle gives rise to expressions such as

> He is at the peak of fitness
> He is in top shape
> Her recovery was so dramatic that she practically rose from the dead
> He fell ill
> She is sinking fast
> She went down with a bug
> Her health went into long-term decline.

It is true that illness and death do literally bring about a downward physical movement as we take to our beds or (in the worst scenario) are lowered into the grave, but when we talk of 'going down with a cold', no actual spatial movement need be entailed. The perception that health equals upwards and illness equals downwards enables us to spin out a whole sequence of meta-phoric idioms that are immediately intelligible within this larger framework. So we could say that 'Brian's health went into sudden free-fall', the idiom, while

not exactly being commonplace, being one whose meaning is readily intelligible.

Orientational metaphors exist across a range of different areas, one such
being that of human relationships. Lakoff and Johnson, for example, describe
several variants on the stock notion that a love relationship is like a journey
taken together by two people:

> We are at a crossroads in our relationship
> Perhaps we should just go our separate ways
> We can't go on like this
> We can't go back now
> This relationship just isn't going anywhere
> We're stuck in a rut
> This is a dead-end relationship
> Our marriage is on the rocks
> This relationship is off the rails

The most common metaphor is that of love's being a car journey ('at a
crossroads', 'stuck in a rut'), though it can be applied by extension to a train
journey ('off the rails') or sea journey ('on the rocks'). Although no one would
claim that such metaphors are highly inventive, this is not to deny their
usefulness in helping us to express the ideas involved.

The orientational metaphors proposed by Lakoff and Johnson are mostly
ones that have become encrusted with cliché. 'Marriage on the rocks', for
example, is a phrase that is itself washed up and on the rocks. The language is
full of worn-out metaphors of this nature: we might sit in a committee room
thinking that one person has a particular 'axe to grind'; another person's
outdated opinions make them a 'dinosaur'; a further person is all too ready to
'tug their forelock to authority'; and the chairperson is prepared to 'ride
roughshod' over everybody else's views. These may be (to speak metaphorically) 'dying' metaphors but should not be classed as entirely 'dead'. They
are still alive in as much as everybody still appreciates the fact of their
being figurative constructions. We ought properly to reserve the phrase 'dead
metaphor' for metaphors that are so bleached out that we can easily forget that
they are figurative. In one sense, indeed, they may no longer be metaphors, since
the non-literal use of the word may have become so common that it may have
acceded to the status of a literal meaning in its own right, recorded as such in
the dictionary. A good example is the word 'star' as applied to celebrities: a literal
sense of the word is now given as 'a leading performer, or one supposed to draw
the public'. Similarly, if we were to say that 'Louise is a pig', you might think
this commonplace insult were based on a metaphoric transference, yet the word
'pig' as meaning a person who is 'dirty, greedy, gluttonous, or cantankerous' is

given in the dictionary as an entirely literal sense. Such instances as this are
legion in the language: when individuals were first declared to be the 'heads' of
organisations (as schools or corporations), the expression was employed in a
metaphoric relation to the physical head, 'the uppermost or foremost part of an
animal's body', but the word has long since acquired the purely literal sense of
'a chief or leader'. Equally, words like 'cock-pit', meaning the confined space in
a vehicle occupied by its pilot or driver, or 'hard shoulder', the hard verge of
a motorway restricted to emergency stopping, are so much part of everyday
usage that we forget altogether how peculiar they are as metaphors.

Dead metaphors differ from live ones because live ones put the language
under duress and bend it in some way, making previously unnoticed connections between concepts, whereas dead ones merely reinforce existing
connections. It would be wrong, though, to suppose that if a poet introduces a
lifeless metaphor, this must damage the poem in which it occurs: indeed, poets
sometimes use such metaphors for conscious effect. As one example, let's take
the first stanza of Geoffrey Hill's (b. 1932) poem 'The Martyrdom of Saint
Sebastian':

> Naked, as if for swimming, the martyr
> Catches his death in a little flutter
> Of plain arrows. A grotesque situation,
> But priceless, and harmless to the nation.

The Christian martyr Sebastian was a third-century AD Roman captain, living
in France, who secretly practised as a Christian. When his favouring of
Christians was brought to the notice of the Roman emperor Domitian, he was
sentenced to be executed by archers. However, his wounds not proving fatal, he
was nursed back to life, though only for the same emperor to procure his death
by other means a short time afterwards. The image of Saint Sebastian's near-
naked body being punctured by a flurry of arrows was reproduced by
numerous Renaissance painters, and has become a powerful statement of
spirituality and eroticism. Hill's poem begins with this image, but treats it, rather
than with solemnity, with a curiously teasing flippancy.

The poem opens irreverently: 'Naked, as if for swimming ...'; Sebastian, like
Christ himself, was stripped, not for swimming, but for a traumatic execution,
and the comparison of the two activities initially jars as maladroit and heartless.
In line 2, however, Hill continues in the same vein of dry mirth, this time
introducing a play on the figurative idea of 'catching one's death'. Being
stripped in the open air, Sebastian might be thought vulnerable to 'catching his
death of cold', but he also catches his death in as much as his body receives
('Catches') the arrows shot into it. The sad scenario of Sebastian's death Hill
describes as 'grotesque' but also 'priceless'. The word 'priceless', here, is curious:

some of the pictorial representations of St Sebastian's death are literally priceless, in as much as it would be impossible to put a definitive figure on their monetary value. But the poem also seems to intend 'priceless' in the modern and figurative sense as referring to some uniquely hilarious incident, as you might say 'It was priceless when Bill's trousers fell down'. The overall effect of the lines is manipulative and unsettling, leaving us unsure of the poem's tone or how we should respond to it. Instrumental in this is a flickering between literality and living and dead metaphors. 'Catches his death', for example, has a certain metaphoric vividness to it (he doesn't literally catch the arrows, nor for that matter literally catch his *death*), but this is compromised and infected by the appallingly clichéd metaphor of 'catch your death of cold'; similarly, we acknowledge the literal significance of 'priceless' in connection with valuable paintings but also can't avoid hearing its figurative sense as applied to comic events. The stanza testifies to how bad metaphors can, in some instances, be as indispensable to the realisation of a poet's intended effect as good ones.

While it is natural for us to say that poetry should avoid cliché, banality, moribund metaphors and so on, all of these evils can be turned to good if they suit the context in which they occur. We want to draw this section to a close by looking at a stanza from a work that in a poll conducted in 1996 was voted the nation's best-loved poem. This is W. H. Auden's 'Stop all the Clocks', a poem which laments the death of a lover. What follows is the third stanza:

> He was my North, my South, my East and West,
> My working week and my Sunday rest,
> My noon, my midnight, my talk, my song;
> I thought that love would last for ever: I was wrong.

If we look coldly on these lines, it is easy to think their figurative content rather threadbare. The tenor of the metaphor is the poet's lover, while its vehicle consists of a list of correlatives ('my North, my South, my East and West'), but we still might feel compelled to ask 'what precisely is the ground of this comparison?' And this is apt to prove a hard question to answer without ending up saying something vapid like his lover 'embraces all the coordinates of the poet's life', or 'constitutes all the points on his emotional compass'. The metaphors, in other words, seem flabby: Auden merely cites lots of phenomena that impact on the poet's existence to express how his lover meant 'everything' to him. There's none of the crisp mapping of concept on concept as when Raine, for example, tells us that a phone is like a baby, or when Eliot compares a fog with a slinking cat. Yet to criticise the stanza's use of metaphor in this way, as it were against a copybook of proper metaphoric technique, is in some respects to miss the point and do the poem an injustice. For the poem is not just about how the *poet* but about how *poetry* mourns the death of the lover.

Auden's metaphors are loose and slushy because poetry itself, and especially its capacity for sharp metaphoric formulation, has faded on the death of the loved one. Metaphor has shrunk to cliché, but it is through such sad clichés that the real pain and poignancy of the poem can assert themselves.

5.7   RIDDLE POEMS

Earlier in the chapter, we approached metaphors mostly as localised effects within poems: we noted, for example, Wordsworth's 'lonely as a cloud' and Stephen Spender's lewd description of telegraph pylons as 'Bare like nude giant girls'. In such instances, the figurative effect flickers down the length of a single line and then comes to a close. Equally, we discussed Marvell's 'On a Drop of Dew', where the *entirety* of the poem is taken up with a single elaborate comparison: the metaphor *is* the poem. In this final section, we want to look at some poems that consist of multiple metaphors, where comparisons are strung together as if in a chain. A homely way of describing such poems is as 'riddles', although not all of them deliberately conceal their subject-matter in the way we normally associate with riddles.

Riddles and metaphors are closely related. What a riddle does is to test whether the listener can deduce a tenor merely from being given a series of vehicles or metaphoric correlations. Here, for example, are two traditional English riddles:

> (1)   A flock of white sheep
>   On a red hill;
>   Here they go, there they go,
>   Now they stand still!

> (2)   As high as a castle,
>   As weak as a wastle [a kind of fine bread];
>   And all the king's horses
>   Cannot pull it down.

The meaning of riddle (1) is the teeth and gums: when we chew, the sideways and up-and-down motion of our teeth resembles a flock of sheep moving back and forth over the red hill of the gums. In riddle (2), the meaning is 'smoke', a substance which rises in high plumes, is fragile and wispy like fine bread, and remains too fugitive for capture or suppression by armies. What you might notice is that the technique of these riddles is identical with that of Craig Raine's 'A Martian', in that we are given the vehicle and ground of a metaphor but are left to uncover the tenor: we can deduce that the entities that are white and move like sheep are teeth; while the thing that is 'As high as a castle, / As weak as a wastle' can be deduced to be smoke.

The riddles above are short and unsophisticated, but many riddles are more elaborate than this. Indeed, the riddle form has long been recognised by poets as providing a useful poetic model. We want to study this interconnection of riddles and metaphors by considering a poem by George Herbert. The poem in question is not exactly a riddle in that both the title and the initial word of the first line name the subject of the poem. We have accordingly suppressed both of these in setting out the poem below:

> [   ] the Churches banquet, Angels age,
>   Gods breath in man returning to his birth,
>   The soul in paraphrase, heart in pilgrimage,
> The Christian plummet sounding heav'n and earth;
>
> Engine against th'Almightie, sinners towre,
>   Reversed thunder, Christ-side-piercing spear,
>   The six-daies world transposing in an houre,
> A kinde of tune, which all things heare and fear;
>
> Softnesse, and peace, and joy, and love, and blisse,
>   Exalted Manna, gladnesse of the best,
>   Heaven in ordinarie, man well drest,
> The milkie way, the bird of Paradise,
>
>   Church-bels beyond the starres heard, the souls blood,
>   The land of spices; something understood.

In spite of there being a full stop tagged on the end, the poem does not conform to a sentence-unit; rather it consists of a string of phrases, each of which encapsulates some aspect of the object described. The word we have lopped off the front of the poem, and that solves the riddle that the poem as a consequence turns into, is 'prayer'. Prayer, so the first stanza tells us, is the 'Churches banquet' because it offers spiritual nourishment; it admits the Christian to a realm of timelessness like the a-temporal condition of angels ('Angels age'); just as God breathes life into man, prayer is a returning back of that breath in an act of supplication; it is an enlargement and discovery of the soul ('the soul in paraphrase'); it is a going forth in pilgrimage to God; and it is like a plumb-line, a builders' instrument for gauging the strict vertical, stretching between heaven and earth.

The whole poem is of this nature – a rapt harping on the single idea of prayer. Although what immediately strikes us is the sheer piling up of analogies, the movement of the poem also admits a sense of development and climax. In the first part of the poem, the comparisons bear witness to a reaching out from man to God, as in 'heart in pilgrimage'; they stress that prayer is an occasion for spiritual striving and supplication, undertaken moreover without certainty of divine sympathy. Yet as the poem draws to its finish, it becomes suffused with a happy conviction that the narrator's prayers will be answered, because it is of the very nature of prayer that God *will* receive and be hospitable to it. The last six lines are positively upbeat, the penultimate line, for example, stressing that prayers are not just like church bells, but like 'Church-bels beyond the starres *heard*' (our emphasis). The final phrase of the poem is also clinching in two respects. In the first instance, it crowns the poem's swelling reassurance that prayers will be answered: indeed, it proposes that we can be so certain of this that we can actually *define* 'prayer' as 'something understood' (that is, 'understood' by God). But the phrase 'something understood' is also signal in another respect: it is literal, not metaphoric. Prayer is not *like* 'something understood'; it *is* 'something understood'. At the end of the poem, spiritual confidence brings also a confidence to speak for the first time literally and plainly.

Riddle poems, it has to be admitted, are not especially common, but the technique on which they are based, that of drawing analogies between dissimilar things, is one of the staple techniques of poetry. Probably the best modern exponent of the riddling art is Sylvia Plath (1932–1963) whose poems 'Balloons' and 'You're' are both fine examples of the genre. Like Herbert's poem, 'You're' consists of a list of analogies, its second stanza running as follows:

> Vague as fog and looked for like mail.
> Farther off than Australia.
> Bent-backed Atlas, our traveled prawn.
> Snug as a bud and at home
> Like a sprat in a pickle jug.
> A creel of eels, all ripples.
> Jumpy as a Mexican bean.
> Right, like a well-done sum.
> A clean slate, with your face on.

This is one riddle that we don't intend to unlock; it is left here for you to work out.

5.8   EXERCISES

Colette Bryce (b. 1970) comes from Derry, Northern Ireland, though she has for some time been based in the North East of England. Her first collection, *The Heel of Bernadette* (from which the poem beneath is taken), came out in 2000, but she achieved greater prominence in 2003 when her poem 'The Full Indian Rope Trick' won the National Poetry Competition. The same work became the title-poem for her second collection published in 2005, which was short-listed for the T. S. Eliot Award. She is currently poetry editor for the influential magazine *Poetry London*.

Wish You Were

Here, an aftertaste of traffic taints
the city's breath, as mornings
yawn and bare this street

like teeth. Here, airplanes leaving
Heathrow scare this house
to trembling; these rooms protect

their space with outstretched walls,
and wait. And evenings fall
like discs in a juke box, playing

a song called *Here*, night after night.
Wish you were. Your postcards
land in my hall like meteorites.

1. Comment on the poem's use of comparisons. Try to identify whether these involve metaphor or simile.

2. Comment on the use of sound effects such as consonance and assonance, especially in the opening stanza.

3. Some of Bryce's poems use the same kind of 'defamiliarising' techniques that we encounter in Craig Raine's 'A Martian Sends a Postcard Home' (see pp. 120–1): that is, they imagine how everyday phenomena might appear to someone entirely unaccustomed to them. Consider Bryce's use of such techniques in this poem. At what points are you most aware of them?

4. What critical observations can you make about the following? (i) The title and its relation to the rest of the poem; (ii) the spelling of 'airplanes' (as opposed to 'aeroplanes') in line 4; and (iii) the relation between lines, sentences and stanzas.

5. Do you like the poem? If so, why?

6. Try to write a poem of your own in the 'Martian' style, by making ordinary things seem unfamiliar through the way in which you describe them.

NOTE

1. George Lakoff and Mark Johnson, *Metaphors We Live By* (Chicago, 1980).

6

The words of poetry

POLONIUS: What do you read, my Lord?
HAMLET: Words, words, words.

6.1   LINGUISTIC DIVERSITY

Britain is to a large extent, and especially in comparison with the United States, a monoglot society: that's to say that the vast majority of people speak and write a shared language – English. Yet even despite this, a marked feature of the language we experience and use remains its diversity. Different speech dialects continue to flourish, even if these are being eroded by the slow drip of our exposure to nationwide television networks; we can discriminate at once between polite and slang verbal usages; we know how to modulate our language in response to the person we are addressing, as when, for example, we talk to young children; and we are sensitive to specialised registers of language enclustering particular activities or professions: legalese, journalese, the formulaic patter of advertising copy and so on. This variability of the language provides an opportunity, but also poses a dilemma, for poets: what should a poet's relation to the language be? and what form of language, given the alternatives, should a poet adopt for his verses? This chapter is concerned with how poets use words but also with how the issue of appropriate language is an explicit theme in many poets' work.

Given that we all share a sense of language's enormous versatility and diversity, how should we account for this phenomenon? To this question, there seem to be two answers. In the first instance, we can point to the sheer numerousness of words in the language. The second edition of the *Oxford*

English Dictionary, for example, contains approximately 750,000 entries, comprising a verbal trove probably twenty times larger than the number of words that even a very sophisticated user will ever need to employ. Of course, a significant portion of the words in the *OED* are 'archaic', having long dropped out of common usage, but, even so, it remains the case that whatever the entity or concept to which we want to refer, the language will always offer us a multiplicity of possible verbal choices. We can demonstrate this point by listing just some of the words and phrases that could be used in place of the expression 'to die':

> to decease, to perish, to pass away or slip away, to give up the ghost, to meet your maker, to go to a better place, to push up the daisies, to turn up or curl up one's toes, to kick the bucket, to kick your clogs, to peg out, to croak, to snuff it.

Whenever we say anything, it is inevitable that we will be choosing our words from a range of alternatives existing to hand; and that different people will select differently, and that we ourselves may select differently on different occasions, is one reason for the general diversity of the language.

It is not, though, the only reason. A good analogy for the way that language works is with the game of chess, especially in as much as chess has a small and finite set of rules from which a nearly infinite number of match situations can develop. We might say of language, in its turn, that from a fairly meagre stock of grammatical rules, a nearly limitless set of structures can emerge compliant with them. To illustrate this point, look at the sentences beneath, all of which are more or less identical in meaning while being dissimilar in structure:

> She put the book on the table.
> The book was put on the table by her.
> On the table, she put the book.

Even though the meaning being expressed is very simple, and though we have kept to the same fixed vocabulary, so flexible is the language that we can formulate the idea in three distinct ways. It should be recognised, too, that language diversity of this kind is a pre-requisite for literature in general. It is only, after all, because language affords such a degree of choice that it becomes possible for a select category of users, poets and other creative writers, to be acclaimed for being unusually adept in exercising such choices.

So far we have represented language diversity to you in neutral terms: we have simply stated that the language always furnishes us with a multiplicity of ways of saying something. But choices that we make between different words or expressions invariably carry social overtones. We tend instinctively to position words along an axis of politeness or colloquialism, formality or abruptness. So, for example, referring to a person's 'passing away' as opposed to 'dying' or 'kicking the bucket' is consonant with a particular tone of address. The first phrase expresses tact and solicitude; the second seems more like a bald statement of fact; the third exudes a detached irreverence. To think that they might be casually interchangeable, as linguistic equivalents of a unified concept, would be socially disastrous.

This distinction between polite and impolite words has long been acknowledged, though the same words have not always been considered in the same way. Whether a word counts as 'posh' or colloquial has less to do with its strictly linguistic properties than with who uses it and in what circumstances. In English, however, the distinction has also fed off the difference between the two major etymological groups constituting the language: the Teutonic and the Romance or Latinate. It is, in fact, one of the most signal aspects of the English language that it derives from two such distinct etymological roots; this is a specialised reason indeed for the superfluity of English vocabulary to which we have already alluded. We can readily think of instances where the language offers us binary alternatives, the one Teutonic, the other Latinate, for the self-same concept as 'think/cogitate, see/perceive, oversee/supervise, understand/comprehend, believable/credible'. The fact that the English language boasts this double etymology is something that poets, as you might expect, have long been familiar with, and indeed have sometimes tried to exploit. A notable example occurs in *Macbeth* II.ii.60–2, when Macbeth fleetingly disavows the idea of assassinating the King, Duncan:

> No, this my hand will rather
> The multitudinous seas incarnadine,
> Making the green one red.

'Incarnadine' is an arcane word derived from French and Italian sources, meaning to 'turn red'; the word is so unfamiliar that Shakespeare has to put into Macbeth's mouth an immediate translation of it: 'Making the green one red'. Given that Macbeth feels obliged to gloss his hard phrasing, why, we might ask, does Shakespeare use the word in the first place? One answer might be to do with the way that both Macbeth and Lady Macbeth, in their envisagement of the assassination of Duncan, constantly veer between vivid imagination and mental evasion. At the moment when Macbeth seems most resolved *not* to carry the deed out, he speaks of it distantly, in an abstract Latinate phrase, as if, both mentally and linguistically, setting the act as far away from himself as possible. The need for this protective idiom disappears as the play goes on and as Macbeth slowly habituates himself to his own barbarity.

There is a long history of people proposing improvements in style through privileging Latinate words over Saxon ones or the Saxon over the Latinate.

Jonathan Swift's *A Proposal for Correcting, Improving and Ascertaining the English Tongue* (1712) is a case in point, identifying the abundance of monosyllables in the language as a regrettable corruption, monosyllabicism being a marked characteristic of words of Anglo-Saxon etymology. The same antipathy towards short Anglo-Saxon words was also felt by Samuel Johnson and underpins some of his critical judgements, not least those on Shakespeare. In his periodical *The Rambler*, for instance, he takes exception to Shakespeare's habit of introducing 'low' words at moments of tragic seriousness, citing the words 'dunnest' (an adjective 'now seldom heard but in the stable') and 'knife', occurring in *Macbeth* I.v.51–2, as particularly disconcerting examples. Yet if for Johnson these curt Saxon monosyllables represent a stylistic aberration, then a major arbiter of style of the twentieth century, George Orwell, has suggested exactly the opposite, that preferring Latinate words to Saxon ones contributes to an artificial and inflated style:

> Bad writers, and especially scientific, political and sociological writers, are nearly always haunted by the notion that Latin or Greek words are grander than Saxon ones, and unnecessary words like *expedite, ameliorate, predict, extraneous, deracinated, clandestine, sub-aqueous* and hundreds of others constantly gain ground from their Anglo-Saxon opposite numbers.

In thinking about how poets use words, then, it is worth recollecting the twin etymological roots from which the English language as now constituted has grown. And it is also worth keeping in mind that not just are writers always faced with stylistic choice, but that the options from which they choose tend not to be value-neutral but instead range themselves along an axis of linguistic prestige. What gives words perceived value may be their etymological derivation; it may be features of their articulation, as Swift's preference for Latinate polysyllabic words on account of their being more mellifluous than harsh monosyllabic ones; or it may be owing to fixed patterns of association, as when Johnson rebukes Shakespeare's introduction of the words 'dunnest' and 'knife' in *Macbeth* because the first word is 'seldom heard but in the stable' and the second has long been overtaken by an association with 'sordid offices'. The vast majority of poems are about something other than merely language, but *all* poems comprise a statement about, and an affirmation of, the true language of poetry. Every poem is, in its own way, an endorsement of a particular view of what the language of poetry ought to be.

6.2   POETIC DICTION

All poems are involved to some degree in fencing in desirable words and fencing out undesirable ones, but some poems strike us as being much more linguistically selective than others. Probably the most important linguistic dilemma that poets must resolve is the relation of their poetic idiom to the language in general. Should poetry be written in a language largely continuous with that of everyday conversation and prose? Or should it instead be committed to a tongue at a remove from, or heightened above and superior to, that of more commonplace linguistic transactions? This question is inevitably one that has been answered differently by different poets, but the general question is one that addresses itself to all poets at all times.

Although such generalisations are unreliable, the idea of a firm demarcation between the language of poetry and that of everyday usage has belonged mainly to earlier poetic cultures. Samuel Daniel, for example, in his *Defence of Rhyme* (1607) defines verse as 'a frame of words confined within certain measure' but also 'differing from the ordinary speech'. The idea, however, is most often associated with the eighteenth century, and is stated in frank terms in Joseph Trapp's *Lectures on Poetry* (1728): 'as Poetry requires a peculiar Way of Thinking, it affects, likewise, a peculiar Manner of Writing and Speaking; that so it may be set off at as great a Distance from Prose as possible'. At this time, the 'peculiar Manner of Writing' to which Trapp alludes becomes synonymous with 'poetic diction': a portfolio of stylistic techniques designed expressly to distance poetry as much as possible from standard prose. This sort of diction is met with in many of the major poets of the early and mid-eighteenth century, but the one to have become most identified with it is Thomas Gray. A good example of the technique in action, as taken from one of his best-known poems, 'Ode on a Distant Prospect of Eton College', is given below:

> Ye distant spires, ye antique towers,
> That crown the watery glade,
> Where grateful Science still adores
> Her Henry's holy shade;
> And ye that from the stately brow
> Of Windsor's heights the expanse below
> Of grove, of lawn, of mead survey,
> Whose turf, whose shade, whose flowers among,
> Wanders the hoary Thames along
> His silver-winding way.

The stanza begins with an apostrophe, or a rhetorical invocation, addressed in this instance to the spires and towers of his old school, Eton College, visible to the poet as he looks down from the hill at Windsor. Invocations of this kind are indicative of a poetry that is consciously affecting to be 'poetic': they are, after all, not something to which we are accustomed in standard prose or everyday conversation. Line 3 shows a similar technique, where the poem again affords itself licence to deviate from the norms of prose and conversation. In the eighteenth century, 'science' meant 'knowledge' or 'learning' in general; 'grateful Science', then, becomes a highly compact metonymy referring to the boys studying (or pursuing 'learning') at Eton and 'grateful' for the opportunity of doing so. There is a dense knottedness of meaning here that we would be startled to encounter anywhere but in a poem. Leaving aside, though, the precise meaning of the words, it is useful to notice that the expression is predicated on a personification. 'Science' is given an initial capital, like a proper noun, and the line ostensibly asserts that the person of 'Science' is grateful. As well as constructions that stand out as deliberately 'poetical', Gray also selects individual words drawn from a narrowly poetic idiom. 'Shade' in line 4, as meaning a 'secluded spot or corner', was a usage almost exclusive to poetry, as were the contracted form 'mead', meaning 'meadow', and 'hoary', meaning 'grey or white with age', applied here to a poetic personification of the river Thames.

When you read a poem written two hundred and fifty years ago, it is difficult to reconstruct how its words and expressions would have sounded to contemporary readers: our overriding experience tends to be one of verbal estrangement. Nonetheless, we know from Gray's own remarks, and the responses of his contemporaries, that his was seen as poetry 'on its tiptoes', a brand of poetry that was deliberately elevated above the common tongue. As well as simply choosing words and phrases with poetic overtones, there is another technique, highly instrumental in poetic diction, that Gray uses to this end, and which can be best illustrated from the third stanza of the *Eton Ode*:

> Say, Father Thames, for thou hast seen
> Full many a sprightly race
> Disporting on thy margent green
> The paths of pleasure trace,
> Who foremost now delight to cleave
> With pliant arm thy glassy wave?
> The captive linnet which enthrall?
> What idle progeny succeed
> To chase the rolling circle's speed,
> Or urge the flying ball?

The device Gray uses here is a specific type of circumlocution called periphrasis. Its technique is that of expressing a meaning in more words than are strictly warranted: it is a form of overwriting or consciously 'writing around'. Yet what a good periphrasis does not admit is redundancy; periphrases properly executed are dense, rather than lax, with meaning. Gray's periphrases typically achieve this sort of density by doubling up as both names and explanations of the concepts to which they refer. Contained in the stanza are four periphrases of note, two subdued and two of a more bravura kind. 'Sprightly race' encapsulates the energy of the little boys but also how they come to the school as successive cohorts or year-groups ('Full many a … race'); and 'margent green' expresses the lushness of the river bank, but also how river banks comprise a 'margin' between earth and water. Next Gray details the activity of swimming as being 'to cleave / With pliant arm thy glassy wave', and a careering hoop as 'the rolling circle's speed'. Though students often complain about the excess verbiage involved in expressions of this kind, in reality it is the absence of linguistic superfluity that is striking. 'Cleave / With pliant arm' describes sparely, even technically, what swimming consists of. It is an exercise in studied literalism. The language may be consciously ornate, but to think of it as slack and redundant would be altogether wrong.

Periphrases were another of those verbal contrivances that made up eighteenth-century 'poetic diction', though the rhetorical technique does not just belong to eighteenth-century poets alone. The underlying philosophy of poetic diction, that poetry should stand at a remove from the language of everyday usage, is summed up in a remark of Gray's in a famous letter to Richard West: 'The language of the age is never the language of poetry.' The point is that the words of poetry ought to be a refined selection from those of everyday usage, but also specifically that they ought to be *older* than those current at the time: the words of poetry belong to the past rather than the present. The practice of writing in a language older than the present day is called 'archaism'. As a poetic technique it rests in part on linguistic nostalgia, the belief that old words are more sterling than newer ones, but also on a belief that, when encountering a poem, we ought always to feel a small shock of estrangement, in particular through encountering modes of language different from those to which we are habituated. Archaism is another of those techniques which we normally parcel up under the name of poetic diction, and Gray's own poetry abounds with old words and with contemporary ones being used in senses that have passed out of common application. In the second of the two stanzas quoted from his *Eton Ode*, for example, he uses the word 'enthrall' to mean 'imprison', a strictly literal understanding of the word that was already being supplanted by the metaphoric one, common to us today, as meaning to 'engross' or 'captivate'; similarly, the very first word of the poem 'Ye', meaning 'you', dates to the medieval period, and by Gray's time had long disappeared from educated parlance.

Although archaism is an important aspect of eighteenth-century poetic diction, its currency as a technique of verse composition goes much wider than this period alone. The inclination to preserve in a modern poem the language of an earlier age may be felt for various reasons. It may be that a type of poetical phrasing becomes so successful that it turns into what is almost a genre in its own right: so, for example, a large body of eighteenth-century poetry adopted the style of Milton's poem *Paradise Lost* (1667) notwithstanding that by the 1700s, in its relation to ordinary language, it had become dusty and antiquated. Or it may be that a writer preserves an older poetic style as a gesture of discipleship towards an earlier poet who had given rise to it. Such is the case with Edmund Spenser's *The Faerie Queene* (1590–6), a Renaissance poem written in a medieval style, and modelled in particular on the phraseology of Chaucer. Here is a stanza from Book 2:

> Eftsoones they heard a most melodious sound,
>   Of all that mote delight a daintie eare,
>   Such as attonce might not on living ground,
>   Save in this Paradise, be heard elswhere:
>   Right hard it was, for wight, which did it heare,
>   To read, what manner musicke that mote bee:
>   For all that pleasing is to living eare,
>   Was there consorted in one harmonee,
> Birdes, voyces, instruments, windes, waters, all agree.

Some of the spellings, strange-seeming to us today, were usual for the time, such as the terminations 'ie' and 'ee' (in 'daintie' and 'harmonee') where we would normally expect a 'y'-ending. But some words would have had a quaint and antique ring to them even in Spenser's day. 'Eftsoones', meaning 'soon afterwards', was a Middle English word already on the lapse; the composite word 'attonce', meaning 'at one time', is a recovered Chaucerianism, as is 'mote' for 'might'; while the term 'wight', meaning a living person, hails from the old English period and is listed by the *OED* as becoming fully obsolete about the time of Spenser's own literary career.

Spenser's recovery of a Chaucerian poetic language is in large part an act of personal apostleship: the process of coming into his inheritance as a poet was closely bound up in his own mind with imitation and emulation of Chaucer. This personal idolisation is not, of course, a necessary factor in a writer's adopting an archaistic style. When Byron chooses to write *Childe Harold's Pilgrimage* (1812–18) in the stanza, and largely in the style, of Spenser, this is much more a case of using the older language to summon up the chivalric atmosphere of Spenser's original and to introduce a slightly estranged relation between the reader and the poem. For the purposes of this section, we have subsumed archaism under the head of poetic diction. It comprises one of those methods by which poets can slew their lines away from the language of everyday usage. The crucial point to realise is that words do not fall naturally to the hands of the poets using them. All poets, in some sense, have to make or define the language of their poems. Should it be contemporary with usage of their own time? Should it be a refinement or heightening of the common tongue? Should it be exclusive or permissive in relation to the language at large? These are questions which we will put down now but take up again later; but we want first to introduce some attitudes to poetic language antithetical to those outlined above.

6.3 POETRY OF THE EVERYDAY LANGUAGE

The idea that the language of poetry ought to stand at a sharp remove from the common tongue has never for long held unchallenged sway over its rival position. John Dryden, for example, in his *Essay of Dramatic Poesy* (1668) recommended that poetry is best composed in 'the most easy language; and is most to be admired when a great thought comes dressed in words … commonly received'. Similarly, as part of the larger Romantic repudiation of early and mid-eighteenth-century poetry, Wordsworth attacked the aesthetic wrong-headedness of earlier poets, especially Gray, who wanted to effect an artificial separation of poetic language from prose language:

> the language of a large portion of every good poem … must necessarily … in no respect differ from that of good prose … Is there then, it will be asked, no essential difference between the language of prose and metrical composition? I answer that there neither is nor can be any essential difference.

It is true that in advocating, and exemplifying in his own poems, a style of poetry made up of 'a selection of the language really spoken by men', Wordsworth was reacting specifically to the ungainliness of the poetic diction proliferating among poets of the era preceding his own. However, the desire to harmonise poetic with 'real' language is one that has been voiced by numerous poets and critics across the ages. We can find, for example, T. S. Eliot, a much later poet who wrote in a very different style, advancing something very similar: namely that 'poetry must not stray too far from the ordinary everyday language which we use and hear'.

Of course, what compliance with such a dictum actually entails is apt to vary enormously from poet to poet. As merely one illustration we propose taking a short poem by William Carlos Williams entitled 'This is Just to Say':

> I have eaten
> the plums
> that were in
> the icebox

and which
you were probably
saving
for breakfast

Forgive me
they were delicious
so sweet
and so cold

The biggest dilemma that the lines pose is whether the reader should approach them as a poem pretending to be something else or as something that is not a poem pretending to be one. What makes it appear like a poem are the existence of a title and the fact that the lines are arranged in three distinct stanzas. But if you look closer, you might decide that neither of these aspects is quite as it seems. The poem's ostensible title, for example, unlike most titles, runs grammatically continuously with the poem itself ('This is Just To Say I have eaten the plums …), as if it really forms part of the poem rather than standing in titular relation to it. Similarly, though the poem is sorted into lines, these do not observe any metrical scheme; what is more, the use of upper case lettering is governed by prose convention rather than that of poetry: a capital is introduced not at the start of each line but only with the initiation of a new sentence. It might also be added that we invariably think of poetry as, perhaps of all modes of writing, the most subject to labour and pained forethought – the very opposite of the breeziness of 'Just to Say'. Poetry, we are used to telling ourselves, is a verbal practice altogether more arduous and grander in pretension than 'Just Saying'.

One factor that makes Williams's poem an exercise in 'just saying' is its conformity to one of the most clichéd mini-genres of co-habitational living: the note left on the fridge door. But it also 'just says' by being painstakingly unpoetic in its idiom: the words may be grouped in stanzaic form but this is the poem's one concession to the rule of 'the poetic'. The poem admits no metaphors or rhetorical tropes: it poses itself as a simple detailing of reality in reality's own words. Yet Williams's lines are not dogmatic in their flatness, for they tease us with the conundrum of what it actually takes for a poem to count as a poem. Some students, in our experience, see the poem as a sort of hoax, a plain real-life utterance that tries to pass itself off as being a work of verbal art. Others find the lines, especially in their sensuous evocation of an absent thing (the eaten plums that were 'so sweet / and so cold'), as fulfilling perhaps a quintessential function of poetry: the use of language to realise to the imagination things and events that do not actually exist. Another group tends to criticise any rigid demarcation of the poetic and non-poetic as a piece of idle didacticism. The key aspect of the poem is perhaps not so much that it answers these questions as that it puts the reader inescapably in mind of them.

6.4   CREATING YOUR OWN LANGUAGE

The questions that we have posed so far in this chapter have concerned lexical selection: which words will poets draw from the store-chest of the language? and which will they elect to set aside as incompatible with the interests of their poem? But to poets, more so than to ordinary language users, there exists a further option: that of actually manufacturing the words that your poem presses into service. The office of a poet often demands putting the language under such stress that words buckle into new meanings or entirely new words are thrown up: this process of coining new words and meanings we call 'neologism'. In Shakespeare's *King Lear*, for example, Edgar says of Lear that 'He childed as I father'd', where the word 'child' is twisted into a new sense as a verb meaning 'to produce children' or perhaps 'to have a relationship with your children'; and in the same play he pities the tattered condition, the 'loop'd and window'd raggedness', of poor vagrants, where 'window'd' is extrapolated as a participial adjective from the more familiar nominal form, and seems to mean 'interspersed with openings', like a building is with windows.

   This technique of converting a word, for reasons of local effect, from one part of speech to another is not uncommon among poets. The Victorian poet Gerard Manley Hopkins, for example, invites Christ into his own and everybody's life by exclaiming 'Let him easter in us' (the noun 'Easter' being transmogrified into a verb); and one of his most spiritually traumatised poems starts 'I wake and feel the fell of dark, not day', where the past tense verb 'fell' carries a nominal meaning, indicating the 'fallenness' or 'fallen state' of the night. But although this technique concerns the generation of new meanings, it doesn't involve the invention of new words. For an example of this latter technique, though, we can turn to Lewis Carroll's 'Jabberwocky', a nonsense poem that first appeared in *Through the Looking Glass* (1872). This is the first stanza:

> 'Twas brillig, and the slithy toves
>   Did gyre and gimble in the wabe:
> All mimsy were the borogoves,
>   And the mome raths outgrabe.

Having read the entire poem, Alice understandably is at a loss, thinking it 'very pretty' but '*rather* hard to understand!', but later on she is able to avail herself of a skilful interpreter in Humpty Dumpty. Humpty Dumpty's main policy for decoding the poem is to have recourse to a concept to which he himself has given name: the 'portmanteau' word, where 'there are two meanings packed up into one word'. So 'slithy' compacts both 'lithe and slimy', as he tells us, and 'mimsy' combines 'flimsy and miserable'. On the same principle 'brillig' seems to effect a marriage of 'brilliant' (as in the sun shining 'brilliantly') and 'broiling'. The combined effect of these constituents is to make the word mean 'four o'clock in the afternoon', a time at which on a summer's day the sun's light is brilliant and at which, according to Humpty Dumpty, 'you begin *broiling* things for dinner'.

Portmanteau words, even though they form the technical mainstay of one of the great works of twentieth-century literature, James Joyce's *Finnegans Wake*, remain an unusual phenomenon. Most of them can be assigned to the category of 'nonce-words', ones, like Carroll's in 'Jabberwocky', that are coined on a precise occasion, without a view to their being widely adopted. Keats, an habitually bad speller, often found his own misplaced letters generating intriguing portmanteaux, as when in a letter to Fanny Brawne he inadvertently penned 'purplue' for 'purple', and then reflected on what a fine appellation this would be for a mixture of purple and blue. In our time, the use of port-manteaux as a way of minting new words has become much more common than previously: we can quickly think of 'smog' (smoke and fog), 'motel' (motor and hotel), 'ginormous' (giant and enormous), 'brunch' (breakfast and lunch), 'guesstimate' (guess and estimate), 'informercial' (information and commercial), and 'herstory' (her and history: for history concerned with women's experience). Portmanteaux, rather than being a specialised poetic technique, have become in our own time one of the main motors of linguistic change in general.

A practice closely related to portmanteaux, though more common, occurs where writers yoke together words in a hyphenated or compound form. This technique is used mainly with adjectives, giving rise to what is known as the compound epithet. In William Cowper's poem 'On the Death of Mrs. Throckmorton's Bulfinch', for example, the poet describes a foraging rat, which is about to devour the bird of the poem's title, in the following terms:

> A beast forth-sallied on the scout,
> Long-back'd, long-tail'd, with whisker'd snout,
>   And badger-colour'd hide.

'Long-back'd, 'long-tail'd' and 'badger-colour'd' here are all compound epithets of this kind. Cowper's predilection for this hyphenation is neither very imaginative nor very neologistic (though the technique in general lends itself to the creation of neologisms). Rather it is part of an erudite joke in which he artificially inflates the gravity of the poem's chief incident by mimicking

Homer's style, compound epithets, like 'wine-dark sea', being one of the most pronounced aspects of Homeric verse. What the individual words do in hyphenated form, and what the aggregative effect of the compound happens to be, depend very much on the individual instance. In Cowper's hyphenation, the first word merely 'modifies', or supplements our knowledge of, the second, as happens when, for example, Dylan Thomas describes a starless night as 'bible-black'. On the other hand, a poet might hyphenate a compound to suggest his interest in two things at once, as with Ted Hughes's 'The Thought-Fox', a poem that is both about a fox and about the act of imagination through which the fox is conjured up. The device, though, can be twisted to stranger and more complex ends, as in the following lines from Gerard Manley Hopkins's poem 'Hurrahing in Harvest':

> SUMMER ends now; now, barbarous in beauty, the stooks rise
> Around; up above, what wind-walks! what lovely behaviour
> Of silk-sack clouds! has wilder, wilful-wavier
> Meal-drift moulded ever and melted across skies.

The relation between the hyphenated items here is a teasing one. 'Wind-walks' refers to the paths followed by the clouds as they scud across the sky, but as well as a sense of smooth consonance between the two words, there is also a feeling of paradoxicality. A walk is by definition earth-bound, and yet these walks are breezy, aerial ones. A similar contradictory effect is generated by 'silk-sack' a little further down: 'sacks' are container bags normally made out of coarse hessian, but here 'sack' is modified by 'silk', a fabric distinctive for its precious texture. 'Meal-drift' is more overtly explanatory, given that 'meal' is the fine part of ground grain; but 'wilful-wavier' is another phrase that has a sharply antithetical ring to it. The *Oxford English Dictionary* comes up with nothing at all under 'wavier', so the nearest option seems to be 'waverer', something or someone whose movements are unfocused, undecided or characterised by mental drift. This seems to agree with what Hopkins has already established about the motion of clouds, but in which case the word sits puzzlingly alongside 'wilful' which implies rather opposite characteristics. Hopkins's special exploitation of the compound form, then, is to fuse together meanings in a way that is neologistic but also sharply antithetical, such as would be difficult to achieve using single words.

6.5   DICTION AND ARGOTS

Making up your own words is one method of departing from standard English, but another is to compose in dialect – in a language that is the preserve of a specific community or region. Take the opening two stanzas of Robert Burns's famous poem 'To a Mouse':

> WEE, sleeket, cowran, tim'rous *beastie*,
> O, what a panic's in thy breastie!
> Thou need na start awa sae hasty,
>   Wi' bickering brattle!
> I wad be laith to rin an' chase thee,
>   Wi' murd'ring *pattle*!
>
> I'm truly sorry Man's dominion
> Has broken Nature's social union,
> An' justifies that ill opinion,
>   Which makes thee startle,
> At me, thy poor, earth-born companion,
>   An' *fellow-mortal*!

Burns began life as an agricultural worker in Ayrshire in the west of Scotland, and his writings in his own native dialect have long become a celebrated part of Scottish culture. The first stanza is indicative of his handling of dialect: famous though the lines are, somebody unfamiliar with Burns's regional idiom, unless perhaps armed with a glossary, would be hard put to understand them. 'Sleeket' we can gloss now as 'sleek'; 'cowran' as 'cowering' or 'fearful'; 'bickering brattle' in line 4 as the sound of the mouse's scampering; and 'pattle' in line 6 as a plough-staff. Nowadays, and perhaps to an extent that cheapens Burns's skill as a poet, his verse tends to be identified with, to be seen as an encapsulation of, this particular dialect. But if we move to the next stanza, these first assumptions stand to be corrected. For this stanza is written entirely in standard English, containing not even a single word that makes us reach for a gloss. This change of language corresponds to some degree with a change in subject-matter; the second stanza opens out to issues of a more abstract kind than those of the first one, especially to do with the relation between man, as sovereign creature, and the rest of the created world. But the larger point suggested here in this is that for Burns, of all British poets the one most associated with a non-standard dialect, the recourse to this dialect was a matter of conscious choice. He could write standard (southern) English, even copying the poetic idiom of Alexander Pope, when he chose; and in one of his best-known poems, 'The Cotter's Saturday Night', he more or less alternates between standard English and dialect. His allegiance to his own native tongue, in other words, was never an habituation.

It is worth, perhaps, underscoring this point. This book is largely concerned with the choices poets make in the process of composing their verses; and it might be objected here that writing in dialect is not strictly a choice, since dialect writers are simply writing in the only language they know to use. Of course, this is in many instances the case; but it remains a fallacy to suppose that such poets are necessarily more linguistically 'authentic' than non-dialect writers, or that rather than deciding how to compose, they are in some unconscious way simply writing out their linguistic birthright. Hugh MacDiarmid, for example, a much more recent practitioner of Scottish dialect verse, is another for whom dialect was a conscious choice rather than a language of habit.

Our use of 'dialect verse' in this section is intentionally a broad one; we include in it poetry written in a regional tongue but also poetry that tries to reproduce regionally specific pronunciation of standard English. A nineteenth-century poet of this latter kind is William Barnes (1801–1886), whose 'My Orcha'd in Linden Lea' provides a good example of this technique:

> 'Ithin the woodlands, flow'ry gleäded,
>   By the woak tree's mossy moot,
> The sheenèn glass-bleädes, timber-sheäded,
>   Now do quiver under voot;
> An' birds do whissle auver head,
> An' water's bubblèn in its bed,
> An there vor me the apple tree
> Do leän down low in Linden Lea.

Barnes was a renowned philologist with reputedly a reading competence in as many as seventy-two different languages. But despite this keen and erudite interest in written words, he was just as much concerned with the sound of words in the spoken tongue. 'Linden Lea' we might see, indeed, as being less a poem written in dialect than a piece of phonological transcription. It contains no words that are not intelligible as part of standard English lexicon: the poem's technique is rather that of mediating the precise Dorset pronunciation for these words, a pronunciation that did and still does deviate markedly from received speech patterns. So Barnes's poetic idiom captures the distinct Dorset burr in words like 'voot' for 'foot' and 'woak' for 'oak'; it uses vocal contractions like ''Ithin' for 'within' and the retrenched participial 'en' termination (for 'ing') as in 'sheenèn' and 'bubblèn'; and it points up the Dorset double vowel pronunciation in 'gleäded', 'bleädes' and so on, where standard English would pronounce as a single harmonised vowel sound or diphthong. Barnes's intentions were both preservatory and aesthetic. He wanted to enshrine permanently the accent of a specific community, but he also wanted to weave these sounds into a rich poetic language.

Barnes's relation towards the language of the poem is complex. He himself was born into the language community of Dorset, so that the tongue represented in 'Linden Lea' is his own native one. Yet his enormous philological erudition meant that he was never imprisoned within this language: his daughter recorded that once in possession of a dictionary he could teach himself to read a new language in a week or two. Our relation to our own local tongue tends to be a very muted one, a sort of flat habituation: we become so accustomed to hearing our own way of speech that it ceases to be audible to us. Barnes, however, subscribed to a lifelong belief that the Dorset dialect constituted a particularly 'pure' Saxon English, comprising a linguistic medium superior to standard English, a tongue that had been corrupted by importations from the Latin and French. A poem such as 'Linden Lea', then, is not just an illustration of the Dorset tongue but a campaigning act on its behalf.

Poems of phonological transcription, however, need not be based on quite such reverential assumptions as those in Barnes's; and one that certainly isn't is Tom Leonard's (b. 1944) parody (or 'derivation' as he calls it), based on a work already cited in this chapter, entitled 'Jist ti Let Yi No (from the American of Carlos Williams)':

> ahv drank
> thi speshlz
> that wurrin
> thi frij
>
> n thit
> yiwurr probbli
> hodn back
> furthi pahrti
>
> awright
> they wur great
> thaht stroang
> thaht cawld

Williams's original poem is an exercise in spare but sharp imagery, and Leonard's is likewise an act of poetic minimalism, composed in a language that studiously resists being poetical. Leonard has appreciated that Williams's original poem poses the question of what exactly constitutes a fit language for poetry, and has experimented by casting his own poem in a strong Glaswegian accent. The poem is not written in dialect (Leonard is not particularly interested in dialect poetry *per se*) but rather consists of a phonetic transcription of Glaswegian speech patterns.

Leonard's imitation takes effect by twinning Williams's original poem, with its sensuous evocation of the cool pristine plums, with the tawdrier culture of Scottish metropolitan life. Here the plums have become 'speshlz' (cans of beer) held back for the 'pahrti', and celebrated here, not like the plums for their sweetness, but for their alcoholic strength. Leonard renders his Glaswegian accent mainly through a series of sharp contractions as 'ahv' ('I have'), 'wurrin' ('were in'), and 'yiwurr' ('you were'). Contractions of a similar sort appear also in Barnes's 'Linden Lea', but whereas Barnes was an unstinting advocate for the expressive potential of his own tongue, Leonard's attitude towards his is rather more wry. The poem, though certainly rich in linguistic authenticity, does not make you feel that great claims are being made for the suppleness or eloquence of Glaswegian speech. In fact, the poem seems happy to acknowledge the banality of its idioms and pronunciations. Williams's mock-apologetic 'Forgive me' is rendered here by the grunting 'awright'; and the mellifluous 'delicious' has been flattened into nowadays that most mundane of honorific words: 'great'. Unlike Barnes, then, Leonard is happy to draw attention to some comically uneloquent aspects of his own speech.

6.6 POEMS ABOUT LANGUAGE

The medium of poetry is language; and language moreover very often provides the subject-matter to which poets find themselves drawn. This may take the form of poems that are concerned with particular linguistic registers, exploring and perhaps poking fun at them, or it may take the form of works analysing the appropriateness within poetry of certain kinds of speech. A poem falling into the first category is Wendy Cope's (b. 1945) 'Lonely Hearts', the first stanza of which runs

> Can someone make my simple wish come true?
> Male biker seeks female for touring fun.
> Do you live in North London? Is it you?

Cope here has both found poetry within, and also made poetry out of, the register of lonely hearts advertisements, where solitary individuals publicise their personal attractions and sketch an identikit of their ideal partner. Her poem, in which each stanza amounts to its own separate ad, is poignantly knowing about the sad parade of eccentricities which is a staple of the lonely hearts genre. The poem, however, also nurtures a sense that habitués of the personal columns are motivated by aspirations shared by all of us, no matter where we acquire our lovers: 'Can someone make my simple wish come true'.

Cope's poem is both comic and plangent at the same time; but it is all the same rather one-dimensional as an exploration of a particular linguistic register. A poem that takes a further step, in intertwining different registers and forcing the reader to tease out the relation between the two, is Henry Reed's (1914–1986) 'Naming of Parts':

Today we have naming of parts. Yesterday,
We had daily cleaning. And tomorrow morning,
We shall have what to do after firing. But today,
Today we have naming of parts. Japonica
Glistens like coral in all the neighbouring gardens,
      And today we have naming of parts.

This is the lower sling swivel. And this
Is the upper swing swivel, whose use you will see,
When you are given your slings. And this is the piling swivel,
Which in your case you have not got. The branches
Hold in the gardens their silent, eloquent gestures,
      Which in our case we have not got.

This is the safety-catch, which is always released
With an easy flick of the thumb. And please do not let me
See anyone using his finger. You can do it quite easy
If you have any strength in your thumb. The blossoms
Are fragile and motionless, never letting anyone see
      Any of them using their finger.

And this you can see is the bolt. The purpose of this
Is to open the breech, as you see. We can slide it
Rapidly backwards and forwards: we call this
Easing the spring. And rapidly backwards and forwards
The early bees are assaulting and fumbling the flowers:
      They call it easing the Spring.

They call it easing the Spring: it is perfectly easy
If you have any strength in your thumb: like the bolt,
And the breech, and the cocking-piece, and the point of balance,
Which in our case we have not got; and the almond blossom
Silent in all of the gardens and the bees going backwards and forwards,
      For today we have naming of parts.

Reed's poem is arranged in five stanzas, each of which is articulated in precisely the same way. The first three and a half lines or so are voiced by an army weapons instructor and relate to a preliminary class in which initiates are taught to name the parts of a rifle. The instructor's words are heard in free direct speech as they register on the consciousness of an army recruit. A faint comedy plays over the scene, since the rifles seem to be old, decommissioned ones with the result that they lack some of the parts whose names the soldiers are supposed to learn. At some point in line 4 the register of military-speak gives way to a markedly different one, one of rich and succulent nature-description. What seems to be happening is that under the drone of the weapons drill, the recruit's concentration wavers and he gazes out at the gardens surrounding the class. The last line of each stanza is a sort of after-echo of what the instructor has just been saying, as the recruit's attention returns to the weapons session in progress.

The poem at first sight seems to maintain a studied equipoise between the two contents of the recruit's split-consciousness. But this is not altogether the case. Although the last line seems to take up the discourse of the early part of each stanza, it also has the effect, at a deeper level, of tying both registers together. The terminal line of stanza 4, for example, 'They call it easing the Spring', seems to echo a previous line about agitating the rifle bolt, but 'spring' of the earlier line has transmogrified into 'Spring', making the line mean something very different. This surreptitious capitalising is, in fact, a clue to a third register of speech that transfuses the poem: the language of sexual intercourse. Sexual intercourse and weapons training have various sorts of affinity. Much like rifles, human sexuality has its 'parts', and education about, or initiation into, sexuality has a lot to do with acquiring their names. Moreover, the physical mechanics of sexual intercourse are easily called to mind by the image of a rifle bolt slipping 'Rapidly backwards and forwards' in the breach. Much gets missed, then, if a reader fails to notice how the weapons training sections are touched with a delicate sheen of sexual innuendo; but it is also the case that the passages describing the gardens are also preoccupied with procreation. It is spring and the blossom is burgeoning on the trees; meanwhile, the fertile bees are going 'backwards and forwards', 'assaulting and fumbling' the flowers. The sexual and seasonal cycle is renewing itself for another year.

The poem is knitted together from three distinct linguistic registers: the military, the natural and the sexual. Over the poem's five stanzas, the stripping of the rifle and naming of its parts takes on the guise of a sexual initiation. The poem's attitude to sex moreover is characterised by lack: after all, being conscripted into the army is likely to bring about a curtailment of sexual opportunities. This same sexual frustration passes obtrusively into the language of rifle training, especially into the refrain 'which in your case you have not got'; and it also accounts for why the gardens (the world outside the military domain) are depicted so pointedly, not as a haven of peace, but as a concourse of busy sexuality. For our purposes here it is crucial to see that the possibility of construing the poem in this way rests on first of all delineating two separate registers of language and then understanding how these are connected: in particular how they meld into a third register, to do with human sexuality, that unites and clarifies the poem.

6.7   POETIC INTERTEXTUALITY

As distinct from fashioning their own languages, poets can also conjure up and revitalise words that have been used by earlier writers. The forms that this takes can vary, encompassing such nearly related techniques as borrowing, **allusion**, direct quotation, parody and even plagiarism. The phenomenon of verbal overlap or chiming between different literary works is referred to in general as **intertextuality**. The next three sections will try to differentiate between and illustrate some of these techniques. As a starting-point, we want to take a passage from Thomas North's (1535–1604) translation of the Roman historian Plutarch's *Lives of the Noble Greeks and Romans* (1579), in which he describes the Egyptian Queen Cleopatra sailing in her stately barge down the river Cydnus:

> When she was sent unto by divers letters, both from Antonius him selfe, and also from his frendes, she made so light of it, and mocked Antonius so much, that she disdained to set forward otherwise, but to take her barge in the river of Cydnus, the poope whereof was of gold, the sailes of purple, and the owers of silver, which kept stroke in rowing after the sounde of the musicke of flutes, howboyes, citherns, violls, and such other instruments as they played upon in the barge. And now for the person of her selfe: she was layed under a pavillion of cloth and gold of tissue, apparelled and attired like the goddesse Venus, commonly drawn in picture; and hard by her, on either hand of her, pretie faire boyes apparelled as painters doe set forth god Cupide, with litle fannes in their handes, with the which they fanned wind upon her.

The passage exemplifies Cleopatra's sheer wantonness and the exorbitance of her rich and refined tastes. She surrounds herself with different sorts of gorgeousness, and the whole pageant forms an exotic banquet of the senses. North imaginatively notes the preciousness of all the accoutrements, the accompanying music, the delicate textures of the coverings and the kiss of the wind upon her body. Later on, he records the 'sweete savor of perfumes, that perfumed the wharfes side'. The sense of dripping lusciousness that the passage generates is assisted by the syrupy repetitions of words or meanings like 'perfumes' and 'perfumed', 'apparelled' and 'attired', and 'fannes' and 'fanned'.

   North's words are, of course, in translation from Plutarch, but there can be no doubting the subtlety and vigour of his own prose style. Yet while North's passage deserves to be lauded in its own right, most students will only ever come across it in connection with Shakespeare's play *Antony and Cleopatra* (1606–7), in which Enobarbus describes the same water-borne procession:

> The barge she sat in, like a burnished throne,
> Burned on the water; the poop was beaten gold;
> Purple the sails, and so perfumed that

The winds were love-sick with them; the oars were silver,
Which to the tune of flutes kept stroke, and made
The water which they beat to follow faster,
As amorous of their strokes. For her own person,
It beggard all description: she did lie
In her pavilion, cloth-of-gold of tissue,
O'erpicturing that Venus where we see
The fancy outwork nature. On each side of her
Stood pretty dimpled boys, like smiling cupids,
With divers-coloured fans, whose wind did seem
To glow the delicate cheeks which they did cool,
And what they undid did.

In a subsequent speech, Enobarbus goes on to describe the waft of 'invisible perfume' reaching the 'adjacent wharfs'.

Shakespeare's rendering of the scene comes across, as one might expect, as more poetically crafted that North's, for all the general liveliness of North's own passage. Shakespeare's version thickens the general lushness into a beguiling sense of paradox: the barge proves so laden with gold that it appears to 'burn' on the water; and the lovely boys simultaneously both cool and enflame Cleopatra's cheeks, cooling them by fanning the air but enflaming them by their amorous conduct. The winds meanwhile are invested with a human yearning, falling love-sick at the scent of the rich perfumes drifting from the barge. Cleopatra's magnetic beauty is captured through a recessive figure of speech in which she is declared to be more beautiful than a picture of Venus, which is itself more beautiful than Venus herself: so Cleopatra 'o'erpictures' 'that Venus where we see / The fancy outwork nature'. In all aspects, the figure of Cleopatra 'beggard all description', so that even Enobarbus's dazzling verbal picture fails to do justice to the full spectacle that she made. Words – even Shakespeare's – are simply unequal to the task.

For all that Shakespeare puts his own imaginative stamp on the scene, the general similarity of his description to North's can hardly be missed. As we might expect, he relies entirely on North's rendering of the circumstantial details: the exotic barge manned by the lovely attendant boys, Cleopatra's precious attire, and the perfumes wafting from the vessel. Yet the similarity between the two passages, their intertextual relationship, goes some way beyond the particularities of the scene, for it also rests in the close repetition of phraseology, such as Cleopatra's 'pavilion' of 'cloth-of-gold of tissue'. It is indubitable that Shakespeare must have had the relevant page of North's *Lives* open before him whilst he drafted Enobarbus's speeches, and that these speeches are in effect poetic translations of North.

One terminology that we can invoke here is to say that North's passage acts as the underlying 'source' for Enobarbus's speeches. It is what the speeches spring from or are based on: they could not possibly have been composed in the same way had Shakespeare not had North's original from which to work. However, it's hard for us now to keep at bay the niggling anxiety that the relation of Shakespeare's text to North's could be expressed in very different terms – as a plagiaristic one – and the very idea of Shakespeare, a poet and dramatist so much venerated for creative originality, being susceptible to such an accusation could seem scandalising in the extreme. Yet, for all that the general level of overlap between Enobarbus's speeches and the passage in North might be sufficient to bring a student essay into disrepute, there are respects in which 'plagiarism' might not seem a readily applicable term to invoke. Shakespeare surpasses North's original in the verbal artistry with which he reproduces the scene; and we should not forget that the medium in which he is working (theatrical production) is far removed from Plutarch's narrative history. As much as Shakespeare appropriates – *borrows* – material from North, he also transmutes it within an entirely different generic context.

We do not intend to pursue here issues to do with poetic sources: our concentration has instead been all along on the way that poems confront their readership and the way that readers engage visually, aurally or imaginatively with the poems they encounter. Sources relate to what is buried beneath a literary work, what may be a pre-condition of the poem's very existence, but what does not necessarily form part of the poem's after-life in the experience of its successive readers or listeners. It might be worthwhile keeping this qualification in mind as we turn to the following lines from the opening of 'A Game of Chess' in T. S. Eliot's *The Waste Land* (1922):

> The Chair she sat in, like a burnished throne,
> Glowed on the marble, where the glass
> Held up by standards wrought with fruited vines
> From which a golden Cupidon peeped out
> (Another hid his eyes behind his wing)
> Doubled the flames of sevenbranched candelabra
> Reflecting light upon the table as
> The glitter of her jewels rose to meet it,
> From satin cases poured in rich profusion.

What stands out immediately is that the first couple of lines ('The Chair she sat in …') clearly echo the beginning of Enobarbus's famous speech in *Antony and Cleopatra*. The passage appears to describe a woman seated at her dressing table surrounded by an array of powders, perfumes and jewellery as she makes herself up. The mention of Cupidons is another specific reference to Enobarbus's speech, in particular to the lovely boys who seem like 'smiling cupids'.

Moreover, the whole passage (longer than the extract we have provided) seems to partake of the same lusciousness and sensory intensity as the lines from *Antony and Cleopatra*.

Yet, this having been allowed, the relation of Eliot's lines to Shakespeare's still seems quite different from the relation of Shakespeare's to North's. The main distinction is perhaps that rather than Shakespeare's lines underlying Eliot's, or being an unstated ingredient within them, they seem importantly constitutive of the effect the passage is designed to have. Eliot referenced Enobarbus's speech when he supplied a set of notes to the work, and it is clear that he wanted the lines from Shakespeare's play to be in some way brought into play within the reader's experience of his own poem. The relation between the two passages is perhaps intended as ironic or mock-heroic: the heroic grandeur of Cleopatra's barge gets replaced with a false, synthetic gorgeousness that seems to epitomise the decay and sickness of the modern world.

Eliot's lines could be described as *alluding* to Shakespeare's play: they direct the reader's attention outside the vicinity of the poem itself to an appreciation of its connection to another text. The fact that Eliot references Shakespeare's original lines relieves us of any need to consider the borrowing in any way underhand, but in any event it clearly forms part of the aesthetic of 'The Waste Land' that the reader should identify and dwell on its dense network of intertextual relationships with other works. The lines at the start of 'A Game of Chess' would be stripped of their resonance were a reader not to pick up the allusion, whereas Shakespeare can hardly have expected that a theatre audience, amidst the onward rush of a live performance, would possibly have recalled the passage from North's *Lives* as significantly related to Enobarbus's speeches.

6.8 FORMS OF ALLUSION

Allusions can misfire in two opposite ways, either through being too obvious or being too obscure. If we were to say that the quandary comes down to knowing whether 'To allude or not to allude', that would comprise in itself an allusion (to Shakespeare's *Hamlet*) of the most inert and clunking variety. Whilst for an allusion to succeed it must first be detected, the ideal allusion is perhaps less something heard than something overheard, or something that registers only faintly, as a mere vibration of the air. For this reason, allusive poetry is often seen as being 'hard' or challenging, like a versified crossword puzzle. It could be argued that the notes Eliot supplied for *The Waste Land* actually detract from the poem's allusions in so far as it makes them (or some of them) obviously explicable, in a way that takes away their scope to act on the reader in a more stealthy way.

The presence of allusions in poems can have the effect of stratifying the readership. Some readers will pick up the allusions whereas others will remain deaf to them. There are those readers who are *au fait* with a range of high cultural references and those who are not. Is the reader who captures all the allusions a better reader of a work? The question is not unlike whether a second reading of a book is always superior to a first reading, in the sense that the second reading is always more knowing than the first. To what extent is a successful reception of a poem that contains allusions contingent on our identifying them?

It should be noted that allusions do not actually form part of the internal fabric of a poem in the way that alliteration and metaphor, for example, do; instead, they concern the *relationship* between one text and another. An imponderable question that inevitably poses itself concerns the degree of chiming or coincidence between texts necessary for us to infer an act of conscious allusion by a poet. Take the first line of Tennyson's poem 'Tithonus' (1860): 'The woods decay, the woods decay and fall'. Tennyson's renowned editor, Christopher Ricks, spies an allusion here to a passage in Wordsworth's *Prelude* (1850): 'The immeasurable height / Of woods decaying, never to be decayed'. We know, from external evidence, that Tennyson was acquainted with, and treasured, this particular part of Wordsworth's poem, and his own lines revive the idea of 'decaying', where decay seems to hint at the weeping of the leaves to the ground on an annual basis as well as the rotting down of timber over long periods of time. Tennyson also repeats not just the word 'decay' but also Wordsworth's uncanny repetition of the same word almost immediately afterwards. Of course, while we are not inclined to doubt that a chiming between the two poems exists, we can't be certain that Tennyson necessarily wants to draw this to the reader's attention, or bring it into play in the context of his own poem. Not everything that echoes within the chamber of the poet's own mind need be intended to echo as well in that of the reader.

The same difficulty of distinguishing between allusion *per se* and a poet's private verbal reminiscence can be seen occurring with this famous stanza from Thomas Gray's 'Elegy Written in a Country Church-Yard' (1751):

> Full many a gem of purest ray serene
> The dark unfathomed caves of ocean bear:
> Full many a flower is born to blush unseen
> And waste its sweetness on the desert air.

The content of these lines has been much mulled over and debated. The stanza addresses the lack of opportunities available in eighteenth-century life to poor people living in the countryside. Given the obscurity of their origins, they never have a chance to fulfil their abilities or to occupy the higher stations that might otherwise have been open to them. The difficulty that many readers encounter with Gray's lines is that they represent this state of affairs in a sentimentally falsifying way. In particular, they depict the state of not being able to achieve life-fulfilment in terms of something actually quite different: that is, the condition of being fully realised in oneself, though in a way that remains invisible to others. So the harshly circumscribed lives of the poor are likened to a gem glowing in an underwater cave or a flower blooming in an uninhabited desert. In so far as such lovely images could seem apt, they make the inhibited lives of the poor seem satisfying and attractive.

Leaving aside the politics of Gray's lines, they are remarkable for their density of poetical allusion. Gray's editor Roger Lonsdale, for example, comes up with a host of texts to which the one image of the flower blooming unseen could be alluding, including the following: W. Chamberlayne's *Pharonnida* (1659), 'Like beauteous flowers which vainly waste the scent / Of odours in unhaunted deserts'; Ambrose Philips's *Fable of Thule* (1718), 'Like woodland flowers, which paint the desert glades, / And waste their sweets in unfrequented shades'; Alexander Pope's *Rape of the Lock* (1714), 'There kept my Charms conceal'd from mortal Eye, / Like Roses that in Deserts bloom and die'; and James Thomson's 'Autumn' (1730), 'A myrtle rises, far from human eye, / And breathes its balmy fragrance o'er the wild −/ So flourished blooming, and unseen by all'. The flower blooming unseen had become by Gray's time a stock poetic image, but it seems likely all the same that he had at the back of his mind one or two actual invocations of the image. The closest analogue seems to be with the lines from Ambrose Philips ('waste their sweets in unfrequented shades') which possesses similar diction along with the same phrasal structure.

The same dilemma poses itself here as with the Wordsworth lines that we looked at above: to what extent is Gray consciously alluding to these earlier poets, inviting the reader to appreciate how they provide a context for his own rendition of the image, or should they be seen instead as merely some of the verbal materials out of which Gray's own work has been manufactured? The problem poses itself differently however in relation to Gray's 'Elegy', simply because the range of possible sources of the allusion is so much wider. Even if we knew that he definitely was alluding, would we know precisely to what?

It should be said that most literary ideas or commonplaces are historically datable, and it must not be assumed, just because we entertain the concept of poetic allusion nowadays, that poets of all previous periods have done the same. Modern critics are fully reconciled to the view that readers, especially through their ability to detect allusive resonances with other poems, can be seen as being actively instrumental in the making of a poem, its effect and meaning. However, it is not clear that this view has always existed, or that readers from earlier generations always understood this to be how poems worked. It might be significant, indeed, that Gray's poetic career was to end prematurely. He stopped writing poetry after 1757 (though he had always been diffident about publishing his works), largely because of being beset by worries that his allusive style of poetry too easily invited the accusation of plagiarism, especially from readers unaccustomed to a brand of poetry that deployed techniques of literary borrowing or allusion.

Gray's image of the flower blooming unseen represents what has been called 'incremental allusion' in that it seems to form part of a chain of allusions. The allusion feels almost like a verbal heirloom, passed down through a sequence of poetic generations. To say this is to acknowledge that some passages of poetry seem to have had the remarkable ability to inspire allusion in other poets. We can see this, for example, with these lines from the ninth book of Milton's *Paradise Lost* which describe Satan's first sight of Eve in the Garden of Eden following his intrepid and arduous journey through the wastes of Chaos:

> As one who long in populous City pent,
> Where Houses thick and Sewers annoy the Aire,
> Forth issuing on a Summers Morn to breathe
> Among the pleasant Villages and Farmes
> Adjoynd, from each thing met conceaves delight,
> The smell of Grain, or tedded Grass, or Kine,
> Or Dairie, each rural sight, each rural sound;
> …
> Such Pleasure took the Serpent to behold
> This Flourie Plat, the sweet recess of *Eve*
> Thus earlie, thus alone.

Satan, concealed in the form of the serpent, feels overawed and momentarily disarmed of his own malice at the sight of Eve. His delight in the new world he encounters – delight that he can't help but feel in spite of his own ruinous intentions towards Adam and Eve – is likened by Milton to the pleasure derived by a city-dweller from a morning walk into the open countryside. Of course, the image of the walker breathing in rural refreshment is mixed in Milton's lines with a powerful sense of foreboding: Satan is intent on despoiling the very thing from which he takes delight. Moreover, the passage might make readers ask just how much we should be gladdened by the gladness of Satan.

So it is worth bearing in mind that Milton's original passage is quite a complex one, consisting of an extended simile that could be viewed as darkly ironic. Several major poets can be found alluding to this passage over the next century and a half, including the following:

> As one who long in thickets and in brakes
> Entangled ...
> (William Cowper, *The Task*)
>
> How many bards in city garret pent
> (Samuel Taylor Coleridge, 'To The Nightingale')
>
> To one who has been long in city pent,
> 'Tis very sweet to look into the fair
> And open face of heaven
> (John Keats, 'To one who has been long')

We do not have space here to discuss the purposes that these poets might have had in alluding to the original passage in *Paradise Lost*, but instead we want to use these verbal echoes to pose a more general question about the 'limits' of allusion. The presence of an allusion directs us to the existence of a relationship between one literary work and another, yet what actually gets imported into a poem when an allusion takes place? Is it merely the words themselves, or is it the whole secondary context that the earlier work provides? When Cowper's *The Task* alludes to a passage in *Paradise Lost*, should that be seen as inviting the reader to interpret the alluding passage in relation to the great themes of *Paradise Lost*: those of sin, loss and self-corruption? Or would that be to risk over-interpreting the allusion, and to place too much semantic emphasis on a mere verbal echo between the two works?

One of the most interesting scholarly treatments of allusion is an essay by Earl Wasserman (1966) on Pope's *The Rape of the* Lock, which considers the repercussions of taking a very broad view of what an allusive context might consist of. Take these lines from the poem:

> But anxious Care the pensive Nymph opprest,
> And secret Passions labour'd in her Breast.

The events of the story are that Belinda (the 'Nymph') has had a lock of her hair cut off by an importunate (but apparently unwanted) suitor, referred to in the poem as the Baron. The lines come shortly after the incident and seem to capture her distress and indignation over it. However, the lines secretly allude to the opening of the fourth book of the Virgil's *Aeneid*: 'But the queen [Dido] long since wounded by anxious cares . . . is torn by secret passion'. These lines refer to Dido's bereavement over her dead husband ('anxious cares') but also her guiltily emerging affection for Aeneas ('secret passion'). What does Pope mean by echoing these lines about secret love in the context of Belinda's sense of affront and violation at having an unwanted suitor take prize of a lock of her hair? Is there a suggestion that actually Belinda is really in the throes of the same emotion affecting Dido: namely a secret love lurking in her heart? The allusion creates a sense of counterpoint, or it runs against the grain of what the poem seems ostensibly to be saying. The allusion, so Wasserman suggests, is one of several which, if explored not just for the narrow verbal coincidence but for the deeper, underlying congruence of ideas, seem to challenge Belinda's public stance of resistance to the Baron's advances and to imply her active collusion with his designs upon her. This is a good example of how an allusion differs importantly from a literary source or analogue, for it can involve the words (and also perhaps meanings) of one literary work being brought creatively into play within the context of another one.

6.9   CREATIVE QUOTATION AND POETIC IMITATION

Allusion often involves quotation of the actual words of another poet. However, it need not necessarily do so, and, when it does, the fact of quotation is likely to be concealed through the omission of speech marks or any explicit reference. Allusion differs in principle from quotation partly because the best allusions tend to be deliberately unobtrusive or ghostly in effect, but also because the words in which an allusion is conveyed belong unambiguously to the alluding poet, whereas quotation involves the public assigning of ownership to another author. Some poets seem to favour quotation, as a polyphonic technique, over allusion. The Romantic poet Charlotte Smith (1749–1806) specialises in poems that incorporate voices other than her own. The first poem in her collection of *Elegiac Sonnets* is about the mixed blessings brought by having a poetic vocation, given that the practice of composing poetry involves just as much pain as delight. The last couplet runs: 'Ah! Then, how dear the Muse's favours cost, / *If those paint sorrow best – who feel it most!*' At the end of the italicised line, Smith footnotes a couplet from Pope's *Eloisa to Abelard*: (1719) 'The well-sung woes shall soothe my pensive ghost; / He best can paint them who shall feel them most'. The quotation is very inexact but, all the same, the slightly clunking footnote to Pope's poem makes the effect seem very different from the delicacy of an allusion as such. The poem resists 'incorporating' Pope's words; it advertises their status as foreign matter.

Poems may quote from other poems (or other literary works in general) for a variety of reasons, some relating to form and some to theme. Let us take the ending paragraph of Eliot's *The Waste Land*:

> I sat upon the shore
> Fishing, with the arid plain behind me
> Shall I at least set my lands in order?

London Bridge is falling down falling down falling down
Poi s'ascose nel foco che gli affina
Quando fiam uti chelidon – O swallow swallow
Le prince d'Aquitaine à la tour abolie
These fragments I have shored against my ruins
Why then Ile fit you. Hieronymo's mad againe.
Datta. Dayadhvam. Damyata.
Shantih   shantih   shantih

Eliot's 'Notes' on *The Waste Land* direct the reader to a list of sources for the mosaic of quotations that makes up the poem's ending. The poem makes no attempt, at this point, to 'fit' these lines smoothly into its own poetic language: instead, the quotations feel like the very 'fragments' that the Fisher King has 'shored' against his ruins. The poem concludes with a babble of jarring, non-synthesised voices, each of which cannot be assumed to understand the other. Despite the paragraph's ending with the repetition of the word 'shantih' ('The Peace which passeth understanding'), the overall effect is one of linguistic melt-down, probably not unrelated to one of the themes that Eliot claimed to have employed in this part of the poem: 'the present decay of eastern Europe'.

The end of Eliot's poem approaches close to the condition of a **cento**: that is, 'A composition formed by joining scraps from other authors' (*OED*). Pure centos are inevitably rare, as befits a highly artificial and specialised creative activity, but that is not to say that more serious poets have always shunned them. The contemporary American poet John Ashbery (b. 1927), for example, has written a notable poem of this kind entitled 'The Dong with the Luminous Nose', the first two stanzas of which are given below:

Within a windowed niche of that high hall
I wake and feel the fell of dark, not day.
I shall rush out as I am, and walk the street
Hard by yon wood, now smiling as in scorn.
The lights begin to twinkle from the rocks
From camp to camp, through the foul womb of night.
Come shepherd and again renew the quest.
And birds sit brooding in the snow.

Continuous as the stars that shine,
When men were all asleep the snow came flying
Near where the dirty Thames does flow
Through caverns measureless to man,
Where thou shalt see the red-gilled fishes leap
And a lovely Monkey with lollipop paws
Where the remote Bermudas ride.

The poem, first appearing in Ashbery's collection *Wakefulness* (1998), draws most of its lines from canonical English poets. The first, for example, comes from Byron's *Childe Harold's Pilgrimage*; the second from a poem by Gerard Manley Hopkins; the third from Eliot's *The Waste Land*; the fourth from Gray's 'Elegy Written in a Country Church-Yard'; the fifth from Tennyson's *Ulysses*; the sixth and eighth are Shakespearean; and the seventh derives from Matthew Arnold's poem 'The Scholar Gipsy'. The second stanza, beginning with a line from Wordsworth's 'Daffodils', proceeds in the same fashion. Ashbery's poem comprises a very strict rendering of the idea of a cento, such that he declines to exercise ownership even over the very title of his work, which is in fact lifted straight from a nonsense-poem by Edward Lear. Nothing in Ashbery's poem, then, other than the particular way that it assembles its fragments, can count as his own creation.

For all this, the poem possesses a strange, surreal loveliness. It only works, of course, in the very limited way that cento poems can work: that is, in the absence of any coherent narrative structure. Instead, we glimpse an indistinct narrator-figure wandering through a sequence of imperfectly realised, shifting, but also evocative settings. The poem may be (inevitably) rather discontinuous with itself, but each line that has been plucked and assembled by Ashbery seems to possess a strange resonance, perhaps made all the greater by the lack of connective logic holding the lines together. Ashbery has confessed to struggling to keep in mind precisely where all the lines have come from, but he has been open about the fact the work was put together as 'a sort of tribute to the period when I used to read nineteenth-century poetry with a sense of awe that great poets could write great poems'.

Allusion and quotation are different techniques through which poets can draw upon words used by other writers, so as to incorporate a second voice within their lines, or indeed multiple voices. Such techniques stand quite closely to imitation (or even perhaps parody) where an author creates a new poem in the image of an old one, possibly in a spirit of mockery but equally likely as a gesture of reverence or homage. Imitation doesn't necessarily involve reuse of the actual words of an earlier poet, but most imitative poems owe some debt to such practices. As a way of concluding this section we want to juxtapose two poems (presented in excerpted form) where the second imitates the first. The first is Christopher Smart's 'My Cat Jeoffry', written after the poet had been committed to a madhouse, which forms one section of his complex religious poem *Jubilate Agno* ('Rejoice in the Lamb'). The second is an amusing work by the contemporary poet Wendy Cope modelled on Smart's original:

My Cat Jeoffry

For I will consider my Cat Jeoffry.
For he is the servant of the Living God duly and daily serving him.
For at the first glance of the glory of God in the East he worships in his way.
For this is done by wreathing his body seven times round with elegant quickness.
For then he leaps up to catch the musk, which is the blessing of God upon his prayer.
For he rolls upon prank to work it in.
For having done duty and received blessing he begins to consider himself.
For this he performs in ten degrees.
For first he looks upon his fore-paws to see if they are clean.
For secondly he kicks up behind to clear away there.
For thirdly he works it upon stretch with the fore paws extended.
For fourthly he sharpens his paws by wood.
For fifthly he washes himself.

My Lover

For I will consider my lover who shall remin nameless.
For at the age of 49 he can make the noise of five different kinds of lorry changing gear
  on a hill.
…
For he supports Tottenham Hotspur with joyful and unswerving devotion.
For he abhors Arsenal, whose supporters are uncivilized and rough.
For he explains that Spurs are magic, whereas Arsenal are boring and defensive.
For I knew nothing of this six months ago, nor did I want to.
For now it all enchants me.
For this he performs in ten degrees.
For first he presents himself as a nice, serious, liberated person.
For secondly he sits through many lunches, discussing life and love and never
  mentioning football.
For thirdly he is careful not to reveal how much his dislikes losing an argument.
For fourthly he talks about the women in his past, acknowledging that some of it must
  have been his fault.
For fifthly he is so obviously reasonable that you are inclined to doubt this.

Smart's affectionate relationship with his cat sustained him during his period of
confinement, and his lines are intently observant of Jeoffry's feline mannerisms.
Jeoffry seems to be imbued with some of the quickness and spirit of life itself:
he incarnates God's creative zest. Yet his characteristics are also highly virtuous,
symbolising forms of exemplary Christian behaviour. His leaping and frisking
are seen by Smart as a sort of feline version of human prayer and thanksgiving.
The poem illustrates how even those most thrust down in the world (as Smart
confined to a madhouse, and Jeoffry consigned to a lowly place in the hierarchy
of creation as a mere cat) can still in their own way reflect the glory of God.

Much of *Jubilate Agno* is structured as a sort of antiphonal chant, with a series of lines beginning with the word 'Let' being answered by corresponding ones starting with 'For', though this structure actually fails to apply to the lines about Jeoffry. Nonetheless, the formal regularity of the lines on Jeoffry, as well as their eccentric religiosity, has rendered them attractive to prospective imitators. Wendy Cope's poem follows the structure of Smart's lines exactly, while turning them to quite another purpose. Her subject is not a favourite pet so much as a new lover, but the poem retains much the same celebratory spirit as in Smart's lines. Just as Smart is enchanted by all Jeoffry's little feline traits, so is Cope by those of her lover. Just as Smart vindicates Jeoffry as a 'servant of the Living God', so Cope vindicates her man as a 'nice, serious, liberated person'. On a more local level, Jeoffry's duty to his maker is matched by the lover's 'unswerving devotion' to Tottenham Hotspur, football (it might be argued) having assumed a position in British society as its modern-day religion.

Cope's poem nowhere formally acknowledges its intertextual relationship with Smart's earlier work: it requires the reader to provide that recognition and the poem will probably be met with perplexity by readers not in the know. As most imitative poems, 'My Lover' improvises within a received framework; Cope does her own thing during most of the lines, but the overarching structure (the repetition of 'For' lines), as well as a small amount of other phraseology, is carried over direct from Smart. As with other intertextual works, the dilemma for the reader is to what extent the meaning of Cope's poem might be shaped by its relationship with the earlier text, to what extent an exemplary reading of it should take due account of potentially a host of ironic parallels, some of which we pointed out above. The previous three sections of this chapter have all been about the phenomenon of words by one poet turning up, or being alluded to, in a poem written by another one. So much, of course, consists with a perception that words or phraseology can be strongly identified with their previous usage by an earlier poet or poets. But we now want to ask whether the English language itself could in some way be seen as 'owned' by, or identified strongly with, a particular section of its users, and what effect this perception might have on the morale and craft of modern-day poets.

6.10   THE QUEEN'S (AND OTHER PEOPLE'S) ENGLISH

There is a poignant poem of Tony Harrison's entitled 'The Queen's English' in which he describes taking a last meal, in the Queen's Hotel in Leeds, with his dying father. However, he is keenly aware of a distance that has grown up between the two of them, and accounts for this in terms of the disparity between his own literate, studious language and his father's indelible Yorkshire dialect: on parting, his father gives him a collection of *Poems from the Yorkshire Dales* to remind him ''ow us gaffers used to talk'. The history of the English language can, in fact, be seen as one of the gradual supremacy over all others of one particular regional dialect, that belonging to the southern counties of England. The process starts early: if we compare the fourteenth-century London-based poet Chaucer with his contemporary William Langland, who hailed from Worcestershire, it is noticeable how much closer to standard English of our own day Chaucer's language seems. That it should seem so is because the process of creating a standard written language throughout Britain entailed the writing habits of educated people in the southern counties fanning out across, and become normative within, the outlying regions. Of course, patterns of speech, unlike those of writing, have never become fully standardised, but it still remains the case that the pronunciatory habits of the southern English have always had greater status and cachet than those of other regions. When foreigners learn to speak English, for example, it is usual for them to be taught the speech-habits of the English southern counties; and even native English speakers can sign up for 'elocution' classes, where they will learn to 'improve' their own speech by appropriating the accent of people living in the south-eastern corner.

Various names have been attached to this south-eastern accent to express its status as a standard: received pronunciation, the Queen's English, BBC English, Oxford English or public school English. Some of these terms, however, are in process of coming to seem anachronistic, as the very *idea* of a speech standard has begun to dwindle. For one thing, the proliferation of television channels has opened up the airwaves to numerous non-standard accents; but also the practice of correcting 'deviant' pronunciatory habits against a linguistic standard has become unfashionable in educational circles. Perhaps most interesting in recent times, however, has been the rise of 'estuary English', a slightly non-standard, supposedly classless, brand of English, which has spread outwards from the Thames estuary partly as a reaction against the élitism of received pronunciation.

A fraught resistance to the tyranny of standard English is obviously felt in a regional poet like Tom Leonard, but another quarter from which opposition to standard English has come is ethnic minority poets. A poem centrally concerned with this issue is John Agard's 'Listen Mr Oxford Don':

> Me not no Oxford don
> me a simple immigrant
> from Clapham Common
> I didn't graduate
> I immigrate

But listen Mr Oxford don
I'm a man on de run
and a man on de run
is a dangerous one

I ent have no gun
I ent have no knife
but mugging de Queen's English
is the story of my life

I dont need no axe
to split/ up yu syntax
I dont need no hammer
to mash/ up yu grammar

I warning you Mr Oxford don
I'm a wanted man
and a wanted man
is a dangerous one

Dem accuse me of assault
on de Oxford dictionary/
imagine a concise peaceful man like me/
dem want me to serve time
for inciting rhyme to riot
but I tekking it quiet
down here in Clapham Common

I'm not a violent man Mr Oxford don
I only armed wit mih human breath
but human breath
is a dangerous weapon

So mek dem send one big word after me
I ent serving no jail sentence
I slashing suffix in self-defence
I bashing future wit present tense
and if necessary

I making de Queen's English accessory / to my offence

The poem is not concerned with Oxford dons as scholars and teachers, but rather with 'Oxford English', with 'Oxford' as a badge for correct English usage. The language of the poem is a phonetic transcription of Anglo–Caribbean pronunciation of English, a language made up, so the reader might think, of multiple deviations from, or corruptions of, standard English. 'Me not' in the first line replaces the more conventional 'I'm not', and in a similar way 'I ent' is a rendering of 'I don't'. Intermingled with these grammatical departures are numerous phonological spellings as 'dem' for 'them', 'yu' for 'your' and 'tekking' for 'taking'.

Much of what the poem is about is contained in the antithetical rhyme 'graduate/immigrate'; the words have like-sounding endings but point to mutually exclusive life expectations: to have immigrated, in practical terms, disqualifies you from, or at least statistically reduces your chances of, graduating. The poem describes the poet's experience of being a linguistic renegade, of fleeing from the long arm of standard usage. Behind him he is conscious of having left a trail of split-up syntax and mashed-up grammar, and of atrocities against prescribed lexicographical usage and correct rhyming practice. All of this bristling linguistic defiance is captured and summed up in the punning slogan: 'I ent serving no jail sentence'.

For the most part, the poet sees himself as under constant harassment and siege by the forces of linguistic convention; his position is invariably defined by negatives: 'not no Oxford don'; 'I ent have no gun' and so on. But at the end, the poem seems to buoy itself up with a sudden perception of its own linguistic emancipation. After all, the essence of the poem is that it has things both ways. It complains about the tyranny of the rules of English while actually in the very process of flouting them. Similarly, the poem reserves for itself the prerogative of falling back on the standard language if and when it suits; this, indeed, seems to be the meaning of the last line about 'making de Queen's English accessory / to my offence'. This remark is one of those that both states a truism and enacts it at the same time. The phrase 'accessory to an offence' comes from legalese, one of the more prestigious registers of English; and Agard intimates that his most subversive act is perhaps not using non-standard English so much as press-ganging this article of polite phraseology into such a linguistically rebellious work.

Agard's poem is a loud interrogation of issues that nearly all poems, however subduedly, have to confront. What is the appropriate language of poetry? What are the linguistic alternatives available to the poet? And what, and how overbearing, are the pressures of linguistic conformity and prestige that might incline a particular writer to use one set of words as opposed to another? These are questions that have always posed themselves to poets, though the exact guise under which they occur is apt to vary from one period to another. However, as our society grows more multiracial and polyglot, much as has been the pattern in the United States, such issues will become ever more prominent and unavoidable.

6.11   EXERCISES

Despite the fact that Thomas Hardy (1840–1928) was best known in his lifetime – as he has been since – as a novelist, he always took greater pride in his poetry, which dominated his literary activity during the last thirty years of his life. He composed the poem below on the death of his cousin, Tryphena Sparks, in whom he had once taken a romantic interest (hence the reference to Phena as his 'lost prize').

Thoughts of Phena at News of her Death

> Not a line of her writing have I,
>   Not a thread of her hair,
> No mark of her late time as dame in her dwelling, whereby
>   I may picture her there;
>   And in vain do I urge my unsight
>   To conceive my lost prize
> At her close, whom I knew when her dreams were upbrimming with light,
>   And with laughter her eyes.
>
> What scenes spread around her last days,
>   Sad, shining, or dim?
> Did her gifts and compassions enray and enarch her sweet ways
>   With an aureate nimb?
>   Or did life-light decline from her years,
>   And mischances control
> Her full day-star; unease, or regret, or forebodings, or fears
>   Disennoble her soul?
>
> Thus I do but the phantom retain
>   Of the maiden of yore
> As my relic; yet haply the best of her – fined in my brain
>   It may be the more
>   That no line of her writing have I,
>   Nor a thread of her hair,
> No mark of her late time as dame in her dwelling, whereby
>   I may picture her there.

March 1890.

1. How would you describe the diction used in the poem? Are there expressions that are unlikely to have formed part of common English usage at the time the poem was written?

2. Comment on the extensive use of verbal suffixes here to create neologisms like 'upbrimming', 'enray' and 'Disennoble'? What effect do they create?

3. Comment in general on the use of interrogatives and negatives in the poem.

4. What effect is created by the virtual repetition of the first four lines at the end of the poem?

5. How successful overall is 'Thoughts of Phena' as a poem of loss, regret and mourning?

6. Try writing a short poem that either (i) makes significant use of archaisms or neologisms; or (ii) makes a self-conscious attempt to form a mental picture of an absent person or thing.

7

Writing poetry

The urge to make poetry is an ancient one. People have composed verse for several thousand years: before writing, before printing, and, indeed, before the development of the modern world itself. The earliest surviving classics of western civilisation, Homer's *Odyssey* and *Iliad* (c. ninth–eighth century BC), for mighty instance, are poetic epics which were composed and passed down orally for centuries before they were recorded in manuscript and well over two thousand years before they first appeared in print. In terms of English literature poetry, in the form of the great Old English verse which survives from tenth-century manuscripts – most notably *Beowulf* and *The Dream of the Rood* (see Chapter 1) – predates the other principal literary forms which we read and study today. Theatre, in its earliest English form, dates back to the medieval drama of the mystery plays, and Anglo-Saxon poetry also pre-exists – by several centuries more – the English novel (which is generally seen as a late seventeenth- and early eighteenth-century phenomenon initiated by such works as Aphra Behn's *Oroonoko* (1695) and Daniel Defoe's *Robinson Crusoe* (1719)).

Though this long-standing desire to compose verse is by no means innate (as expressive language itself seems to be among humans), poetry is one of those age-old accomplishments like music or art which seem common to almost all societies in however rudimentary or sophisticated form. The following pages, in which we move from the reading of poetry to the writing of poetry, offer advice on the composition of verse. Dylan Thomas once jocularly described writing poetry as 'an incurable disease', and, whether scourge or blessing, the desire to create poetry, which spans four millennia and more, is still a vital one. Whether one writes for publication or for one's own pleasure – or is prompted by a combination of the two – the act of writing a poem is, for many people, one of the most rewarding of artistic endeavours.

Writing poetry can be a hugely enjoyable process, though it can also seem a frustrating and thankless task at times. This chapter, which aims to maximise the former sentiment and minimise the latter, is intended to offer practical advice to those moved to write verse. After an initial discussion of why poets write, it offers practical advice on composing poetry, on creative writing classes and poetry workshops, and on how to get one's poetry published. Practitioners frequently have much to say about their craft and the 'Poets on Poetry' mini-anthology also included below offers useful insights into the manner in which poets have written about their craft over the last century or so. The chapter concludes with a series of practical exercises on writing poetry.

7.1 WHY WRITE POETRY?

Poetry is a channelled form of self-expression which can offer profound personal rewards to its author, and – if done well – to its readers or listeners. It has many motivations. To some, Wordsworth's notion of verse as the 'spontaneous overflow of powerful feelings' encapsulates the point and purpose of poetry while others believe, with the Modernist critic T. E. Hulme (1883–1917), that poetry does not always 'mean a bringing in of some of the emotions', and that unemotional, 'accurate, description is a legitimate object of verse'. Poetry can describe, can clarify a vague idea, can capture a moment felt deeply, and express emotions – from love and desire to scorn and contempt. It can do many other things: move, amuse, arouse, persuade, shock and even simply answer the need to cover a blank sheet of paper.

There are no hard and fast rules about what poetry should address or what it should ignore. Poetry does not always have to be high toned, or moral or profound. It can be intellectually combative, wounding or satirical; it can be nonsensical, whimsical and take delight in wordplay. It can celebrate virtue or shed light on the darkest areas of human consciousness; as Keats said of Shakespeare, the 'poetical character ... has as much delight in conceiving an Iago as an Imogen'. The purpose of art is not always to speak to or from the heart, and writing verse can also involve the cultivation of a persona or allow us to imagine the minds of others remote from us, whether in time or terms of individual morality. The poet Browning, for instance, had no personal knowledge of murder, high politics or madness but in his *Dramatic Lyrics* (1842) was able to venture into the world of Machiavellianism, psychosis and abnormal mental states in such works as 'My Last Duchess' and 'Porphyria's Lover'.

Poetry can, with the Romantics Wordsworth and Coleridge, privilege an expressive model of poetic creation, or, with the neoclassicists Pope and Swift, engage in public debate or satirical point scoring. It can also do neither and repudiate both, and endorse a poetry devoted to formal excellence or beauty for their own sakes, what C. B. Cox and Michael Schmidt called in 1973 a 'practice of clearly formal writing, a common bridling at vacuous public and private rhetoric'. It can, with the 'Liverpool poets' of the 1960s – Adrian Henri (1932–2000), Roger McGough (b. 1937) and Brian Patten (b. 1946) – and in more recent performance poetry adopt an anti-academic model of clarity of expression and attempt to address a wide audience, believing, as Adrian Mitchell (1932–2008) put it in 1964, that 'Most people ignore most poetry / because / most poetry ignores most people'. It can also cultivate a mandarin aloofness and difficulty, as in the work of the contemporary English poet J. H. Prynne (b. 1934). Here are three stanzas from Prynne's recent pamphlet 'Streak ~~~ Willing ~~~ Entourage *Artesian*' (2009) as illustration of this willingness to baffle and challenge:

> Fix out gaze on this, on virtue. Acknowledge
> skid forward or same plastic fervid embankment
> her link antler, rising and driven. Above his
> anthem converge tall preening slips to axial
>
> Image dilation eager for size, steep-side per
> macro run by dozen oh warship gauge silent
> elated regimen. See the same hold for top flit
> margin payout, grab on eyes wide to ever fade,
>
> Total extensor bin. Hold your to me ligate for
> free ply employ random either way countenance
> rebel gate, gate far over enter attracted win
> worn cumber ask, dazzle so profile ply to play.

Poetry, it is clear, is complex in its nature and its motivations. That said, however much one qualifies and problematises the notion, much – though by no means all – modern poetry is prompted by a desire for self-expression and by a sense that writing verse is somehow a voyage of personal discovery. This conviction, it might be said, is nothing new. As least as far back as the Anglo-Saxon period, in 'The Wanderer' and 'The Seafarer' (which, though doubtless written earlier, survive in the Exeter Manuscript which was given to that city's cathedral in the year 940), poets have described themselves metaphorically as travellers and voyagers and have used verse as a means of expressing personal feelings about the nature of existence and of their own life's journey. Rather more recently, the American poet Robert Frost (1874–1963) once remarked that 'I have never started a poem yet whose end I knew. Writing a poem is discovering'. Now plainly it is perfectly possible to write any number of poems where one knows the 'end' of those works in advance of their writing, but this is useful counsel in terms of writing verse. Composing poetry is not often like a motorway journey, where the destination is clear at the point of departure. The art of verse, rather than being motivated by a clear need to express a previously fixed idea, can be seen as a way both to articulate and to 'discover', to use Frost's terminology, one's feelings. (The Irish poet Michael Longley remarked in 2010 that 'If you know exactly where you are going in writing a poem, what's the point of doing it? If you can't surprise yourself, then what's the point of poetry?')

This is not say, of course, that poetry should be an unvarnished and unmediated record of personal feeling or circumstance (if such a thing is possible, given the ambiguities of language and – on the other hand – the fact that a writer imposes a measure of order on lived experience, then a diary is the best place for it). Poetry submits emotion, opinion and sentiment to formal discipline. Some of the most powerful poetry, in articulating individual feelings, thoughts and experiences, uses the narrowly personal – from the painful and traumatic to the exalted and exhilarating through to the mundane and commonplace – and transforms individual utterance into something of more general significance and appeal. In 'My November Guest' (1913), for example, Frost takes the universal emotion of sorrow, which we have all experienced, and personifies it into a female companion, someone at once familiar and strange. The very plainness of his idiom serves the emotional power of the verse:

> My Sorrow, when she's here with me,
>   Thinks these dark days of autumn rain
> Are beautiful as days can be;
> She loves the bare, the withered tree;
>   She walks the sodden pasture lane.

Thomas Hardy's post-Romantic notion of verse as 'emotion put into measure', which evokes a sense of poetry as a combination of expressive feeling with a controlling intelligence and formal skill, certainly applies to Frost's lyric. One might also see a similar sentiment informing some of the most darkly elegant and expressive poetry of the second half of the post-Freudian, post-Wordsworthian twentieth century in the work of Frost's successor Robert Lowell (1917–1977) and his disciples, Sylvia Plath (1932–1963) and Anne Sexton (1928–1972), both of whom lived troubled lives. In the work of these poets, it is often argued, poetry acted as a form of confessional writing, even as – albeit ultimately unsuccessful – therapy. We see perhaps the most remarkable manifestations of this cultural tendency in the posthumous collection published after Plath had killed herself, *Ariel* (1965), and in the powerful lyrics gathered in Sexton's *All My Pretty Ones* (1962), which appeared ten years before that poet's own suicide.

Sexton's 'The Abortion', for instance, first published in 1961, describes the poet's feelings when, after a termination, she travels, almost without purpose, up into the Blue Mountains of Pennsylvania where she drives over dark lands from which the coal has been roughly hewn out. The analogy is troubling, and powerfully obvious:

> its roads sunken in like a grey washboard;
> where, in truth, the ground cracks evilly,
> a dark socket from which the coal has poured,
>
> Somebody who should have been born is gone.

Sexton's poem, the skilfully worked-up expression of personal feeling, is despairing yet curiously exhilarating. Here verse is both darkly personal and manages to transcend immediate circumstance.

The above notwithstanding, a poet can also achieve poetry of force and resonance by understating and suppressing emotion. Poetry is a rich art and its effects can sometimes be contradictory. Lowell's American contemporary William Stafford's 'Travelling Through the Dark' (1962), for example, is rendered compelling by the narrative voice's very reluctance to give in to emotion. Like 'The Seafarer' and like 'The Abortion', this is a poem prompted by 'travelling'. Stafford (1914–1993), who himself described poetic composition as a journey in 1971 ('I keep following this sort of hidden river of my life, you know, whatever the topic or impulse which comes, I follow it along trustingly'), describes a nocturnal car ride in which the narrative voice tells, baldly, of finding the carcass of a deer, dead at the side of the road by the Wilson River in Oregon. In such circumstances (male) drivers normally threw the animals' bodies 'down the canyon', and into the river, to prevent accidents. As the poet, unmoved, stoops to do this, he notes that the roe, though cold, was 'large in the belly'. The side of the animal, he discovers, is still warm:

> My fingers touching her side brought me the reason –
> her side was warm; her fawn lay there waiting,
> alive, still, never to be born.
> Beside the mountain road I hesitated.
> ...
> I thought hard for us all – my only swerving –
> Then pushed her over the edge into the river.

Both Stafford and Sexton derive the emotional impact of their poems through reference to the unborn. However, while Sexton's poem comments directly and makes its emotional position clear, Stafford's rigorously simple and artfully artless (some readers would say heartless) work relies on spare description, with the reader supplying the emotion from which the narrator, indeed, seems to be struggling to escape.

While the criteria of authenticity and sincerity are clearly associated with the writing of self-expressive verse, the best poets in this tradition hone and polish their technique, no matter how natural or unmediated it might seem. Robert Lowell himself wrote in 1974 that 'From the beginning, I was preoccupied with technique, fascinated' by it. In Sexton's abrupt turning away from metaphor into blunt threnody, and in Stafford's studied poetic refusal of poeticality, we see poetic skill and technique at work, the one giving the effect of poetic interiority, the other attempting to maintain a surface veneer of the un-impassioned while simultaneously hinting at – in his reference to his 'only swerving' – a suppressed emotion. Writing poetry is an art as well as a means of self-expression and patterning human experience into the meaningful.

We will conclude this section by examining the opening section of Adrienne Rich's (b. 1929) philosophical poem 'Transcendental Etude' (1971) as a work which offers an example to aspirant poets of the capacity to combine T. E. Hulme's descriptive manner with a post-Romantic register of emotion. This too, like Sexton's and Stafford's poems, was prompted by the mundane experience of driving, and Rich also uses that everyday circumstance to engage with larger notions of the maternal, and of life, and of death:

> This August evening I've been driving
> …
> my car startling young deer in meadows – one
> gave a hoarse intake of her breath and all
> four fawns sprang after her
> into the dark maples.
> Three months from today they'll be fair game
> for the hit-and-run hunters
> in a weekend's destructive power,
> triggers fingered by drunken gunmen, sometimes
> so inept as to leave the shattered animal
> stunned in her blood. But this evening deep in summer
> the deer are still alive and free
> nibbling apples from early-laden boughs
> so weighted, so englobed
> with already yellowing fruit
> they seem eternal.

This is a version of the ancient literary form of pastoral, and as in Milton's *Paradise Lost* or Blake's 'The Lamb', its Edenic vision contains, even at the moment of its inception, the portent of death, the sense of a Satanic intruder lurking without. But however portentous and inescapable that knowledge, here at least is an idyllic moment, in the Keatsian language of the 'apples from early-laden boughs', 'englobed / with already yellowing fruit', before the apple – as it does in *Paradise Lost* – becomes a witness to the Fall. Once again the deer and its fawn are both deer and fawn and something much more resonant, in symbolic terms, allowing Rich to meditate on the maternal, the frequent and unthinking cruelty of men, and the fact that life, infancy and innocence will always, eventually, perish. Once again, here is a poem which takes the commonplace sight and makes it heavy, 'weighted', with meaning. Whether consciously poetic, as in Rich's work, or unadorned in idiom, as in Stafford's, good poetry frequently possesses different levels of meaning, speaking to the incident or emotion being described, but also to much more besides.

7.2   WRITE A POEM

For newcomers to poetry, often the best advice *is* to address one's own feelings and personal experiences. Write a poem prompted by either of these ineluctable and interrelated things. Make this from the raw materials of that which you know or that which has happened to you, as did Rich, Sexton and Stafford before you. Begin writing by thinking about the things which surround you, about the emotions that touch you closely, or about the world – be it lived in metropolis, village or town – which you experience in everyday life. Almost anything will do to make a poem, from the huge events of human life to the mundane and trivial. Indeed the humdrum, perhaps paradoxically, can be made striking in a poem. Consider as an example the manner in which Phillip Larkin's '*Vers de Société*' (1974) takes the everyday experience of being asked to a social event which one doesn't quite fancy and transforms it into a magnificent poem. The work opens by coarsely and scornfully paraphrasing the unwelcome invitation to a provincial dinner party:

> 'My wife and I have asked a crowd of craps
> To come and waste their time and ours: perhaps
> You'd care to join us?' In a pig's arse, friend.
> …
> And so '*Dear Warlock-Williams: I'm afraid*' –

After the mordant wit of these opening lines, the poem mutates into a meditation on how human life is full of such unwanted moments of social intercourse ('Funny how hard it is to be alone'). 'I could spend half my evenings', laments Larkin, 'holding a glass of … sherry' and listening – the poet comments rather uncharitably – 'to the drivel of some bitch'. When Larkin could have been reading or writing and being enliveningly alone, he often found himself gathered round the trough with the likes of the Warlock-Williamses:

> Just think of all the spare time that has flown
> Straight into nothingness by being filled
> With forks and faces, rather than repaid
> Under a lamp, hearing the noise of wind.

However, as he thinks of this once-fond solitude in his late middle age, the poet realises that it no longer offers consolation or imaginative succour. Now sitting 'by a lamp more often brings / Not peace, but other things', writes Larkin mournfully: 'Beyond the light stand failure and remorse'. So the poet finds himself, in the end, writing '"*Dear Warlock-Williams: Why, of course* …"'.

Good poetry – we repeat – can be made by associating commonplace matters with things of more elevated, even timeless, significance. A lesson to be learnt from '*Vers de Société*' is to be unafraid of the familiar. Philip Larkin wrote that he admired, and wanted, to cultivate in his work what S. T. Coleridge called William Wordsworth's 'minute accuracy in the painting of local imagery'. So, write a poem derived from your 'local imagery' – not on Larkin's Hull, or Wordsworth's Lake District, or Stafford's Oregon – but on the world which surrounds you, whether in terms of your particular sense of place or in terms of a deep-felt emotional circumstance, or indeed, both. We examine above (in Chapter 5) Craig Raine's famous 'Martian' poetry of the 1970s, in which something as ubiquitous as a telephone or a visit to the lavatory could be described in a manner strange and striking. The particular and charming notion of looking at the commonplace through totally alien eyes has something of the pony with one trick about it, but those twin imperatives of making it new and describing the familiar are things to which someone new to writing poetry can usefully aspire. Look at your surroundings and try to describe them in a poem, and perhaps in so doing you will discover some previously unseen significance or pattern in your everyday experience. Write your own poem of place and maybe you will capture some wider resonance for your readers, introduce them to something outwith their own experience or, indeed, make them identify with yours. At the very least the journey might be an interesting one.

On the principle of practising what we preach, the poem below, John Strachan's 'Of Sunderland, and its Vicinities', addresses our own 'local imagery'. The present authors both used to travel to work from Newcastle-upon-Tyne in the North East of England to the nearby coastal city of Sunderland via the Metro (a light railway). The final stops on this journey were pleasingly alliterative – Seaburn, Stadium of Light, St Peter's and Sunderland – and each one had particular literary or cultural associations: with the author of *Alice's Adventures in Wonderland*, C. L. Dodgson ('Lewis Carroll') who spent much time at the seaside village of Seaburn as a young man; with the local football stadium, the Stadium of Light; with the ancient eighth-century monastic settlement of the Venerable Bede at St Peter's at the mouth of the Wear; and finally, with the city itself, where one arrives via a subterranean railway platform.

> There is a symmetry about the stations
> As the Metro moves alliteratively on.
> A northern sibilance:
> Seaburn, Stadium of Light,
> St Peter's, Sunderland.
>
> Seaburn, the beach where
> The sea is not on fire. Not boiling hot.
> And yet so it seemed to Charles Dodgson
> In that bright heat of his mind as he walked there.
> The Walrus was from Wearside.
>
> There is a certain arc at the North West Upper
> Where the light refracts down
> Through the metal girders of the stand
> Flickers white – and red – below.
> Gleaming, a trace of transcendence.
>
> The Saxon tower, the church,
> The place where Bede's young monks scrivened,
> Where the wind on the headland
> Was shut out and the word's light
> Shone, lasting: *scínon, langsum.*★
>
> At the central station, the light falls down
> Through the yellow liveries of the stairs
> And escalator, reflected by the glass
> Of Greggs' window. All lit up –
> The sea, the light, the saint, the land.
>
> ★ 'Shone', 'lasting' (Old English)

We give this as a practical example of observing one's surroundings and fashioning verse from them. This, too, is a journey poem, and one which builds on a number of linguistic associations pertaining to the taxonomy (the names) of the places alluded to – the words 'burn', 'light', 'sea', 'land' and 'sun' in particular – and develops them in its account of the cultural resonance of each stop on the journey being described. Not all of its particular allusions (that Sunderland's football team play in red and white, that Lewis Carroll wrote a poem whimsically imaging the sea as 'boiling hot', or that Greggs is a chain of sandwich shops) will be familiar to everyone who reads the poem (though these, like many initial obscurities in verse, can be easily established via an internet search), but we hope that its thematic notion of the interconnectedness of the past with the present is clear.

It is principally for the reader to assess 'Of Sunderland, and its Vicinities' in terms of its particular meanings for them, but on reading the work after its own 'journey' of composition was completed, it seems to us that the poem attends to both the particular nature of the city which it describes, from ancient learning to modern food-to-go, and, arguably, hints at some bigger issues: the continuities and dislocations of history from the Anglo-Saxon period to the twenty-first century (the span of surviving English verse itself, it might be pointed out); the notion, perhaps, that sport, especially football, occupies a place close to that which religion once possessed in English society; and the changing, but at the same time constant, nature of transcendent experience and joy. So, following this example, write about your own environs and, to borrow William Stafford's phrase, 'whatever the topic or impulse which comes ... follow it along trustingly'.

7.3 FEEDBACK ON YOUR POETRY: CREATIVE WRITING CLASSES, POETRY WORKSHOPS AND WRITERS' GROUPS

Try not to think of poetry as a lonely art. The old stereotype of the solitary genius writing in a garret never had much truth about it. Chaucer read his poetry aloud to enthusiastic court audiences, Wordsworth and Coleridge in their pomp worked very closely together and T. S. Eliot's *The Waste Land* was heavily edited by that poet's eccentric friend Ezra Pound. Poetry is shaped by its listeners, critics and audiences. New poets should find theirs. Especially valuable are informed and receptive readers who can offer useful advice and criticism on your work. Everyone likes a pat on the back, of course, and you might very well receive warm accolades on your poetry from friends, family and loved ones. That said, feedback from more disinterested sources is of more practical value to an aspiring poet. There are several places where poets can receive detailed criticism and advice on their verse: at creative writing classes, at poetry workshops run by more experienced poets, and at writers' groups of varying degrees of formality.

You will not be attending, it should be pointed out, to make your fortune. 'No man but a fool', as Dr Johnson might have said were he alive in the twenty-first century, 'ever wrote poetry for money'. People compose for love rather than for money, as writing poetry should not be confused with the road to riches. Even the most well-known poets – unlike best-selling novelists and successful screenwriters – do not make a fortune from their craft and only a tiny number of people in the UK and North America make a living from writing verse and giving readings alone. Indeed, most poets would agree with T. S. Eliot's 1959 remark that 'Obviously a poet has got to find a way of making a living apart from his poetry'. The present British poet laureate, for instance, Carol Ann Duffy, also earns a crust as a professor of creative writing, while her predecessor, Andrew Motion, is both a professor of the same discipline and also a distinguished biographer. In like manner, some of the most notable contemporary poets, Derek Walcott, Seamus Heaney, Paul Muldoon and Charles Wright among them, work or have worked as university teachers. Even Ted Hughes, Sir Andrew's great immediate predecessor as laureate, was children's author, translator, anthologist and great poet in simultaneity.

The facts that the present and previous British poets laureate are both university teachers of creative writing – and that Ted Hughes, a man from a previous generation, was no such thing – is symptomatic of the rise of creative writing courses, in a university context and elsewhere, in the United Kingdom over the last three decades. Many undergraduate programmes in English now have creative writing elements, joint honours degrees in English and Creative Writing abound and there are a number of postgraduate masters degrees. Almost all of these courses feature poetry (their quality can vary, of course, and university guides will help you in choosing the appropriate programme; as will asking questions of, and seeking testimonials from, admission tutors in advance of starting a class). The conviction, widely held in the past, that an ability to write poetry was a gift rather than an art which could be taught, is no longer the consensus in modern academia. Though some poets consider formal creative writing courses in the form of lectures and workshops as a waste of time and as likely to produce samey, formulaic verse, opinion among students tends to differ. Classes on writing poetry, whether part of a formal degree or taught within a non-examined adult education syllabus, are popular and can prove invaluable to those seeking to learn more about writing poetry.

Poetry workshops and writers' groups, which appeal to some precisely because they lack the element of formal assessment evident in most creative writing courses, also offer opportunities to study the craft of poetry and receive criticism upon one's work. In the former, an experienced poet, generally with a number of existing publications, will debate poetic composition in an informal context, discussing examples from his or her own work and also offering comments on work by workshop participants. Local writers' groups, on the other hand, see like-minded people gathering together to share their work and discuss it. The majority of these groups include prose writers as well as poets, though there are also a number of specific poetry groups. There might be one principal facilitator at these occasions, or there might be a number of people who take turns to chair proceedings. They have the virtue, to some, of not making poetic composition 'examination fodder' (as some of their members consider university creative writing courses) and they also possess flexibility, given that attendance is not directed towards academic qualifications.

Learning about writing in a group context, whether in a college or university course or in a more informal writers' group or poetry workshop, can be very important in developing one's poetry. However, students should arrive at class prepared to receive criticism and advice on their work with good grace, whether sourced from tutors in oral and written feedback or from fellow members of their group. Given the often personal nature of poetry, it is understandable that poets tend to be more defensive of their work than short story writers or dramatists, who tend to write from a third-person perspective. Given these sensitivities, criticism, however constructively meant, can sound withering. Nonetheless, it is not generally intended as such and students of poetry should attempt to view criticism as constructive. Indeed, writers should try, though this is not easy of course, to learn from both positive and negative criticism. Even if feedback on your work seems unnecessarily discouraging, think it over at length and consider whether, in the end, it might prove to be useful advice. Finally, console yourself with the fact that literary criticism is not a precise science. What one teacher might applaud another might find great fault with, and what one tutor sees as unclear and confusing another – more willing to applaud obscurity – might praise as challenging and innovative verse.

As well as seeing which creative writing courses and workshops are available to you, it is also useful to find out about local poetry readings in your area. Attend as many as you can. These are not classes as such, of course, but they can teach you a great deal about poetry. Local periodicals have arts listings in their 'What's On' pages. You can also look for local poetry events via internet search engines. If any of the poets you hear particularly impress you, buy some of their books, pamphlets or broadsheets (these will generally be on sale at these events) and try to work out exactly how their poetry works. When you develop skill and proficiency in writing poetry you might try participating in readings yourself (though do not volunteer until you have a body of work which has been published in poetry magazines or has at the very least been well received in your writing group or creative writing class). There is of course nothing to stop you from hosting a poetry event, however small, at which you could participate (or, indeed, a writing group of your own). Poetry readings are also good opportunities for networking with people who are interested in poetry, who might suggest further activities in your area. If you are on social networking sites there is the chance to be in contact with a great many poetry groups, from fan groups of poets well-known and obscure, through to organisations who exchange their work on line and host poetry readings.

7.4   PUBLISHING YOUR POETRY

Some great poets, Emily Dickinson for instance, have not written for publication, and others did not publish in the usual sense of canvassing a publisher – most notably William Blake who wrote, illustrated and printed his own work. However, these are exceptional cases; most writers want their verse to be read by as many people as possible and publication is the best way to achieve this. In the twenty-first century, you can publish yourself instantly and cheaply on the internet and some people are content with doing so in the hope that their work will find readers in cyberspace. There are also internet-only poetry 'ezines' to which you can submit your work, though at the moment such magazines lack the cachet of those published in the more conventional manner (but this may change, in time). If you have enough poetry to make a book, then one option is self-publishing via such companies as Amazon's CreateSpace (www.createspace.com), Lightning Source (www.lightningsource.com) and Lulu (www.lulu.com). These concerns will allow you to design, edit and market your own volume of poetry. Even so, there remains a feeling in some quarters that self-publishing a book indicates that it is not worthy of publication by a commercial press. This is certainly the common opinion of 'vanity presses', companies which indiscriminatingly publish anything offered them, on receipt of the requisite amount of cash. It is generally unwise to pay for your poetry to be published by a press which asks you to 'invest' in your own work. This will actually damage your reputation with what are generally seen as the best places to publish new verse: poetry magazines and prestigious poetry presses.

The most highly thought-of poetry is not self-published. It is assessed or refereed by an external publisher who, after accepting it following a review process, produces it, after judicious editing, at its own cost. For individual poems, this means specialist poetry magazines; for books, publishers which specialise in poetry. That said, if you decide you want to pursue these routes, then be realistic in your aspirations. A new artist would not take his or her first canvases down to the Tate Modern in the expectation of seeing them exhibited there, so it is not a good idea to send your first efforts to the poetry editor at the *Times Literary Supplement* or your first book proposal to Faber & Faber (unless, of course, you have a longish record of publication in highly thought-of journals before doing so).

If you are serious about publishing your verse, the best place to start is to approach specialist poetry magazines, from *Agenda Poetry Magazine* and the *American Poetry Review* onwards. The best place to find out about British and Irish journals is the 'Poetry Magazines' listing section of the *Writer's Handbook* (published by Macmillan), which has been issued annually since the mid-1980s and is to be found in many local libraries (the venerable *Writers' and Artists' Yearbook*, founded over a century ago, also includes sections on publishing poetry and listings of influential poetry organisations such as the Poetry Society and the Poetry Book Society). It is important to familiarise yourself with the journals and poetry magazines to which you intend to submit your work. Visit the magazines' websites for details and subscribe to those which interest you most and which might be the best place for your poetry. Expect rejections, especially in the early part of your poetic career, but do persevere, and if you are offered feedback on your work, try to treat it as useful free advice rather than a slap in the face. Learn to have confidence in editorial judgements unless they seem utterly eccentric; as Paul Muldoon wrote in 2010, 'I trust my editors to tell me if a poem is bad. You can bet that in a collection of thirty-nine poems, if thirty-eight are okay and one is a stinker, it's the stinker that everyone will talk about'.

If you have published a good number of poems in highly rated magazines and perhaps won or have been highly commended in a prestigious poetry competition (for monthly listings see the Poetry Library's website, http://www.poetrylibrary.org.uk/), then you might consider approaching a poetry publisher to see if they will publish a book of your poetry. Generally you will need to submit a proposal, saying why your work would suit the particular list of the house concerned and what you have published previously, along with a writing sample (rather than a full manuscript). Don't dismiss regional publishers. Their print runs can be as large as national ones and their local distribution network is deep, if not wide.

Editors of poetry presses often wearily portray themselves as deluged by hundreds of unwanted manuscripts from would-be poets (Faber & Faber's website, for instance, declares that 'Every week our Editors are inundated with manuscripts') and to get them to take a new author seriously it is essential that you have an established track record in terms of placing individual poems in magazines and anthologies or in publishing pamphlets or broadsheets (which feature a single-page poem or small number of poems). The submissions policies of some of the most notable British poetry publishers tell their own stories and are revealing (these will change in time and you should check the websites of the individual companies should you wish to approach them).

Enitharmion Press, for instance, declare bluntly that 'we are not in a position to look at unsolicited work', while only slightly more encouraging, but more informatively, Arc maintain that

> If your work has never been published, or if you have not built up a 'track record' of publication in specialist poetry magazines and journals, it is extremely unlikely that your work will be suitable or acceptable for publication in book form. With any submission you should, therefore, send a list of where you have already been published.

The highly rated firm of Bloodaxe resort to ill-tempered capitals to offer the same message: 'IF YOU HAVE NOT YET PUBLISHED POEMS EITHER IN REPUTABLE LITERARY MAGAZINES OR IN A PAMPHLET FROM A REPUTABLE SMALL PRESS, DO NOT SEND US YOUR WORK'.

If, however, you have built up the requisite 'track record' of individual publications, then publishing a book is the next step, though it is by no means an easy one to achieve. Research a company before you approach it. Carcanet's advice is useful in stressing to its prospective authors the need for familiarity with its list: 'Writers wishing to submit poetry should familiarise themselves with Carcanet's books and then, in the first instance, send between six and ten pages of work' ('and', they write less encouragingly, 'a stamped and self-addressed return envelope'). Be honest in introducing yourself and your work; don't make inflated claims about what you have already produced; as the Two Ravens Press puts it,

> There is little we dislike more than submissions from people who try to pretend they're something they're not … Don't oversell yourself or your work or exaggerate – it doesn't help. We want honest submissions from writers with integrity.

Two Ravens, like many poetry publishers, only says 'yes' or 'no' to a book proposal rather than offering detailed critiques of the work it has been sent, so do not expect expansive reasons why your verse has been turned down. Its reasons are informative:

> We are a small independent publisher, not a publicly funded agency or a writing consultancy … There are lots of literary consultancies who will happily offer you such appraisals for a fee. In addition, due to an astonishing number of disgruntled, argumentative and often plain offensive e-mails from people for whom we've taken the time to give honest, albeit necessarily brief, reasons for turning down their work, we find that the most pleasant route is to provide no comment at all.

The above might seem discouraging, but if you have developed a readership for your poetry via well-established magazines, then it is possible that you will, in the end (after developing a thick skin about rejections), find a publisher willing to produce a book of your verse (around 40–60 poems is usual). Poetry presses will not publish many new poets in any given year, but if they are convinced that your work is exceptional they will take it on. This all said, there are few pleasures to be had from composing poetry that are better than seeing an individual poem one has written appearing in print, and publishing a book of verse is certainly not the be all and end all of writing poetry.

7.5 POETS ON POETRY

In Chapter 1 of this book, we examined the way in which a number of the most notable poets in the tradition of English literature defined poetry and wrote about the art of composition, from the Renaissance through to the early twentieth century, and from prosaic notions of poetry such as Samuel Johnson's 'the art or practice of writing poems' through to such idealistic formulations as Thomas Hardy's 'emotion put into measure'. The short anthology below collects more recent remarks on the nature of poetry, principally by American, British and Irish poets, all of which were made since the end of the First World War. Insightful, provocative, impassioned and sometimes witty, it offers much invaluable – if sometimes contradictory – advice on how to write verse by some of the last century's most notable practitioners.

Genuine poetry can communicate before it is understood.
(T. S. Eliot, 1920)

The truth of poetry is imaginative, not literal.
(Amy Lowell, 1921)

Poetry is simply made of metaphor.
(Robert Frost, 1931)

Perfect understanding will sometimes almost extinguish pleasure.
(A. E. Housman, 1933)

For God's sake, don't try writing poetry in my style … Try your own style.
(Dylan Thomas, 1933)

There's a fountain of clearness in everyone.
(Dylan Thomas, 1933)

A poet writes always of his personal life.
(W. B. Yeats, 1937)

Just as among the literary arts poetry shows the highest degree of concentration, so the reading of poetry calls for an attention not demanded by the literature legitimately designed for the amusement of tired minds.
(John Drinkwater, 1938)

[Poetry] has to be living ... learn the speech of the place.
(Wallace Stevens, 1942)

The time to read poetry is before you start to write it; after you start to write it you are afraid to read other people's poetry.
(Wallace Stevens, 1945)

Poetry is the language in which man explores his own amazement.
(Christopher Fry, 1950)

As a poet I still believe in writing for the page, but I also think that some poems – not all – should be heard.
(Louis MacNeice, 1952)

Poetry is ordinary language raised to the nth power. Poetry is boned with ideas, nerved and blooded with emotions, all held together by the delicate, tough skin of words.
(Paul Engle, 1957)

I don't think good poetry can be produced in a kind of political attempt to overthrow some existing form. I think it just supersedes. People find a way in which they can say something. 'I can't say it that way, what way can I find that will do?' One didn't really *bother* about the existing modes.
(T. S. Eliot, 1959)

A man innocently dabbles in words and rhymes and finds that it is his life.
(Patrick Kavanagh, 1961)

I certainly never intended to write poetry. That never came into my head. And now, too, I think each time I write that it may be the last time; then I'm charmed by something and seem to have to say something. Everything I have written is the result of reading or of interest in people, I'm sure of that. I had no ambition to be a writer.
(Marianne Moore, 1961)

Inside is the place where poems come from.
(Anne Sexton, 1962)

Poetry generally is like a rhythmic articulation of feeling. The feeling is like
an impulse that rises within – just like sexual impulses, say; it's almost as definite
as that. It's a feeling that begins somewhere in the pit of the stomach and
rises up forward in the breast and then comes out through the mouth and
ears, and comes forth a croon or a groan or a sigh. Which, if you put words
to it by looking around and seeing and trying to describe what's making you
sigh – and sigh in words – you simply articulate what you're feeling. As simple
as that.
(Allen Ginsberg, 1966)

Do one thing.
   That one thing is to imagine what you are writing about. See it and live it.
Do not think it up laboriously, as if you were working out mental arithmetic.
Just look at it, touch it, smell it, listen to it, turn yourself into it. When you do
this, the words look after themselves. Like magic.
(Ted Hughes, 1967)

In constructing [a] world which was only inhabited by me, I was already
beginning to learn how poetry is written.
(W. H. Auden, 1974)

Deprivation is for me what daffodils were for Wordsworth.
(Philip Larkin, 1979)

I have never separated the writing of poetry from prayer. I have grown up
believing it is a vocation, a religious vocation.
(Derek Walcott, 1986)

Even the simplest poem / May destroy your immunity to human emotions.
(Elma Mitchell, 1987)

My poetry is often quite impersonal, and may suffer because of it. I rarely
put my most ardent and suffering self into it … The poetry tends to be
observational.
(John Updike, 1987)

When all the powers of the soul are focused on what is final, and cannot be
altered, even though it is horrible, the anguish, it seems, is indistinguishable

from joy. The moment closest to extinction turns out to be *the* creative moment.
(Ted Hughes, 1989)

Poetry is music written for the human voice.
(Maya Angelou, 1989)

One has to write poorly before one can write well.
(Charles Wright, 1989)

Literature still takes shape in the mouth and finds its resting place in the ear.
(Michael Longley, 1992)

Whether there is much that any editor can do with a poetry manuscript, I'm not sure. I'm about as prickly as anybody when it comes to having my lines rewritten for me, where verse is concerned. One may cringe momentarily on being queried, but if the query is valid, one swallows hard and takes account of it.
(Amy Clampitt, 1993)

Sometimes when I haven't written in some time, I really decide I'm going to work toward getting the requisite fever, and this would involve, oh, reading a few favorite poets intensively: Hardy, for example, John Donne, Herbert, Basil Bunting – any one of a number of my favorites. I try to get their tunes going in my head so I get a tune of my own.
(Thom Gunn, 1995)

In a good poetry reading – good for you, the poet, that is – you retrieve some of the quickening that you got when you first wrote the thing. The surprise and gratitude are with you again for a moment – the old sense of having been supplied with the words you needed to summon. You have an obligation as a poet not to betray the reality of that. You have been mysteriously recompensed by the words and you owe some fidelity to the mystery.
(Seamus Heaney, 1995)

Poetry is everlasting. It is not going away. But it has never occupied a sizable portion of the world's business and probably never will.
(A. R. Ammons, 1996)

It's a great mystery. When you consider how boring and painful nearly all poetry readings are, it's a wonder anyone shows up. And, wisely, few people do.
(A. R. Ammons, 1996)

Why does music, why does poetry have to address us in simplified terms, when if such simplification were applied to a description of our own inner selves we would find it demeaning? I think art has a right – not an obligation – to be difficult if it wishes.
(Geoffrey Hill, 2000)

Never ask an editor for comments and criticisms unless you are willing to take them. I have often been asked for 'a serious appraisal'. When work seems genuinely interesting I offer detailed advice, and often receive back angry letters or defences of work I have risked commenting upon.
(Michael Schmidt, 2007)

[There is] a postmodern poetic school led by J. H. Prynne whose purpose is to be difficult – emulatively difficult. (Not difficult to be difficult, actually.) And this take on modernism has created the critical idea of a 'new poetic' – essentially the notion that the reader shouldn't expect anything in the way of conventional 'meaning' since the poetry was anyway fetched up from the dark womb of the poet's unconscious.
(Craig Raine, 2008)

When poetry is *obscure* this is chiefly because information necessary for comprehension is not part of the reader's knowledge ... Finding out this information may dispel much of the obscurity. When poetry is *difficult* this is more likely because the language and structure of its presentation are unusually cross-linked or fragmented, or dense with ideas and response-patterns that challenge the reader's powers of recognition ... Alexander Pope's *The Dunciad* (1728–43) is now obscure but not especially difficult. [Such poems as] Eliot's *The Waste Land* (1922) are hard for readers because they are obscure and also difficult; indeed, their difficulties are deliberate and integral to poetic method.
(J. H. Prynne, 2009)

If I knew where poems came from I'd probably go and get more of them than I have already.
(Simon Armitage, 2010)

The best poetry has always come from what Auden called the small group – poets writing for themselves and each other, which a larger audience is welcome to read or listen in, but not specifically courted.
(Harry Clifton, 2010)

Poetry is basically personal.
(Michael Longley, 2010)

7.6   FORTY PRACTICAL TIPS ON WRITING POETRY

1. Many poets see truth in the somewhat intangible notion of 'inspiration', the lines that seem to come from nowhere or the idea for a poem that arrives seemingly unprompted by the conscious mind. When such moments occur, don't waste them − note them down immediately and use them as the base from which to compose the rest of the poem.

2. That said, do not always wait around for inspiration to descend, but work at composition as you would practise a newly taken-up hobby, sport or − perhaps the best analogy − a musical instrument. Better to write 'little and often' − as the music teachers say about practising the piano or the violin − than for a much longer time very infrequently, and better to write for ten to fifteen minutes four or five times a week rather than for a whole afternoon every three or four weeks.

3. A related point: though there is such a thing as a natural aptitude for writing verse, poets are made, through practice and sustained dedication, as well as born.

4. If inspiration seems a long way away when you want to write poetry, cultivate its opposite by writing about something or somebody − a person, an experience, an emotion − in a highly deliberate manner. Put down in prose bullet points everything that you know about them. Be precise in your description and try to be as precise in your depiction of your emotions. After doing so, try to make a poem from the raw material which you have recorded.

5. It is not always necessary to write poetry about personal feelings, experience and emotions, but much of the greatest verse has used these as starting points for poetic composition.

6. Throw unsatisfactory drafts away, or, if anything seems worth saving from an abortive writing session, save a few fragmentary lines. If you've written a poem with which you are not satisfied, but which has one or two good lines, then, at some point in the future, they might become the sand in the oyster to make a new poem.

7. Dispose of a completed poem if it seems to you a failure rather than keeping

something which is second rate by your own standards. There is a story about the artist Francis Bacon once leaving a completed oil painting, with which he was dissatisfied, in a friend's European apartment which he had borrowed for a holiday. Over a decade later he saw the canvas in the window of a Bond Street art dealer's, and saw that it was up for sale, and to the not inconsiderable tune of £50,000. Bacon went into the shop and paid for the painting by cheque. He then went outside, jumped up and down on upon it till it was smashed beyond repair and dumped the broken fragments of the canvas in the nearest dustbin. This is a commendable attitude.

8. Often *starting* a poem is the hardest part of its composition. Get down to work.

9. It is nonsense to say that poetry has absolutely no connection with reason or thought; even the Romantic idealist Wordsworth insisted that a poet, though 'a man … possessed of more than usual organic sensibility' was someone who has 'also thought long and deeply'.

10. Show your work to other people, informed friends or members of a writing group, before you send it to a poetry magazine. Indeed, always let others read your work. And always remember, as Louis MacNeice wrote in 1952, 'It is a gamble entrusting a poem to a reader, but it is a worthwhile gamble'.

11. Though it is tempting to react to adverse criticism or a perceived slight on your poem as you would to someone mocking your child's appearance, try to get away from this quasi-parental attitude. Treat informed criticism constructively and endeavour to take it with good grace.

12. If you've written a bad poem, whether you throw it away or put it in a drawer to see if some of its bones might make a passable stew later, either way you will have learned from it as a chef who has spoiled a meal does from that experience.

13. You *must* read poetry to write it. Reading informs writing.

14. You *should* listen to poetry, to your own and to other people's; listening trains the ear to the sound of verse and to the cadence of both written and spoken language.

15. Buy, and keep about your person, a notebook into which you should write lines of verse and stray thoughts that might one day feed into a poem.

16. If you don't keep a diary, start one, with the intention of mining it for your poetry.

17. Think about what you are aiming to do by a poem. Why are you writing those particular words? *What* is your poem for, *who* is it for and *why* are you writing it?

18. Read examples of the kind of poetical work you have in mind to start your own creative juices flowing. For instance, if you want to write introspective, self-contemplative verse about feelings of loss or rejection, read Sylvia Plath or Anne Sexton rather than the limericks of Edward Lear or the nonsense verse of Lewis Carroll.

19. Self-mortification and the confessional mode can inspire great poetry, as in the case of Sexton and Plath. It can also be mawkish and embarrassing; a catalogue of pain and misery is simply painful to read if it is not converted into language of emotionally charged beauty and resonance.

20. If you want to write about a particularly painful episode in your life in verse but the experience is too raw to address directly, try writing about it in the third person ('He' or 'she' ...) or the second person ('You' ...).

21. If you decide to send your verse to a particular magazine or poetry press, familiarise yourself with what they already publish. How is your work similar? How is it different?

22. Decide how much or how little you want to explain in your poem. Walter de la Mare wrote of reading verse in 1931 that 'It is always good, so far as is possible, to *understand* what one reads. A deep and vivid understanding only adds to the joy it gives'. On the other hand, not everything in a poem needs to be explained. A decade or so later, in 1942, E. B. White maintained that 'A poet's pleasure is to withhold a little of his meaning'. Indeed, some poetic purists such as J. H. Prynne maintain that it is not the duty of a poet to capture shared or unique experience and deliberately set out to cultivate difficulty. All of these are perfectly respectable intellectual positions; choose your place on this spectrum of difficulty and ease.

23. Write for yourself first and your readers second. The latter group will make up their own minds about your work.

24. Always read what you have written aloud to yourself and, if you are pleased

with it, to others. This allows you to hear the rhythmical patterns of your work and allows the *sound* of your poem to express itself alongside its *meanings*.

25. Poems in stanzas are not, of course, academic essays, but there should usually be a reason – as there is in a university assignment – why they are structured, with a beginning, middle and end. Why is your first stanza before the second, and the second before the third, and so on?

26. Though it isn't a crime, you don't have to rhyme, not all the time.

27. Don't always write in non-metrical free verse. Experiment in writing metrical poetry, from a simple ballad stanza to a villanelle, from a limerick to blank verse.

28. Musicians develop 'muscle memory', where their fingers automatically go to the right notes from long and sustained practice. When you become accustomed to writing in metrical rhythms something similar will manifest itself for your own poetry.

29. When you feel like putting off writing, or finding an excuse not to compose poetry, use composition as an excuse to avoid doing something you haven't been looking forward to, perhaps something necessary but less than pleasurable (reading bank statements and so on).

30. 'I think I am going to have a heart attack' might be a vivid and arresting way to begin an e-mail, but it is not going to make a striking opening to a poem. Take a familiar phrase and make it less conventional: 'My heart attack waits / Behind my back, and counts the hours ...'

31. Many poets, from Geoffrey Chaucer in the fourteenth century, to S. T. Coleridge in the eighteenth, to Charles Causley in the twentieth, have used dreams as the basis for verse. Do the same. Keep a dream diary and write poetry based on what you have dreamt.

32. Learn from the poets whom you most admire. Don't just wallow uncritically in their verse (or at least don't always) – try to understand in interpretive terms how it works and what it is about it that moves you.

33. An arresting opening is less important in a poem than in a novel, which generally needs to grab its reader warmly by the throat in an attempt to engage his or her attention from the first page. Poems are generally shorter.

Nonetheless, writing an intriguing and suggestive first line of a poem is a talent to be cultivated.

34. 'Improvise', as the renowned American poet John Ashbery wrote in 2010, 'and don't worry about what the neighbours will think'.

35. Go to a creative writing class, or participate in a poetry workshop or writers' group and, eventually, read your verse at a poetry reading.

36. In a poem dealing with intense emotion, try replacing direct references to something abstract with, instead, an object or thing which suggests it; a spent firework might intimate sexual frustration, for example, or a closing door the sense of impending death. T. S. Eliot wrote in 1919 that 'The only way of expressing emotion in the form of art is by finding an "objective correlative"; in other words, a set of objects [or] a situation … which shall be the formula of that *particular* emotion'. This is useful, if somewhat overstated, advice.

37. Don't give up. You will improve in time. John Keats's second book of poetry, *Endymion* (1818), was laughed to scorn and remains somewhat indigestible; his third, *Lamia, Isabella, The Eve of St Agnes, and Other Poems* (1820), is almost universally seen as one of the most important collections of the last two hundred years.

38. Don't provide too much detail, even in a descriptive poem. Leave something to the reader's imagination.

39. Those who *want* to understand you *should* do so – albeit sometimes with effort. Those who *do not* want to understand you *will not*.

40. You can say a lot in a little.

7.7   EXERCISES

1. Read a random line of verse to see if it sparks you to creation of your own:

Out of the dark, man comes to life and into it. (Eavan Boland)

This is the cactus land. (T. S. Eliot)

Nobody heard him, the dead man. (Stevie Smith)

But not the stars; the stars came otherwise. (Robert Browning)

He remembered spiders and frogs. (Eiléan ní Chuilleanáin)

And *you* offer me happiness? (Louis MacNeice)

These lines were taken at random and out of context from anthologies of poetry. Do the same. Open a book of verse at arbitrary pages and see if the stray lines which you encounter prompt you to composition.

2. Describe a vivid, frightening or strange dream which you have experienced. First do so in prose. Then make a poem from this source material.

3. Try some word association. Think of something at random and then write down anything and everything that comes to mind. Do this as fast as you can, writing the words down on a piece of paper or keying them into your computer. Then see what you have written. This might, of course, have produced gibberish but it could, on reflection, have prompted something which you can use in your verse.

4. Try writing a poem from an entirely different point of view and idiom (language) from your own, perhaps in a narrative soliloquy delivered by an imaginary speaker. For example, compose a poem which envisages a morally corrupt person speaking, and let the speaker's defence of his or her own depravity produce the dramatic irony which condemns them. The Victorian dramatic monologues of Robert Browning are models of this approach (read, for example, his 'My Last Duchess' (1842)).

5. Ezra Pound famously edited and heavily pruned T. S. Eliot's *The Waste Land* (1922) and S. T. Coleridge and William Wordsworth made instructive comments on each other's poetry in the late eighteenth century. Learn from these exalted examples. Ask a friend to rewrite one of your poems. Alternatively, and less drastically, ask them to suggest changes to your poem as if they were the editor of a poetry magazine or a creative writing tutor.

6. Although Robert Frost maintained that 'I have never started a poem yet whose end I knew', even for that poet starting with a vague idea for a poem was better than none at all. Take such a half-formed notion – a thing, an emotion, a person – and then write its name down on the middle of a blank sheet of paper. Cover the rest of the page with ideas and reflections prompted by it. See if these can provide the building blocks for the first draft of a poem. If it does, revise and revise it till it feels *right*.

7. Write a poem about poetry, about what it means to compose verse and what you hope that your poetry will achieve. Try to make this poem's form reflect its meaning, as per this poem by John Strachan, 'Fourteen', a free verse sonnet which, nonetheless, ends in the traditional final couplet of the Shakespearean sonnet to suit the argument of the poem:

> I am going to write a sonnet, in the hope
> That something of its essence might touch you
> In a manner that I no longer can,
> Touch you in a gentler way than I
> Latterly could manage. A free sonnet –
> Shorn of rhyme and structure, the comfortable
> Patterning that we no longer have.
> But freedom is not always a good thing,
> Not in verse, not in music, not in life –
> The necessary shape and structure
> Is abandoned for a bold chimera.
> *Vers libre* – free verse – is emptiness.
> I need it back, the metre and the art,
> That shapes the measure of my line and heart.

8. Exercise with regular metrical forms. Begin by writing a haiku, a limerick and a ballad. After that, try more complex patterns (all of these terms are defined in the glossary below): a Petrarchan sonnet, terza rima, a villanelle. They will initially seem challenging, but will come much more easily with practice.

A glossary of poetical terms

Cross-references to other entries are in bold. Terms are not illustrated in the Glossary where examples have been given in the chapters above (the Glossary gives the relevant page references).

acatalectic   A verse line where the final **foot** conforms to the prescribed number of **syllables** in terms of the metrical **frame**. An alternative term is 'complete'. Lines where the final foot is short by a syllable are **catalectic** (or 'curtailed'). See examples on p. 79.

accent   *See* stress.

accentual   Methods of metrical analysis which pay sole attention to **stress** rather than **syllable**-counting are called 'accentual systems'. English metrical analysis, which addresses both stress and syllable, is **accentual-syllabic**.

accentual-syllabic   A metrical system which attends both to a line's **syllable** count and the placing of **stress** within the line. English metrical analysis is thus accentual-syllabic (as opposed to being solely **syllabic** or **accentual**).

acephalous   A 'headless' line which omits the first **syllable** of the first **foot**. It is found most commonly in the **hexameter** and the Chaucerian **iambic** line: 'If gold ruste, what shall iren do?'.

acrostic   A poem in which the first letters of each line, taken in sequence, spell a word or sentence.

alexandrine   In English **metrics**, an **iambic hexameter** line (a twelve-syllable line of six feet in **rising rhythm**). Though whole poems have been composed in alexandrines, the line is most common as the final line of a **Spenserian stanza**. See example on p. 101.

allegory   An extended **metaphor** in which a narrative refers to a subject other than its literal subject. Allegorical writing offers a disguised but sustained parallel between the superficial events of the story and some other veiled theme, leaving the reader to infer the 'hidden' meaning. Allegorical writing is particularly common in the medieval and Renaissance periods. Much poetical allegory uses abstract **personification**, where ideal or vicious qualities are granted human form (as in Langland's *Piers Plowman* and Spenser's *Faerie Queene*).

alliteration   The commencement of adjacent or closely related words with the same sound or letter. Alliteration was the defining characteristic of Old English verse and that of the **alliterative revival**, but is now generally confined to occasional use for poetic embellishment or unusual effect. See examples on p. 48.

alliterative revival   A term used to describe the medieval revival of the alliterative poetic method of Old English poetry. Its supreme poetic products are the fourteenth-century poems *Sir Gawain and the Green Knight* and *Piers Plowman* (by William Langland). Some scholars argue that the tradition never actually disappeared and that the term 'alliterative survival' is more appropriate.

allusion   An indirect reference made by one literary text to another one. The reference will often involve coincidence of phraseology, and may be designed to alert the reader to the way that the meaning of the text is shaped by its relation to the other work.

amphibrach   A **trisyllabic foot** where the **stress** falls in the middle of the foot, as in the word 'important'. It is an occasional device of **modulation** in English verse. See examples on p. 96.

amphimacer   *See* cretic.

anacrusis   The insertion, for the sake of the sense, of a **syllable** at the beginning of a line before the formal **metre** resumes. See example on p. 89.

anapaest   A metrical **foot** which consists of three **syllables**, with two unstressed syllables followed by a stressed one, as in the word 'intercede'. A poem where the foot predominates is in 'anapaestic verse', or simply 'anapaests'. The foot is also an occasional device of **modulation**. See examples on p. 94.

anaphora   The repetition of the same word or phrase in several successive clauses, sentences or lines, most commonly at the beginning of verse lines.

anticlimax   The conscious fall from the sublime to the ridiculous, or from the important to the trivial (in contradistinction to **bathos**, the unintentionally abrupt shift in register). The device is often used in **burlesque**, and is demonstrated in the address to the Queen in Pope's *The Rape of the Lock*:

> Here thou, great ANNA! whom three realms obey,
> Dost sometimes counsel take – and sometimes tea.

antistrophe   In Greek poetry, and in some English neoclassical verse, the second section of certain choral and lyrical **odes**. It follows the opening **strophe** and repeats its metrical structure.

antithesis   An opposition or contrast. Poetical antithesis generally involves the use of contrasting or opposing words in two adjacent sentences or clauses, as in Pope's 'A very heathen in the carnal part / Yet a sad, good Christian at her heart'.

apostrophe   An exclamatory, generally eulogistic address to a person or abstraction, as in Milton's apostrophe to light at the start of *Paradise Lost*, Book III: 'Hail, holy light, offspring of heaven first-born'. *See also* invocation.

assonance   The recurrence of the same vowel sound, especially within stressed **syllables**, in neighbouring words. The repetition of sound may occur in spite of variability in spelling, so that the words 'nation' and 'traitor' show assonance. Assonance differs from **rhyme** in that the final consonants of assonant words differ. See discussion on p. 48.

aubade   A poem or song on the subject of the day's dawning, dealing in particular with the need for two lovers to part. The aubade is a medieval French form, but has occasionally been adapted by English poets, as in Act III of Shakespeare's *Romeo and Juliet*:

> It was the lark, the herald of the morn,
> No nightingale. Look, love, what envious streaks
> Do lace the severing clouds in yonder east.

ballad   An ancient form of folk song or **oral poetry** which was common in the Middle Ages, but has often been imitated since. Ballads are usually **narrative** or **lyrical**. See examples on p. 36 and p. 39. *See also* ballad stanza.

ballad metre   *See* ballad stanza.

ballad stanza   The most notable English form of the **quatrain**. The ballad stanza alternates four-stress lines (**tetrameters**) with three-stress lines (**trimeters**) rhymed *abab* or *abcb*. See examples on p. 39.

ballade   A complex medieval French **lyric** which was particularly associated with the poet François Villon. It was borrowed by English medieval poets, most notably by Chaucer, and was occasionally used by Victorian poets. The ballade employs three **octets** rhymed *ababbcbc* and an *envoi* rhymed *bcbc* (as in Swinburne's 'Ballade of the Lords of Old Time'), or three ten-line **stanzas** rhymed *ababbccdcd* and a six-line *envoi* rhymed *ccdccd* (as in Swinburne's 'A Ballad of François Villon').

base   *See* frame.

bathos   An unintentional and ludicrous shift in tone from the elevated to the commonplace. Poetic **anticlimax** is related, but differs in that it is a conscious rather than an undesired effect. Two lines from Wordsworth's 'The Thorn' are often cited as an example of the bathetic:

> I've measured it from side to side
> 'Tis three feet long, and two feet wide.

blank verse   **Continuous iambic pentameter** verse lines which are unrhymed. See examples on p. 83 and p. 84. Blank verse is perhaps the most important metre of English poetry. It provides the **base metre**, for example, of Shakespeare's dramas, of Milton's *Paradise Lost* and of Wordsworth's *The Prelude*.

blazon   A poetic catalogue, most notable in sixteenth- and seventeenth-century love **lyrics**, of virtues or excellences, especially female virtues and excellences.

book   A term sometimes used for the main divisions, or **cantos**, of a long poem.

break   A pause in a verse line, generally indicated by punctuation. The **caesura** is a specific form of break which occurs near the middle of a line. See examples on p. 84.

broken rhyme   The splitting of a word to facilitate a **rhyme**, generally for comic effect, as in George Canning's 'Song. By Rogero':

> Whene'er with haggard eyes I view
>   This dungeon that I'm rotting in,
> I think of those companions true
>   Who studied with me at the U
>   -niversity of Gottingen,

It is important to realise that it is a word that is broken rather than an actual rhyme.

burden   The chorus or **refrain** of a poem or song. The term is also (though infrequently) used to refer to a poem's chief idea or theme.

burlesque   A form of **parod**y which exploits the comic differential between a trivial subject-matter and an elevated poetic form, describing mundanities in a highly-wrought fashion. The most notable example in English poetry is Pope's *The Rape of the Lock* which applies **epic** conventions to everyday circumstance:

> And now, unveil'd the *Toilet* stands display'd,
> Each Silver Vase in mystic Order laid.
> First rob'd in White, the Nymph intent adores
> With Head uncover'd, the *Cosmetic* Pow'rs.

See also mock epic.

Burns stanza   A **sestet** rhymed *aaabab* with lines 1, 2, 3 and 5 four-stressed and lines 4 and 6 two-stressed. Though the **stanza** is named after Burns, it is actually an ancient form, having been used in medieval **narrative poems**.

cacophony   Words which sound discordant and jarring, as in a tongue-twister. Cacophony is occasionally exploited for poetic effect, as in Swinburne's cacophonic internal **rhymes** in his 'A Ballad of François Villon': 'Villon, our sad bad glad mad brother's name'. The term is also sometimes used by critics in antipathetic mood who wish to deride the sound effects of a particular poem as badly executed.

cadence   The unsystematic **rhythm** of **free verse** and prose, as opposed to the more or less regular patterning of **metrical** verse.

caesura   A pause around the middle of a metrical line, often associated with a pause in the sense or the ending of a clause or a sentence. A caesura which follows a **stress** is said to be 'masculine' whilst one which follows an unstressed **syllable** is 'feminine'. See discussion on pp. 82–5. *See also* break.

canto   A main division of a long poem. *See also* fit, book.

carol   A Nativity or Easter hymn. In the Middle Ages, however, a carol could be a secular song, often composed for a round dance. The most common form of this type of carol is an *aaab* **quatrain** with a two-line **refrain**.

carpe diem   'Seize the day', an aphorism quoted from the Roman poet Horace. A significant number of love **lyrics** dwell on the *carpe diem* theme of the mutability of human existence, urging a beloved person to seize the moment. A noted example is Herrick's 'To the Virgins, to Make Much of Time' (quoted above on p. 40).

catalectic   A metrical line where the final **foot** is short by a **syllable**. An alternative term for the short foot is 'curtailed' (the term 'defective' is also used). The catalectic line is most common in the **trochaic tetrameter**.

cento   A literary work assembled from fragments of other texts placed in a new order.

chiasmus   A rhetorical device in which the order of words in one of two parallel clauses is inverted or approximately inverted in the other, mirroring the other in a back-to-front way, as in Coleridge's 'Flowers are lovely, love is flowerlike'.

choriamb   A four-syllable Greek metrical **foot**, the first and last **syllable** long, the others short. The foot has been adapted in English poetry (though very occasionally) as a foot which consists *de facto* of a **trochee** followed by an **iamb**. Swinburne's experimental 'Choriambics' is a rare example.

clerihew   A form of humorous verse introduced by E. Clerihew Bentley (1875–1956). Generally biographical and gently **satirical**, the clerihew is composed of two couplets of uneven length. The subject's name is usually part of the first line. The biographical snippet contained in the clerihew is, of course, singularly absurd or overstated:

> The poet Wordsworth
> Or as Lord Byron called him 'Turdsworth',
> Got his thrills
> From contemplating daffodils.

closed couplet A **couplet** which reaches a break in sense at the end of its second line. In other words, one which would make sense if abstracted from its context and left to stand alone. The term is most associated with **heroic couplets**. The effect is achieved both through the sense of the lines and through metrical effects (the use of **end-stopped** lines, the lack of **enjambement**). See examples on p. 82.

common measure A label sometimes applied to the *abab* variant of **ballad stanza**. The term 'common metre' is synonymous.

complaint A plaintive lyric, generally on the theme of lost or unresponsive love.

complete *See* acatalectic.

conceit An extended and highly wrought **metaphor**. Conceits tend to involve comparison of entities that, at first sight at least, are very dissimilar. Conceits are particularly associated with the seventeenth-century 'school' of poets known as the '**metaphysicals**', but can be found in poems of all periods. See examples on p. 124.

consonance The repetition between neighbouring words of consonantal sounds, generally where the vowel sounds are different, as in the term 'dark work'. See examples on p. 48. *See also* assonance.

continuous Poetry which is not divided into **stanzas** and is printed in successive lines, as in **blank verse** and **Hudibrastics**. *See also* stichic.

conversation poem A term coined by the poet Coleridge as the subtitle of his poem 'The Nightingale' and which critics apply to several of his meditative **blank verse** poems of the late 1790s. These are addressed to friends and family and generally see the poet move from a confined, domestic setting to a contemplation of the landscape and its imaginative significance.

coronach In Celtic cultures, a funeral song, **dirge** or lamentation. Sir Walter Scott's 'He is gone on the mountain' is the most notable literary example.

couplet A pair of linked verse lines which are generally of the same length and which are linked most particularly by **rhyme**. The most notable manifestations of the two-line couplet are found in **continuous** verse, the **heroic couplet** most particularly, rather than in **stanzaic** poetry.

cretic A Greek **foot** with a short **stress** between two longs which has occasionally been adapted for metrical **modulation** in English poetry as a foot of a stressed **syllable** between two unstressed syllables (as in the words 'bold as brass'). The foot is also known as an 'amphimacer'.

crisis lyric A term used to describe certain key introspective Romantic **lyrics**

where the poet meditates upon a sense of loss and, very often, the demise of his poetic vision. Wordsworth's 'Immortality Ode' and Coleridge's 'Dejection' are notable examples.

crossed rhyme   The rhyming of a word at or about the middle of a line of verse with one at or about the middle of the next line, as in Poe's 'The Raven':

> While I nodded, nearly napping, suddenly there came a tapping,
> As of some one gently rapping, rapping at my chamber door –

crown   A series of **sonnets**, though occasionally other forms of **lyrical** poetry, in which the last line of the first poem becomes the first line of the next one and so on. The last line of the final poem in the crown repeats the first line of the first poem.

curtailed   *See* catalectic.

dactyl, dactylic   A **foot** consisting of a stressed **syllable** followed by two unstressed ones, as in the word 'negative'. Poetry where the dactylic foot predominates is referred to as 'dactylic verse' or simply as 'dactyls'. The foot is also used for the purposes of **substitution**. See examples on pp. 92–3.

defective foot   *See* catalectic.

diæresis   A **prosodological** term occasionally used to refer to the division made in a poetic line when the end of a **foot** coincides with the end of a word.

dimeter   A two-**foot** metrical line. See examples on pp. 98–9.

dirge   A poem of lamentation, generally for a dead person. The dirge is generally a less highly wrought poetic exercise than the formal **elegy**.

dissonance   Inharmonious or harsh poetic sound, either for conscious effect to suit a poet's purpose, or, less happily, as an inadvertence.

distich   Two lines of verse, which are generally rhymed and make sense in isolation, as in many **couplets**.

disyllabic   Consisting of two **syllables**, as in the **iambic** and **trochaic feet**.

doggerel   Originally a term applied to **burlesque** poetry which used highly irregular **rhythms**, the word doggerel is now used as a term of abuse about poetry considered – by the user of the term at least – to be clumsy, inept and badly written. The one poet to have made his name by the unwitting production of doggerel is the Scottish poet William McGonagall (see example on p. 86).

double rhyme   *See* feminine rhyme.

dramatic monologue   A poem where the poet assumes the voice of a particular historical or fictional person talking to a particular listener or listeners. The form is particularly associated with the Victorian poet Robert Browning.

dramatic poetry   Poetry originally composed for theatrical production, as in the **blank verse** commonly used in Shakespeare's plays. The term has also been used more loosely to apply to poetry not written for the theatre but which involves the poet assuming the voice of a particular person or character, as in the **dramatic monologue**. *See also* verse drama.

dream vision   An **allegorical narrative poem** which tells a story experienced by the narrator in a dream. In English poetry, it is particularly associated with the medieval poets Chaucer, Langland and the *Gawain*-poet.

duple metre   Verse where the poetic frame has two **syllables** (is **disyllabic**), i.e. **iambic** and **trochaic** metre.

eclogue   A pastoral poem, especially one in the form of a dialogue. English eclogues (such as those by Spenser and Pope) are neoclassical variants of the **pastoral** poetry of Theocritus and, especially, Virgil.

Elegiac couplet   A **dactylic hexameter** followed by a dactylic **pentameter**. The elegiac couplet is extremely common in Greek and Roman verse but is rare in English poetry.

elegiac stanza   *See* heroic stanza.

elegy   A **lyrical** and generally meditative poem which commemorates a deceased person, as in Milton's *Lycidas* (1637) and Shelley's *Adonais* (1821).

emblem poem   Poetry written to explain the meaning of an **allegorical** picture, as in the notable seventeenth-century pattern books which feature illustrations with accompanying verse by Francis Quarles (*Emblems*) and John Bunyan (*Divine Emblems*).

encomium   A highly-wrought expression of praise and admiration. *See also* eulogy, panegyric.

end-rhyme   Where a word placed at the end of a line rhymes with a similar-sounding word at the end of another line.

end-stop   A line of verse which reaches a pause or **break** (signalled by punctuation) at its end. *See* enjambement.

enjambement   Poetry running over the line-end or sequence of line-endings without pause or punctuation. It is most common in blank verse. See examples on pp. 85–6.

envelope   A poem or **stanza** which opens and closes with the same line or stanza (or a near-identical line or stanza).

envoi, **envoy**   A poetrical device most common in medieval poetry such as Chaucer's *Troilus and Criseyde*, in which a poet bids farewell to his work, often commending its progress in the world.

epic   A **narrative poem** on a grand scale which describes the adventures of some great person or persons. The form is ancient, dating back to Homer's *Iliad* and *Odyssey* (eighth century BC). Its most notable English manifestation is Milton's *Paradise Lost*.

epic catalogue   A convention of **epic** poetry which offers a poetic list, often of the participants in some battle (as in Milton's catalogue of the devils in *Paradise Lost* Book I).

epic simile   A **simile** which is extensive and sustained. It is **epic** in both scale and genre, given that it is frequent in epical poetry from Homer and Virgil through to Milton (indeed, it is sometimes referred to as the 'Homeric simile').

epigram   A comic poem which is short, condensed and pithy, as in Byron's epigram on the suicide of the Tory politician Castlereagh:

> So *He* has cut his throat! – He! Who?
> The man who cut his country's long ago.

epistrophe   The use of the same phrase or word at the end of successive lines (or occasionally clauses).

epithalamion   A Greek nuptial song originally intended to be sung on a wedding night. The form was imitated by several key Renaissance poets, notably Edmund Spenser in his 'Epithalamion'.

epode   That part of an **ode** which traditionally follows the **strophe** and **antistrophe**.

eulogy   A poem which expresses praise or admiration. *See also* encomium, panegyric.

euphony   A somewhat imprecise term which is used to describe what the user of the term sees as a pleasing and musical poetical manner.

exemplum (plural **exempla**)   An **allegorical** medieval tale which points a spiritually improving moral. The most notable example in English poetry is Chaucer's 'Nun's Priest's Tale'.

eye rhyme   A **rhyme** more apparent to the eye than to the ear where the spellings of rhymed words imply rhyme but the pronunciation of those words do not (as in the words 'laid' and 'said').

fabliau (plural **fabliaux**)   Medieval French comic **narrative poems**, generally of a bawdy and **satirical** nature, which deal with lower-class or bourgeois life, and offer a more recognisably realistic setting than the other-worldly **romance**. Chaucer adapts the fabliau to brilliant effect in the *Canterbury Tales*, most notably in the tales of the Miller and the Reeve.

falling rhythm   Metrical verse where the characteristic **foot** of the poetic **frame** 'falls' from a stressed **syllable** to an unstressed syllable or syllables (as in **trochaic** and **dactylic** verse).

feet   *See* foot.

feminine ending   The placing of an extra unstressed **syllable** at the end of a verse line. The device is most common in **blank verse** and there involves the **hypercatalectic** addition of an extra syllable (which is unstressed) to the ten-syllable **frame**. See example on p. 87.

feminine rhyme   An **end-rhyme** on two **syllables** where the first syllable is stressed and the second unstressed. The device is also known as 'double rhyme'. *See also* masculine rhyme.

fit   The Old and Middle English term for a section of a long poem or song. The usual post-medieval terms are **book** and **canto**.

foot   A metrical unit composed of a group of **syllables** with a particular and fixed **stress** pattern. See discussion on pp. 74–97. *See also* amphibrach, anapaest, dactyl, iamb, pyrrhic, spondee, trochee.

fourteener   A **trochaic** or, more usually, an **iambic heptameter** is sometimes labelled a 'fourteener' on account of the standard number of **syllables** in the line. See example on p. 103.

frame   The basic **metrical** structure of a poem (its characterisation according to **stress**-patterning and line-length into, for instance, **iambic pentameter** or **trochaic tetrameter**).

free verse   Verse which does not conform to the regular sound-patterning of **metrical** poetry. See discussion on pp. 104–7.

georgic   A poem on the subject of farming and the activities of rural life (named after Virgil's *Georgics*). The georgic is preoccupied with more prosaic and day-to-day affairs than the more idyllic and idealised **pastoral** and **eclogue**.

graphic scansion   The process of marking lines of verse according to their **metrical** sound-pattern (in contradistinction to the **scansion** of **rhyme scheme**, into *abba* and so on). Divisions between feet are marked |, **stressed syllables** $^{/}$ and unstressed syllables ^{x}.

graveyard poetry   A term sometimes applied to eighteenth-century poetry on **elegiac**, mournful themes of human mutability, as in the work of Edward Young, Robert Blair and the Thomas Gray of the 'Elegy Written in a Country Church-Yard' (quoted above on pp. 40 and 76).

haiku   A form of Japanese poetry, developed in the sixteenth century, which normally consists of seventeen **syllables**, set in three unrhymed lines of five, seven and five syllables. Originally a comic form, the haiku is now more usually used to offer a concise reflection upon a particular theme or scene:

> Evening falls slowly,
> The river softly murmurs
> In gentle moonlight.

half-rhyme   A **rhyme** in which final consonants rhyme but final vowel sounds do not, as in the words 'dig' and 'log'. *See also* pararhyme.

hemistich   A half-line, as divided by a **caesura** or **break**; or, less frequently, a shorter line than that of the **frame**.

hendecasyllabic   A verse line of eleven **syllables**.

heptameter   A seven-**foot** verse line. Most heptameters are **iambic** or **trochaic** and, as a consequence, the term **fourteener** is sometimes used.

heroic couplet   A pair of consecutive **iambic pentameter** verse lines which **rhyme**. See examples on p. 82.

heroic line   A ten-syllable **iambic** verse line, the basic line of both the **heroic couplet** and **blank verse**.

heroic stanza   A five-stress **iambic quatrain** rhymed *abab*. It is sometimes referred to as the 'elegiac stanza' after its use in Thomas Gray's 'Elegy Written in a Country Church-Yard'.

hexameter   A verse line which contains six **feet**. The most significant hexameter line is the **iambic** hexameter, which is generally referred to as an **alexandrine**.

homostrophic   Stanzaic poetry comprised of **stanzas** which are formally similar in terms of line-lengths, rhyme scheme and number of lines. Most stanzaic forms are homostrophic, but the label is most commonly used to differentiate regular **odes** from **irregular odes**.

Horatian ode   A type of **lyric** poem named after the Roman poet Horace (65–8 BC), who wrote in subtle, elegant and metrically sophisticated four-line stanzas. The form has been adapted by English poets in a variety of simpler metres, for instance in Andrew Marvell's 'An Horatian Ode upon Cromwell's Return from Ireland' (1650).

Horatian satire   A form of **satire** which is tolerant, urbane and gently amused at the follies of human nature, rather than offering fierce denunciations of human viciousness. It is named after the Roman satirist Horace. It is generally used in contradistinction to **Juvenalian** satire which employs an acerbic and vitriolic manner.

Hudibrastics   Comic verse in sustained octosyllabic **couplets** with ingenious comic **feminine rhymes**. The form is named after Samuel Butler's seventeenth-century poem *Hudibras* (quoted above on pp. 62 and 87), which uses it extensively.

hymn   A song of praise to the Almighty which is generally intended to be sung at a service of religious observation. Poets occasionally use the term in the looser sense of an address to an individual or to a natural or abstract phenomenon (as in James Thomson's 'Hymn to the Seasons' and Shelley's 'Hymn to Intellectual Beauty').

hyperbole   From rhetoric, a figure of speech consisting of an exaggerated or extravagant overstatement which is not meant to be understood literally ('I've told you a million times').

hypercatalectic   A verse line which possesses a **syllable** more than the number conventionally demanded by the metrical **frame**.

iamb, iambic   An iamb is a two-**syllable** poetic **foot** which consists of an unstressed syllable followed by a stressed syllable. 'Iambic verse' is poetry which uses the foot as its **frame**. Iambic poetry, notably the **iambic pentameter**, is perhaps the most significant metre in English poetry. See examples on pp. 80–8.

iambic pentameter   A ten-**syllable** five-**foot** line in **rising rhythm**. It is arguably the most important line in English poetry. The most significant iambic pentameter **metres** are the **heroic couplet** and **blank vers**e. See examples on pp. 81–4.

ictus   The **stress** falling on a particular **syllable** in a metrical **foot**, in contradistinction to the syllable itself.

idyll   A short poem which describes some picturesque incident, generally in some idealised rustic setting.

imagery   A general term applied to the entirety of a poem's images, whether figurative (its **metaphors**, **similes** and so on) or literal (its scenes, characters and settings). The phrase is somewhat imprecise, referring to the objects described or suggested by a poem rather than its meditative, abstract or contemplative themes.

imperfect rhyme   *See* half-rhyme, pararhyme.

incremental repetition   The near-repetition of lines or **stanzas** within a poem. The device is particularly common in the **ballad**:

> O who will shoe my bony foot?
>   Or who will glove my hand?
> Or who will bind my midle jimp
>   With the broad lilly band?
>
> O who will comb my bony head
>   With the red river comb?
> Or who will be my bairns father
>   Ere Gregory he come home? ('Fair Isabell of Rochroyall')

internal rhyme   A **rhyme** between words within a verse line (rather than the more usual rhyming of line-endings). See example on p. 60. Its most common form is where a word in the middle of a line rhymes internally with the final word of the line (a **leonine rhyme**).

intertexuality   A word sometimes used to express the general relatedness of texts, especially literary ones, to each other. Often used as a generic name for specific forms of inter-textual reference or appropriation such as **allusion**, quotation, **parody**, etc.

inversion   The replacement of a **foot** within a line in one **base metre** with one in another diametrically opposed metre. The most common manifestation is the replacement of an **iamb** with a **trochee**. See example on p. 78. *See also* substitution.

invocation A form of opening **apostrophe** where a poet summons the assistance of a **muse** or a deity in the composition of the work. It is most common in **epic** and follows the conventions of Greek and Roman epic poetry. Milton, for example, begins *Paradise Lost* by invoking a 'heavenly muse'.

ionic A metrical **foot** used in the analysis of Greek poetry which consists of two short **syllables** followed by two long ones (ionic *a minore*) or vice versa (*a majore*). The English equivalent is a foot of two unstressed syllables followed by two long ones or vice versa. In practice, such a foot is indistinguishable in English metrics from two feet where one is a **pyrrhic** and the other a **spondee**.

irregular ode An **ode** where the **strophes** vary in length, as in Wordsworth's 'Ode. Intimations of Immortality'.

Italian sonnet *See* Petrarchan sonnet.

Juvenalian A form of **satirical** writing which is highly acerbic, offering clear moral condemnation of its targets. The term is generally used in contradistinction to **Horatian satire**, which is generally seen as more tolerant, urbane and amused. If Horatian satire attends to human folly, Juvenalian satire attends to human vice. It is named after the Roman satirist Juvenal (AD c. 60–c. 136) whose most characteristically denunciatory manner is well captured in his declaration that his 'heart burns dry with rage'.

lai *See* 'lay'.

lament A song of grief and lamentation, notably one composed to be sung or recited at a funeral or burial.

lampoon An acerbic and scurrilous attack, most generally of a **satirical** nature, upon an individual. The most notable English lampoon is perhaps the seventeenth-century poet John Dryden's 'Mac Flecknoe'.

lay (occasionally 'lai') A medieval French poem of a **narrative** or **lyrical** kind, the most notable of which were the twelfth-century Breton lays of Marie de France which were adapted by a number of English poets, including Chaucer.

leonine rhyme An internal **rhyme** where the final **syllable** or word of a verse line rhymes with a syllable or word at or about the middle of the line (as in Poe's 'Once upon a midnight dreary, while I pondered, weak and weary'). It was originally a form of medieval Latin verse which consisted of **hexameters** (or alternate hexameters and **pentameters**) in which the final word rhymed with the word immediately before the **caesural** pause, but now has the wider meaning.

limerick A five-line non-stanzaic humorous poem in **anapaests** which rhymes *aabba*. The limerick generally offers a brief comic description of the idiosyncrasies of a particular individual. One of the earliest examples is this poem by Richard Scrafton Sharpe, which dates from 1821:

> As a little fat man of Bombay
> Was smoking one very hot day,
> A bird called a snipe
> Flew away with his pipe,
> Which vex'd the fat man of Bombay.

The use of the same rhyming word at the end of the first and last lines is now generally ignored. The form is particularly associated with the later nineteenth-century **nonsense** poetry of Edward Lear. The limerick is the verse of choice for many obscene and anonymous poetical wits.

litotes   A figure of speech occasionally used by poets in which something is expressed indirectly by denying its opposite, as in the phrase 'I am not averse to a drink'. The device is exemplified in Wordsworth's 'Not useless do I deem':

> Not useless do I deem
> Those shadowy sympathies with things that hold
> An inarticulate language:

lyric   A short poem which expresses a poet's (or an assumed character's) own feelings, thoughts and sentiments, whether they be of love, loss or grief. Certain key poetic forms are 'lyrical': the **sonnet**, **ode** and **elegy**.

macaronic   Poetry where two or more languages are intermingled. The term originally denoted a form of Renaissance **burlesque** in which vernacular words were introduced into poetry otherwise composed in Latin or Greek for humorous effect. The term is sometimes used to describe poetry where occasional lines in foreign languages are introduced for thematic effect (as, frequently, in the work of T. S. Eliot).

madrigal   A **lyric** written to be sung by three or more (usually five or six) unaccompanied voices.

masculine ending   A verse line where a **stress** falls on the final **syllable** of the final foot, as in all regular **iambic** feet and as in **catalectic trochaic** lines: Regular iambic: 'Felt in the blood, and felt along the heart' (Wordsworth); Catalectic trochaic: 'Tyger, tyger, burning bright' (Blake).

masculine rhyme   A **rhyme** which falls on **stressed syllables**. See discussion on p. 63. *See also* feminine rhyme.

measure   A historical, now decidedly obsolete, term for **metre**.

metaphor   A figure of speech in which one thing is referred to by reference to another thing in a comparison which is not meant to be taken literally. Unlike the more qualified **simile** which acknowledges its figurative nature by using the words 'as' or 'like', the metaphor directly associates **tenor** and **vehicle**. Thus 'I am burning with love' is metaphorical whilst 'My love burns like a fire' uses a simile. See discussion on p. 113.

metaphysical poetry A label applied to a number of seventeenth-century poets (Donne, Marvell, Cowley, Herbert and others), whose work is often characterised by the use of **conceits**, paradoxes and striking and unlikely **metaphors**.

metonymy A figure of speech which replaces something with an object which is closely associated with it, as in the phrase 'he's hit the bottle again', where the word bottle is a metonym for alcoholic drinks in general. See discussion on pp. 115–17.

metre The measurable sound pattern evident, in varying degrees of regularity, in a line of poetry. This sound-patterning is analysed in terms of **feet** and **syllables**. A poem's 'metre' is another name for its poetic **frame**. See discussion and examples on pp. 73–104.

metrics A synonym for **prosody**.

Miltonic sonnet A variant on the **Petrarchan sonnet** most associated with the sonnets of John Milton in which the *volta* is delayed until around the tenth line.

mixed metre The use within a poem in a given **metre** of a line which uses an entirely different metre. It is most often an occasional device of variation. Nonetheless, sometimes whole poems are composed in mixed metre. See examples on p. 91 and p. 94.

mock epic A particular form of **burlesque** which applies the conventions of **epic** poetry to some trivial or mundane subject, as in John Philips's 'The Splendid Shilling' and Alexander Pope's *The Dunciad*.

mock-heroic, mock-epic Adjectival terms for **mock epic**.

modulation **Metrical** deviation from the poetic **frame**. An extensive number of different modulations are discussed and exemplified on pp. 77–97. *See also* substitution.

monologue A poem, or extended speech in verse drama, spoken by one person or character and expressive of his or her feelings or attitudes.

monometer A verse line consisting of a single **foot**. See example on p. 97.

mosaic rhyme A form of **feminine rhyme** or **triple rhyme** in which at least one of the rhyming units consists of more than one word, as in Byron's *Don Juan*:

> We have all seen him in the pantomime
> Sent to the devil, somewhat ere his time.

muse A source of poetic inspiration, named after the nine muses of classical myth who were patrons of various branches of the arts. Much epic poetry in English begins with an **invocation** to the muse. Poets have also referred to a beloved as a muse.

narrative poem   A poem which tells a story. One of the principal forms of poetry, alongside **lyric** and **dramatic poetry**. Narrative poetry is common in much pre-twentieth-century poetry, in a variety of different forms: **epic**, **fabliau**, **romance**, **ballad**.

neologism   A new word.

nonce-word   A word invented for a particular occasion or purpose, without a view to its being widely adopted. See examples on p. 148. *See also* neologism and portmanteau words.

nonmetrical verse   An alternative term for **free verse**.

nonsense verse   A poem which derives its effect from the use of **nonce words** and illogical turns of thought. It is particularly associated with the Victorians Lewis Carroll and Edward Lear. See example on p. 147.

occasional verse   A poem written to mark a particular occasion. Examples are found in most poetic forms, but occasional verse is most commonly manifested in the **ode** and **elegy**.

octameter   A rare metrical line comprising of eight feet. See examples on pp. 103–4.

octave   The first eight lines of a **Petrarchan sonnet**. The term is very occasionally used to describe an eight-line **stanza**.

octet   An eight-line **stanza**. The term **octave** is sometimes used. The most significant octet form in English verse is the *ottava rima*.

octosyllabic   A line of eight syllables, as in the **iambic** and **trochaic tetrameter**. It is perhaps most notable in **ballad stanza**, the trochaic **lyric** and in the **continuous Hudibrastic** couplet.

ode   In Graeco-Roman literature, a poem intended or adapted to be sung. The ancient ode and some neoclassical English odes are often divided in a tripartite manner; into **strophe**, **antistrophe** and **epode**. In English poetry, an ode is generally an elevated, rhymed address to a person, abstraction or thing. *See also* Pindaric ode.

onomatopoeia   A word formed by the imitation of the sounds which it designates, as in the words 'hiss' or 'cuckoo'. See discussion on pp. 51–4.

oral poetry   Poetry originally composed to be sung or recited rather than to be written down, as in songs, **hymns** and some **lyrics** and **ballads**.

ottava rima   An eight-line **stanza** with an **iambic pentameter** base, rhyming *abababcc*. The stanza is adapted from a Renaissance Italian **metre** and is most notable in the **satirical** work of Lord Byron (see example on p. 43).

oxymoron   A paradoxical linking of two contradictory terms, as in Shakespeare's 'O heavy lightness, serious vanity'.

paean   A song or **hymn** of praise.

paeon   A metrical **foot** used in the analysis of Greek poetry. It has four **syllables**, one long and three short. The paeon is denominated according to the position of the long syllable as a first, second, third, or fourth paeon. The foot is most rare in English poetry, but this line from Shakespeare's *As You Like It* has been cited as an example of a second paeon:

$$\text{You fool|ish shep|herd, where|fore do | you } \overset{x\ \ /\ \ x\ \ x}{\text{follow her}}$$

However, the line might as easily be seen as a six-foot **alexandrine** which ends with an **iamb** followed by a **pyrrhic**:

$$\text{You fool|ish shep|herd, where|fore do | you } \overset{x\ \ /}{\text{foll}}\text{|}\overset{x\ \ x}{\text{ow her.}}$$

palinode   A poetical recantation of a position taken by the poet in a previous work.

panegyric   A laudatory or adulatory celebration. *See also* encomium, eulogy.

pararhyme   A near-**rhyme**, which manifests the same consonantal pattern, but where the vowels vary (as in the words 'hat' and 'hot'). English pararhymes are particularly associated with Wilfred Owen. See example on p. 64. *See also* half-rhyme.

parody   The imitation of a particular cultural form to comic, generally **satirical**, effect. Parody often achieves its effect through stylistic exaggeration of that which it parodies.

passus   A medieval term for a main division of a story or poem, as in William Langland's fourteenth-century *Piers Plowman*.

pastoral   A poem in which the lives of shepherds and shepherdesses are idealistically portrayed. The term is also sometimes extended more generally to refer to poems dealing with simple, rural life. The pastoral offers a more **idyllic** and idealised account of rusticity than the more day-to-day descriptions of the **georgic**. *See also* eclogue.

pathos   An attempt to effect the compassionate emotions of sympathy and pity in the reader.

pattern poetry   A poem which is set on the page in an unusual fashion in a way which echoes the sense of the poem. The most notable English example is George Herbert's 'Easter Wings' (quoted above on p. 26).

pentameter   A five-**foot** verse line. Though there are examples in **trochaic** and in **triple metre**, its most significant form in English poetry is the ten-syllable **iambic** line, which is often referred to as the 'heroic' line.

performance poetry   Poetry written in the first instance for performance rather than for publication and to be heard by an audience rather than studied on the page. Building on the engaging poetry recitals in the United Kingdom, from the 1960s onwards, of the Liverpool poets (see p. 176) and Michael Horowitz (b. 1945, the founder of the Poetry Olympics and other public events) and the work in America of Hedwig Gorski (b. 1947, generally seen as the originator of the phrase), performance poetry events are often held in 'non-literary' venues, in pubs, comedy clubs, pop concerts and so on. It is frequently, though by no means always, characterised by wordplay and wit, as in the work of John Hegley (b. 1953) and the 'verbal riddums' of Benjamin Zephaniah (b. 1958). Other performance poetry draws upon the popular cultural forms of rap and hip-hop, such as the 'choreo-poetry' of London-born Jonzi D (David Johns, b. 1969). Performance poets such as Zephaniah frequently portray their work as politically subversive, a radicalism summed up in Johns's aim to articulate 'the voice of the underclass in capitalist society'.

periphrasis The expression of meaning in more words than are strictly warranted. Periphrasis was much cultivated by eighteenth-century poets who saw circumlocutory phrases such as 'woolly tribe' as possessing more **poeticality** than the word 'sheep'.

personification The granting of human or animalistic qualities to abstract concepts. The device is common in **allegorical** poetry such as Langland's *Piers Plowman*, but is not infrequent in other forms of poetry, notably **lyrical** poetry. It is particularly associated with medieval and neoclassical English poetry. See example on p. 141.

Petrarchan sonnet A **sonnet**, named after the fourteenth-century Italian poet Petrarch, which is divided into an eight-line **octave** and a six-line **sestet**. The **turn** between the octave and sestet is known as the *volta*. The octave rhymes *abbaabba* and the sestet most commonly *cdecde*. The Petrarchan sonnet is also known as the 'Italian sonnet'. *See also* Shakespearean sonnet.

Pindaric ode A kind of **ode** named after the Greek poet Pindar which is divided into three sections: **strophe**, **antistrophe** and **epode**. The form has been adapted by English poets such as Abraham Cowley, Thomas Gray and Robert Southey.

poem, poetry See Chapter 1.

poetaster A bad or trashy poet, especially one with literary pretensions which exceed his or her talents.

poeticality The quality or style of poetry, as opposed to that of prose.

poetic diction In the widest sense, the language and figures of poetry. Most particularly, however, the phrase is used as a critical label to denominate the highly-wrought and specialised language of eighteenth-century poetry (in such poets as Thomas Gray), language which stands at a remove from the language of everyday usage and is characterised by archaisms, **periphrasis** and **personification**. See example on p. 141.

poetics The theoretical study of the general principles of poetry.

portmanteau word A term invented by Lewis Carroll and defined by him as where 'there are two meanings packed up into one word'. See examples on p. 148.

poulter's measure   A metre where **iambic hexameter** lines alternate with iambic **heptameters**. It was pioneered by the sixteenth-century poet Sir Thomas Wyatt and taken up by his follower the Earl of Surrey. It is exceedingly rare since. See example on p. 103.

prosody   The art of versification, in particular the analysis of **metre**, **rhyme** and **stanza**. Prosody is most notably concerned with the analysis of the rhythmical patterning – the arrangement of poetic lines into **stressed** and unstressed **syllables** – evident in almost all pre-twentieth-century English verse. The term metrics is synonymous.

prothalamion   A wedding song. The term was coined by Edmund Spenser in his 'Prothalamion; or a Spousal Verse made in Honour of the Double Marriage of the Ladie Elizabeth and the Ladie Katherine Somerset' (1596). *See also* epithalamion.

psalm   The sacred songs of the Hebrews which are collected in the biblical book of Psalms. The term is also used more widely to describe **hymns** and poems of a sacred or devotional nature.

pyrrhic   A **foot** composed of two unstressed **syllables**. It is a device of variation and is only used for such metrical **modulation** in poems which employ one of the metrical **frames**. See example on p. 96.

quantitative verse   A metrical system which is founded upon the analysis of **syllable** length, as in the study of Greek and Roman poetry.

quatrain   A four-line **stanza**. The quatrain is one of the most important stanzaic forms. Its most notable manifestation is the **ballad stanza**. See examples on pp. 38–40.

quintain   A five-line **stanza**. It is sometimes referred to as a quintet. See examples on pp. 40–2.

quintet   *See* quintain.

recessive accent   A poetic **stress** on the first **syllable** of a **disyllabic** word which in everyday speech would be pronounced with the emphasis placed upon the second syllable. Recessive accents are generally marked in a text by an acute accent over the first letter of the syllable. For instance, the word 'extreme' in everyday speech is stressed on its second syllable. However, in the prologue to the second act of *Romeo and Juliet* it is sounded with a stress on the first syllable: 'Tempering extremities with éxtreme sweet'. Recessive accents are prompted by the needs of the **metre**, though in some cases it is probable that poets were employing alternative pronunciations of the words which were admissible in their day. Recessive accents are a particular form of **wrenched accent**.

refrain   A form of words which recurs at the end of a **stanza**.

repetend   An irregularly recurring line, phrase or word (in contradistinction to the regular **refrain**).

rhopalic verse   A line where each successive word has a larger number of **syllables**, as in John Clare's trimeter line: 'The quagmire overgrown'. The term is sometimes used for a **stanza** where each successive line is a foot longer than its predecessor. A notable example is found in Richard Crashaw's 'Wishes to His (Supposed) Mistress':

> Whoe'er she be,
> That not impossible she
> That shall command my heart and me.

rhyme   Sound repetition involving an identity of sound between **syllables** which normally falls at the end of a verse line. See discussion and examples on pp. 56–9. *See also* broken rhyme, crossed rhyme, end-rhyme, eye rhyme, half-rhyme, internal rhyme, leonine rhyme, masculine rhyme, mosaic rhyme, pararhyme, rhyme scheme, triple rhyme.

rhyme royal   A seven-line iambic **pentameter stanza** which rhymes *ababbcc*. It is sometimes referred to, after its inventor, as the 'Chaucerian stanza'. The stanza was taken up by Chaucer's imitators, but after its use in Shakespeare's *The Rape of Lucrece* (1594), it is rare, superseded in **narrative poetry** by the **heroic couplet**, **blank verse** and the **Spenserian**. See example on p. 42.

rhyme scheme   The arrangement of **end-rhymes** in a pattern. Each **rhyme** is given an alphabetical letter *a*, *b*, *c*, and so on, facilitating analysis of rhyme pattern, from the straightforward **couplet** (*aa*) to the complexities of ornate **stanzas** such as the **Spenserian**.

rhythm   A pattern of sounds. In much English poetry, sound-patterning is ordered according to a regular pattern (a **metre**) and in the study of metrical poetry the terms metre and rhythm are close to being synonymous. However, the term rhythm has a wider literary application and can be applied to the irregular sound-patterning of **free verse** and the unsystematic **cadence** of prose. See discussion on p. 72.

rising rhythm   A **metre** which employs a basic **foot** which 'rises' from an unstressed **syllable** (or syllables) to culminate in a **stressed** syllable, as in the **iambic** and **anapaestic** metres.

romance   A **narrative poem** on some other-worldly theme, generally involving a chivalric setting. The form is most common in English medieval poetry, notably in Chaucer and *Sir Gawain and the Green Knight*, but has been adapted by later poets such as Spenser and Tennyson.

rondeau   A medieval French **lyrical** form which English poets have used occasionally. It is **octosyllabic**, and generally consists of thirteen lines divided into three **stanzas**. There are only two **rhymes** and the opening words form a **refrain**.

roundel   In medieval times, a roundel was a synonym for **rondeau**. In the nineteenth century, however, the term was borrowed by Swinburne to denominate a particular rondeau of his devising: a two-rhyme, eleven-line poem divided into three **stanzas** of four, three and four lines. The poem's opening becomes a refrain in lines 4 and 11.

Sapphics   An unrhymed **quatrain** verse form in which the first three lines contain eleven **syllables** and the fourth only five. There is also a rhythmic pattern: the first three lines have five **feet** and generally scan **trochee**, trochee (or **spondee**), **dactyl**, trochee, trochee (or spondee). The final line uses a dactylic foot followed by a trochee or a spondee. Isaac Watt's 'The Last Judgment' is an example of English Sapphics:

> Hark! the shrill outcries of the guilty wretches!
> Lively bright horror and amazing anguish
> Stare through their eyelids, while the living worm lies
> > Gnawing within them.

The form is rare in English poetry, but has been used by Sidney, Southey and Swinburne. It is adapted from the Greek metre associated with the poet Sappho.

satire   A form of comic writing which has a moral purpose: the condemnation of folly or vice. The two principal forms are **Horatian** and **Juvenalian** satire. Though figures as diverse as Chaucer and Byron have written virtuoso poetic satire, the form is particularly associated with English neoclassical poetry in the work of Dryden, Pope and Swift.

scansion   The analysis of poetic patterns of **stress** (**graphic scansion**) and of **rhyme** (*see* **rhyme scheme**).

separation   A term sometimes applied to verse lines in **continuous** poetry which resemble self-contained units (as in the **closed couplet**).

septet   A **stanza** of seven lines. The stanza has occasionally been referred to as a 'septuary'. The most notable form of the stanza is the **rhyme royal**. See example on p. 42.

septuary   *See* septet.

sestet   The second part of a **Petrarchan sonnet**, i.e. the last six lines, which follows the **octave**. Six-line **stanzas** are also known as sestets. See example on p. 41.

sestina   A poem which employs six **stanzas** of six lines (**sestets**) followed by a three-line *envoi*. The line-endings of the initial stanza are repeated, though in a different order, in the other five stanzas. The form is a Renaissance Italian adaptation of French troubadourial poetry, and was introduced into canonical English poetry in Sir Philip Sidney's *Arcadia* (1590). The most notable modern adaptation of the form is Swinburne's 'Double Sestina', 'The Complaint of Lisa' (1878).

Shakespearean sonnet   A **sonnet**, named after its most notable practitioner, which consists of three **quatrains** and a **couplet** rhymed *ababcdcdefefgg*. The Shakespearian sonnet is also known as the 'English sonnet'. *See also* Petrarchan sonnet.

short measure   A form of **quatrain** rhymed *abcb* or *abab* which uses **trimeters** in lines 1, 2 and 4, but a **tetrameter** in line 3:

> My former hopes are fled,
> My terror now begins;
> I feel, alas! that I am dead
> In trespasses and sins. (Cowper)

sibilance   A poetic device involving the close proximity of sibilants, i.e. 'hissing' sounds ('s', and 'sh' most notably, but also 'ch' and 'zh'). Sibilance need not necessarily involve initial consonants and can be used anywhere in a word:

> The sun burns sere and the rain dishevels
> One gaunt bleak blossom of scentless breath. (Swinburne, 'A Forsaken Garden')

See also sigmatism.

sigmatism   A narrow form of **sibilance** which involves the marked repetition of 's' sounds (as opposed to the full range of sibilants), as in Langland's 'In a somer seson whan soft was the sonne'.

simile   A comparison of one thing with another thing which, unlike the **metaphor**, uses the qualifying terms 'as' or 'like'. See examples on pp. 113–14.

slam poetry   Poetry recited at a competitive **performance poetry** event.

sonnet   A fourteen-line rhymed **lyrical** poem in **iambic pentameters**. There are two major patterns: the **Petrarchan** and **Shakespearean**. The sonnet is an Italian import and is particularly associated with the poetry of the Renaissance (in the work of Sidney, Shakespeare and Milton) and the Romantic period (in that of Keats and Wordsworth).

Spenserian stanza   A nine-line **iambic stanza** named after its pioneer Edmund Spenser. The first eight lines are **pentameters** and the last is an **alexandrine**. The rhyme scheme is generally *ababbcbcc*. See examples on pp. 43–4.

spondee   A **disyllabic foot** consisting of two **stressed syllables** together. Spondees are only used for metrical **modulation**; there is no such thing as 'spondaic verse'. See examples on p. 95.

sprung rhythm   A term coined by the Victorian poet Gerard Manley Hopkins to denominate a **metre** which supposedly approximates to the rhythm of everyday speech, in which each **foot** is in **falling rhythm**, consisting of one stressed **syllable** either singly or followed by a varying number of unstressed syllables.

squib   A short **satirical** poem, most usually of the nature of a **lampoon**.

stanza   A subdivision or section of a poem. A poem's stanzas generally share the same line-length, **rhyme scheme** and poetic **metre**. See examples and discussion on pp. 33–44.

stave   A rare variant of the term **stanza**.

stichic   Verse which consists of **continuous** successive lines in the same metrical form is stichic (as opposed to stanzaic). **Blank verse, Hudibrastics** and the heroic **couplet** are normally stichic.

stress   The relative emphasis placed upon a **syllable** as it is pronounced. English **prosody** examines the patterning of poetry into stressed and unstressed syllables.

strophe   In Greek poetry, and some English neoclassical verse, the first section of certain choral and lyrical **odes**. The metrical structure of the strophe is repeated by the following **antistrophe**. The term is also sometimes used as a synonym for **stanza**.

substitution   A metrical term for the insertion of a **foot** which differs from the **base metre** into a line of poetry. See examples on p. 78 and pp. 95–7. *See also* modulation.

syllabic   A method of **metrical** analysis which pays sole attention to **syllable** count (as opposed to **stress** (**accentual** metrics) or stress and syllable count combined (**accentual-syllabic** metrics)). The metrical analysis of French and Spanish poetry and that of several other European languages is generally syllabic.

syllable   A word, or portion of a word, made by a single effort of the organs of speech.

symbol   A thing which denotes something else. A symbol has a rather less explicit relationship to that which it symbolises than the exact correspondences of **metaphor** and the sustained metaphors of **allegory**. Whilst a metaphor explains its **tenor,** a symbolic meaning is suggested less forcefully and in many cases can be ambiguously interpreted. Thus, for example, the albatross slain by the mariner in Coleridge's 'The Rime of the Ancient Mariner' is generally seen as a symbol, but many different accounts of the significance of that symbol have been offered. See example on p. 56.

synecdoche   A figure of speech in which something is referred to indirectly, by an association of the whole of something with a part of it or vice versa, as in the phrase 'Many hands make light work'. See discussion on pp. 115–16.

tenor   The thing a **metaphor** or **symbol** is actually about (as opposed to the object with which it is compared (the 'vehicle'). See examples on p. 119.

tercet   Three successive lines bound by **rhyme**. Three consecutive lines of the same length which rhyme together *aaa* are called **'triplets'**, but there are other variants: see *terza rima* and **villanelle**. Though there are examples of

continuous tercets, the stanzaic tercet is more common. See pp. 36–7 for examples.

terza rima   Tercets linked in a particular **rhyme** pattern: *aba bcb cdc* and so on, closed by a line (occasionally two) which rhymes with the second line of the final **tercet** (*ded e* or *ded ee*). See example on pp. 36–7.

tetrameter   A four-foot verse line. Tetrameters are common in English poetry. They are found in the **iambic** tetrameter and in **stanzaic quatrains** and have also not infrequently been used for sustained **continuous** iambic composition, notably in **Hudibrastics**. The tetrameter is still more important in **trochaic** verse and provides the most common form of trochaic line (though many lines are **truncated**).

threnody   A poem or song of lamentation, in particular a **lament** or **dirge** for a dead person.

tone   A somewhat imprecise term used to describe either a poem's atmosphere or the stance taken by the poet.

topographic poetry   Verse which portrays a particular place, whether city, town or landscape. Topographic poetry generally also includes meditative sections in which the poet describes his or her reaction to the topography. Dyer's 'Grongar Hill' (quoted on pp. 89–90) is an example.

trimeter   A line of verse composed of three poetic **feet**. See example on p. 100.

triolet   A **stanza** composed of eight lines, built around two **rhymes**. The first line of a triolet is repeated as the fourth and seventh, and the second line is repeated as the eighth. The rhyme scheme is *abaaabab*. The form is imported from medieval French poetry. Though it is not common in post-Renaissance poetry, it was revived by a number of Victorian poets.

triple metre   Verse where the metrical **frame** is **trisyllabic**, i.e. **anapaestic** and **dactylic** poetry.

triple rhyme   A **rhyme** on three **syllables**, of which the first is **stressed** and the others unstressed. See examples on p. 94.

triplet   Three successive lines of the same length which **rhyme** together *aaa*. See example on p. 36.

trisyllabic   Consisting of three syllables, as in the **anapaestic** and **dactylic feet**.

trochaic   A **falling rhythm** where a single **stressed syllable** is followed by an unstressed one. The basic metrical unit is the trochaic foot, the **trochee**. After **iambic** verse, trochaic verse (sometimes referred to as 'trochaics') is the commonest metre of English poetry.

trochee   A single foot which consists of a stressed followed by an unstressed syllable. A poem in trochaic metre is sometimes said to be written 'in trochees'. The foot is also often used in **substitution** in **iambic** verse.

truncation   The shortening of a verse line by a **syllable** less than the norm demanded by the poetic **frame**. Truncation is distinct from the use of a **catalectic** foot in that it can occur in any foot in a verse line.

turn   A rapid change in the course or argument of a poem, most notably in the **sonnet**. *See also volta.*

typography   The appearance and arrangement of words as they are printed on a page (discussed extensively in Chapter 2 above). Poets have sometimes exploited typography for particular effect, as in **pattern poetry**.

vehicle   *See* tenor.

verse drama   Drama composed predominantly in verse. Though verse drama has been used in the twentieth century by such figures as T. S. Eliot (in *Murder in the Cathedral* and other plays), contemporary drama generally uses prose. However, much pre-twentieth-century drama is in verse: in **blank verse** (as in the work of Shakespeare, Marlowe and Jonson) or, less commonly, in **heroic couplets**.

verse paragraph   The irregular (as opposed to regular, **stanzaic**) subdivisions of **stichic** verse, notably blank verse. *See also* **dramatic poetry**.

versification   The art, techniques and principles of composing verse, most particularly in the practical utilisation of **metre**, **rhyme** and stanzaic form.

vers libre   The French term, sometimes used in English critical writing, for free verse.

villanelle   A poem, generally **lyrical** or **pastoral**, consisting of an odd number (but normally five) of three-line **stanzas** and a final **quatrain**. The villanelle has only two **rhymes**, with the first and third lines of the initial stanza repeated alternately in the succeeding stanzas as a **refrain**, and brought together as a final couplet in the quatrain. A French sixteenth-century import, the form was used most particularly in the Victorian period. A noted modern example is Dylan Thomas's 'Do not Go Gentle into that Good Night' (quoted above on p. 37).

volta   The Italian word for 'turn'. It is applied to a change in the course or argument of a **Petrarchan sonnet** between the **octave** and the **sestet**.

weak ending   The placing of an unstressed monosyllable (generally a preposition or conjunction) at the end of an **iambic** line, in the place where a **stress** normally occurs (the tenth syllable). See example on p. 86. *See also* feminine ending.

wrenched accent   A poetic **stress** on a **syllable** in a verse line which in everyday speech would be unstressed, or some other form of poetic over-ruling of the pronunciation of a word (particularly in the forming of two syllables where there would normally be only one). Wrenched accents are sometimes marked by a symbol over the syllable, a grave in final syllable of a word, an accent elsewhere:

> Thy bosom is endearèd with all hearts (Shakespeare)
>
> Gliding metéorous, as evening mist (Milton)

Wrenched accents are prompted by the needs of the **metre**, though in some cases it is likely that poets were employing alternative pronunciations of the words which were admissible in their day. *See also* reccessive accent.

Metre exercise: answers

Here are our answers to the exercises on metre set in Chapter 4 ('Metre and Rhythm'), subsection 13. We have noted the foot breaks in the first line of each extract and occasionally thereafter to illustrate metrical variation or points of note.

```
 /     x  |  /     x   | /    x  | /
Haste thee nymph, and bring with thee
```

```
 /    x   /    x  /    x | /
Jest and youthful joll | i | ty,
```

```
 /     x    /    x  /   x  | /
Quips and Cranks, and wanton wiles,
```

```
 /    x   /    x    /   x | /
Nods and becks, and wreathed smiles.
```
   (John Milton, 'L'Allegro')
Base metre: Trochaic
Line type: Tetrameter
Note that the final foot in each line is 'short' by a syllable, or 'catalectic' (see glossary).

```
 x  /  | x   /  | x   /  | x / | x  /
The western sun now shot a feeble ray,
```

```
 x   /   x  / |  x   x | x  /   x  /
And faintly scatter'd the remains of day:
```

x /   x   /   x / x   /   x /
Ev'ning approach'd; but oh what hosts of foes

x   / x /   x /   x   /   x   /
Were never to behold that ev'ning close!
   (Joseph Addison, 'The Campaign, A Poem')
Base metre: Iambic
Line type: Pentameter
Note the pyrrhic foot (see glossary) in line 2.

x / | x / | x / | x   /
If e'er thy breath with freedom glow'd,

x   /   x / x   /
And spurned a tyrant's chain,

/   / |x   / |x /   x   /
Let not thy strong oppressive force

x   / x   /   x /
A free-born mouse detain.
   (Anna Barbauld, 'The Mouse's Petition')
Metre: Iambic
Line types: Tetrameter (1, 3), followed by trimeter (2, 4). This pattern in quatrain stanza is known as 'ballad stanza'.
Note the spondaic substitution (see glossary) in the first foot of line 3.

x x /| x   x   / | x   x   / | x   x /
The Assyrian came down like the wolf on the fold,

x   x   / x   x   /   x   x   /   x x /
And his cohorts were gleaming in purple and gold;

x   x   /   x x   /   x   x   /   x x /
And the sheen of their spears was like stars on the sea,

x   x   /   x   x   /   x x   /   x x /
When the blue wave rolls nightly on deep Galilee.
   (Lord Byron, 'The Destruction of Sennacherib')
Metre: Anapaestic
Line type: Tetrameter

/   x x| /   x   x x|/ x x|/   x
Just for a handful of silver he left us

/   x x / x   x /   x x l /
Just for a ribbon to stick in his coat –

/   x x / x x   /   x x l/ x
Found the one gift of which fortune bereft us,

/   x x   / x x l/   x l/ x
Lost all the others she lets us devote.
   (Robert Browning, 'The Lost Leader')
Metre: Dactylic
Line type: Tetrameter
Note the extensive use of metrical substitution here: the trochees which conclude lines 3 and 4, the one syllable curtailed foot at the end of line 2 and the two trochees which conclude line 4.

x   / l /   x l x / l x /
The boy stood on the burning deck

x   / x / x /
Whence all but he had fled;

x   /   x / x / x   /
The flame that lit the battle's wreck

x   /   x /   x   /
Shone round him o'er the dead.
   (Felicia Hemans, 'Casabianca')
Metre: Iambic
Line types: Ballad stanza (iambic tetrameter followed by iambic trimeter)
Note the trochaic substitution in the second foot of line 1. Further note that the following reading of line 1 is also possible (we quote it as an illustration of how metrical scansion is not a precise science):

x / l x   / l x / l x /
The boy stood on the burning deck

x   x / l x x   / l x x   / l x x   / x
When the castle's rich chambers were haunted and dreary,

x   /   x x / x x /   x x /
The poor little hovel was still and secure;

x   x / x x / x x / l x   x / x
And no robber e'er enter'd, nor goblin nor fairy,

x   x   /   x   x   /   x   x   /   x x   /
For the splendours of pride had no charms to allure.
   (Mary Robinson, 'The Poor, Singing Dame')
Metre: Anapaestic
Line Type: Tetrameter
Note the 'extra' syllables at the end of lines 1 and 3 ('hypercatalectic' feet – see glossary) and the iambic substitution in the first foot of line 2.

x   / | x   / |x   / |x   / | x   / |x   / | x   /
I sang of leaves, of leaves of gold, and leaves of gold there grew:

x   /   x   /   x /   x   /   x   /   x   /
Of wind I sang, a wind there came and in the branches blew.

x   /   x   /   x   /   x   /   x   /   x   /   x   /
Beyond the Sun, beyond the Moon, the foam was on the Sea,

x /   x   /   x/   x   /   x   /   x /   x   /
And by the strand of Il | mar | in there grew a golden Tree.
   (J. R. R. Tolkein, 'Song of Eldamar')
Metre: Iambic
Line type: Heptameter

x   x   / | x   x   / |x   x   / |x   x   /
It was noon, and on flowers that languish'd around

x x / | x   / |x   x /   x x   /
In silence repos'd the voluptuous bee;

x   x   /   x   x   /   x x   /   x   x   /
Every leaf was at rest, and I heard not a sound

x   x   /   x x /   x   x / x   x   /
But the woodpecker tapping the hollow beech-tree.
   (Thomas Moore, 'Ballad Stanzas')
Metre: Anapaestic
Line type: Tetrameter
Note the iambic substitution in the second foot of line 2.

/   x   x | /   x   x |/   x   x |/   x   x
Woman much miss'd, how you call to me, call to me,

/   x   x   /   x x   /   x   x   /
Saying that now you are not as you were.
   (Thomas Hardy, 'The Voice')
Metre: Dactylic
Line type: Tetrameter
Note the catalectic nature of the second line.

／   x ｜／   x｜ ／ x
Teach me half the gladness

／   x   ／   x   ／
That thy brain must know,

／   x   ／   x ／   x
Such harmonious madness

／   x ／   x ／
From my lips would flow.
  (P. B. Shelley, 'To a Skylark')
Base metre: Trochaic
Line type: Trimeter

Note that lines 2 and 4 are curtailed.

Further reading

CHAPTER 1: THE KEY WORDS OF POETRY

There are several excellent general anthologies of English poetry that are representative of the thousand years of verse discussed in this chapter. The venerable *Oxford Book of English Verse,* which first appeared in 1900, when its editor Sir Arthur Quiller-Couch ('Q') declared his intention to 'range over the whole field of English Verse', remains the most well known and it has most recently been revised under the editorship of Christopher Ricks (1999). Another substantial and enjoyable canonical anthology is Paul Keegan's *The Penguin Book of English Verse* (2001). The most commonly used classroom anthology is the *Norton Anthology of Poetry* (5th edition 2005; edited by Margaret W. Ferguson, Mary Jo Salter and Jon Stallworthy), which first appeared in 1970 (though many lecturers use all or part of the huge, chronologically arranged, multi-volume *Norton Anthology of English Literature*, first published in 1962, which contains prose fiction, drama and essays as well as poetry). Cambridge University Press and Wiley Blackwell both publish a valuable series of *Companions* to the various epochs of poetic history, from Old English verse to the Renaissance, from Romantic poetry to Modernism and beyond.

In terms of the periods of English poetry, Bruce Mitchell and Fred C. Robinson's *A Guide to Old English* (1986; 6th edition 2001) is the most widely used textbook on Anglo-Saxon poetry and culture (and Mitchell and Robinson also edited *Beowulf: An Edition with Relevant Shorter Texts* in 1998). Peter S. Baker's *Introduction to Old English* (2003) is also very useful. On medieval literature, good introductions include J. A. W. Bennett and Douglas Gray's *Middle English Literature* (1986), Elizabeth Solopova and Stuart D. Lee's

Key Concepts in Medieval Literature (2007) and Christopher Cannon's *Middle English Literature: A Cultural History* (2008). In terms of fourteenth-century literature, the high point of middle English verse, J. A. Burrow's *Ricardian Poetry: Chaucer, Gower, Langland and the 'Gawain' Poet* (1971), remains a valuable study.

There are a number of comprehensive anthologies of Renaissance verse, including *The New Oxford Book of Seventeenth Century Verse*, edited by Alastair Fowler (1991), and *The Penguin Book of Renaissance Verse: 1509–1659*, edited by H. Woudhuysen and David Norbrook (2005). A useful specialised anthology is *Kissing the Rod: An Anthology of Seventeenth Century Women's Verse*, edited by Germaine Greer et al. (1988). The most widely used anthology of eighteenth-century verse is *Eighteenth-Century Poetry: An Annotated Anthology*, edited by David Fairer and Christine Gerrard (2nd edition 2004), and Gerrard has also edited a wide-ranging collection of essays, *A Companion to Eighteenth-Century Poetry* (2006), to stand alongside the anthology. The best introductory study is David Fairer, *English Poetry of the Eighteenth Century 1700–1789* (2003).

For Romanticism, the most widely used anthology is Duncan Wu's *Romanticism: An Anthology* (3rd edition 2006). In critical terms, Marilyn Butler, *Romantics, Rebels and Reactionaries* (1982) is the most notable work of recent decades. Jane Moore and John Strachan's *Key Concepts in Romantic Literature* (2010) is the most up-to-date and comprehensive textbook on the Romantic period. Also useful are Aidan Day, *Romanticism* (1996), Jane Stabler, *Burke to Byron/Barbauld to Baillie, 1790–1830* (2001) and Sharon Ruston, *Romanticism* (2007). The best theoretical comparative account of neoclassicism and Romanticism remains M. H. Abrams's *The Mirror and the Lamp: Romantic Theory and the Critical Tradition* (1953).

In terms of the later nineteenth century, for texts see *The New Oxford Book of Victorian Verse*, edited by Christopher Ricks (1990) and Francis O'Gorman's *Victorian Poetry: An Annotated Anthology* (2004). Isobel Armstrong's *Victorian Poetry: Poetry, Politics, Poetics* (1993), Joseph Bristow's *The Cambridge Companion to Victorian Poetry* (2000) and *A Companion to Victorian Poetry*, edited by Richard Cronin, Alice Chapman, and Anthony H. Harrison (2002) are significant critical introductions. In terms of modernism, good general books include Peter Nicholls's *Modernisms: A Literary Guide* (1995), *A Concise Companion to Modernism*, edited by David Bradshaw (2003), Jane Goldman, *Modernism, 1910–1945* (2004) and Tim Armstrong, *Modernism* (2005). The most comprehensive anthology is *Modernism: An Anthology*, edited by Lawrence Rainey (2005).

CHAPTER 2: THE SHAPE OF POETRY

Ernest Haublein's *The Stanza* (1978) is a helpful introduction to stanzaic kinds. For more general treatment of verse form, see Philip Hobsbaum, *Metre, Rhythm and Verse Form* (1996) and Nigel Fabb, *Language and Literary Structure: The Linguistic Analysis of Form in Verse Structure* (2002). There are some useful comments on page layout in John Lennard, *The Poetry Handbook* (1996).

CHAPTER 3: THE SOUND OF POETRY

Rhyme, as well as other sound effects, is discussed in nearly all studies of poetry. However, you might consult in particular John Hollander, *Rhyme's Reason: A Guide to English Verse* (1981), Philip Davies Roberts, *How Poetry Works* (1986) and Ronald Tamplin, *Rhythm and Rhyme* (1993). An older, but still influential, book is Anne Cluysenaar, *Introduction to Literary Stylistics* (1976).

CHAPTER 4: METRE AND RHYTHM

There are a number of informative books on metre. Perhaps the most notable is Derek Attridge's polemical monograph, *The Rhythms of English Poetry* (1982). More accessible to a student audience, however, is the same author's later textbook, *Meter and Meaning: An Introduction to Rhythm in Poetry* (2003), co-written with Thomas Carper. See also *The Scissors of Meter: Grammetrics and Reading* by Donald Wesling (1996) and the useful collection by fourteen poets and critics to be found in *Meter in English: a Critical Engagement*, edited by David Baker (1996).

CHAPTER 5: COMPARISONS AND ASSOCIATIONS

There are numerous books concerned with metaphor as a rhetorical device, as a linguistic phenomenon, as a philosophical conundrum, or as a defining aspect of poetic writing. See Terence Hawkes, *Metaphor* (1986), George Lakoff and Mark Johnson, *Metaphors We Live By* (1980), and David E. Cooper, *Metaphor* (1986). A more recent overview is Zoltán Kövacses, *Metaphor: A Practical Introduction* (2002).

CHAPTER 6: THE WORDS OF POETRY

For treatment of the language in which poems of different periods are written, see Geoffrey N. Leech, *A Linguistic Guide to English Poetry* (1969), Richard Bradford, *A Linguistic History of English Poetry* (1993) and Mick Short, *Exploring the Language of Poems, Plays and Prose* (1996). For a very fertile discussion of literary allusion in practice, see Christopher Ricks, *Allusion to the Poets* (2002).

CHAPTER 7: WRITING POETRY

A number of annuals offer valuable advice to writers of poetry. *The Poetry Writers' Yearbook,* edited by Gordon Kerr and Hilary Lissenden, includes information on poetry workshops, magazines and publishers. The 'Poetry Magazines' listing section of the *Writer's Handbook* is also very useful (see p. 187), as are the *Writers' and Artists' Yearbook* sections on approaching publishers and its listings of influential poetry organisations (see p. 187). A. & C. Black, publishers of the latter book, also publish John Whitworth's *Writing Poetry* (2001), an introductory handbook on writing and publishing poetry. Stephen Fry's *The Ode Less Travelled*: *Unlocking the Poet Within* (2005) is an accomplished (and witty) guide to writing poetry, especially metrical poetry.

Those UK readers interested in writing poetry should consider joining the Poetry Society whose 'mission is to advance the study, use and enjoyment of poetry'. It publishes the *Poetry Review* and *Poetry News* and runs poetry competitions, 'surgeries' and readings. Also worth investigating are the Poetry School, a registered charity devoted to the teaching of poetry (http://www.poetryschool.com/) and the National Association of Writers' Groups (NAWG), which among other things offers details of UK writing groups arranged by region (see http://www.nawg.co.uk/writing-groups/).

A GLOSSARY OF POETICAL TERMS

For wider glossaries of general literary and theoretical terms, see Chris Baldick's *Oxford Dictionary of Literary Terms* (1990; 3rd edition 2008), M. H. Abram's *Glossary of Literary Terms* (1957; 9th edition 2006, now co-authored by Geoffrey Galt Harpham) and John Anthony Cuddon's *Penguin Dictionary of Literary Terms and Literary Theory* (formerly *A Dictionary of Literary Terms and Literary Theory* and first published 1977; new edition 2004, revised by Claire Preston).

Index

Note: Entries appear in word-by-word alphabetical order. Page references in **bold** type indicate Glossary entries. In entries for specific poets, thematic subentries are followed by works cited.

acatalectic (complete) lines, 78, 79, 91, 104, **201**
accent
  recessive, **219**
  wrenched, 219, **225–6**
  see also stress
accentual analysis, **201**
accentual–syllabic analysis, **201**
acephalous lines, **201**
acrostic, **201**
Addison, Joseph, 'The Campaign, A Poem', 108
Advent Lyrics, 14
aesthetics of print, 23–4
Agard, John, 'Listen Mr Oxford Don', 169–71
Agenda Poetry Magazine, 187
alexandrine, 83, 100–1, **201**, 211, 217
  and Spenserian stanza, 43–4, 81, 101, 201, 222
allegory, **201–2**, 20; *see also* emblem poem;
  exemplum; personification
alliteration, 5, 15, 48–51, 61, 63, 64, **202**
  alliterative revival, **202**
allusion, 156, 159–64, **202**, 212
  and creative quotation, 164–8
  incremental, 162
  and source, 157–9, 164
alphabet, phonetic, 48
American Poetry Review, 187
Ammons, A. R., 192
amphibrach, 96–7, **202**
amphimacer *see* cretic
anacrusis, 89, **202**
analysis, metrical, 73–7
  accentual, 77, **201**
  accentual–syllabic, 77, **201**
  syllabic, 77, **223**
anapaest, 94–5, 96–7, **202**, 213, 220, 224
anaphora, 31, 107, **202**

Angelou, Maya, 192
Anglo-Saxon *see* Old English
Anstey, Christopher, *New Bath Guide*, 95
anticlimax, 43, **202**; *see also* bathos
antistrophe, **203**, 216, 218, 223
antithesis, 171, **203**
apostrophe, 21, 141, **203**; *see also* invocation
appearance, visual *see* visuality
Arc (publisher), 188
archaism, 5, 10, 143–4, 172–3, 218
Ariosto, Ludovico, 16
Armitage, Simon, 193
Arnold, Matthew
  and definition of poetry, 8, 12
  'Dover Beach', 123–4
  'The Scholar Gypsy', 165–6
Ashbery, John, 198
  'The Dong with the Luminous Nose', 165–6
assonance, 48–9, 61, 135, **203**
Auden, W. H., 64, 191, 193
  'Stop all the Clocks', 131–2
Augustanism, 17, 85
Ayton, Sir Robert, 'When thou did thinke I did not
  love', 40

Bacon, Francis (artist), 195
Bacon, Sir Francis (statesman), 16
  'Of Death', 76–7
ballad, 200, **203**
  and incremental repetition, 212
  and stanzaic couplet, 36
ballad stanza, 39–40, **203**, 206, 216, 219
ballade, 19, **203**
Barbauld, Anna, 'The Mouse's Petition', 108
bard, 13–14
Baring-Gould, S., 'Onward, Christian soldiers!', 88

Barnes, William, 'My Orcha'd in Linden Lea', 151–2, 153
base *see* frame
base metre, 9, 72, 73, 84, 108, 204, 212, 223
bathos, 43, 202, **203–4**; *see also* anticlimax
The Battle of Maldon, 14
Bayly, N. T. H., 95
Beattie, James
    and definition of poetry, 11
    and stanza, 44
Beaumont, Francis and Fletcher, John, 16
Behn, Aphra, *Oroonoko*, 174
Benson, A. C., 'Land of Hope and Glory', 88
Bentley, E. Clerihew, 205
Beowulf, 14, 174
Binyon, Lawrence, 'For the Fallen', 39
Blair, Robert, 210
Blake, William, 18, 186
    'The Fly', 99–100
    'Jerusalem', 38
    'The Lamb', 180
    'The Tyger', 91
blank verse, 4, 43, **204**, 206, 208
    and amphibrach, 96
    and feminine ending, 87, 209–10
    and heroic line, 87, 211
    and iambic pentameter, 81, 83–8, 212
    and overrunning lines, 84–6
    as stichich, 223
    see also enjambement; verse drama
blazon, **204**
Bloodaxe (publisher), 188
Boccaccio, Giovanni, 15, 16
Boland, Eavan, 198
book, **204**; *see also* canto; fit
Boswell, James, *Life of Johnson*, 7
break, 82–3, 84, 86, **204**; *see also* caesura; end-stop
Browning, Robert, 19, 198, 207
    'Before', 101
    Dramatic Lyrics, 175
    'How they brought the good news from Ghent to Aix', 95
    'The Lost Leader', 109
    'My Last Duchess', 199
Bryce, Colette
    'The Full Indian Rope Trick', 134
    'Wish You Were', 135
Bunyan, John, *Divine Emblems*, 208
burden, **204**
Burgum, E. B., 18
burlesque, 88, **204**
    and anticlimax, 202
    and mock epic, **215**
    see also doggerel; macaronic verse
Burns, Robert
    'The Cotter's Saturday Night', 150
    'My Luve is like a Red Red Rose', 119
    'To a Mouse', 42, 150
Burns stanza, 41–2, **204**

Butler, Samuel
    and rhyme, 61–3
    Hudibras, 62–3, 87–8, 211
Byron, George Gordon, Lord Byron, 20–1, 209
    and metre, 81, 101
    and *ottava rima*, 43, 81, 218
    Beppo, 81
    Childe Harold's Pilgrimage, 44, 144, 165–6
    'The Destruction of Sennacherib', 109
    Don Juan, 43, 215
    The Prophecy of Dante, 36–7
    and rhyme, 61
    and satire, 218, 221

cacophony, **205**
cadence, 195, **205**, 220
    and prose, 9
caesura, 82–3, 84, 204, **205**; *see also* break
Canning, George, 'Song. By Rogero', 204
canto, 204, **205**; *see also* book; fit
Carcanet (publisher), 188
carol, **205**
carpe diem, **205**
Carroll, Lewis, 182, 183, 216, 218
    'Jabberwocky', 147–8
    'The Mouse's Tale', 24–5
Castiglione, Baldassare, *The Book of the Courtier*, 16
catalectic (curtailed) lines, 79, 104, 201, **205**
    and anapaestic metre, 94–5
    and dactylic metre, 93–4
    and iambic metre, 86
    and trochaic metre, 79–80, 89, 91, 100
catalogue, epic, **209**
Causley, Charles, 197
cento, 165–6, **205**
Chamberlayne, W., *Pharonnida*, 161
Chapman, George, and Homer's *Iliad*, 102
Chaucer, Geoffrey, 14, 197, 220
    and ballade, 203
    Chaucerian stanza, 42, 220
    and dream vision, 208
    and heroic couplet, 43, 85
    influence on Spenser, 144
    and satire, 221
    and standard English, 169
    Canterbury Tales, 15, 42, 209
    The Parliament of Fowles, 42
    Troilus and Criseyde, 42, 208
chiasmus, 29, **205**
choreo-poetry, 218
choriamb, **205**
Christianity, and Old English poetry, 14
Clampitt, Amy, 192
Clare, John, 220
clerihew, **205–6**
cliché, and metaphor, 129, 131–2
Clifton, Harry, 193
Clough, Arthur Hugh, 'Amours de Voyage', 102
Coleridge, S. T.
    and definition of poetry, 8, 11–12

and dream, 48, 197
and metre, 78
and Wordsworth, 183, 199
'Dejection', 19, 207
'Flowers are lovely, love is flowerlike', 205
'Kubla Khan', 48–9, 51
'The Rime of the Ancient Mariner', 9–10, 39, 94,
    96, 223
'To The Nightingale', 163, 206
common measure, 206
comparison, 5; *see also* conceit; ground; metaphor;
    simile; symbol; tenor; vehicle
complaint, **206**
conceit, 5, 123–7, **206**, 215
concrete poems, 24–8
consonance, 48–9, 61, 66, 135, 149, **206**
content, and form, 10, 23–33, 35, 39, 90, 92, 101,
    106
context, historical, 4, 6, 8
continuous verse, **206**
conversation poem, **206**
Cope, Wendy
    'Lonely Hearts', 153
    'My Lover', 166–8
coronach, **206**
couplet, **206**, 220, 222
    broken, 35
    closed, 82, **206**, 221
    elegiac, **208**
    heroic, 206, 223, 225
        in Chaucer, 43, 85
        and iambic pentameter, 43, 81–5, **211**, 212
        in Pope, 59, 82–3, 85, 90
    octosyllabic, 88, 90, 211, 216
    stanzaic, 35–6, 38
    see also distich
Cowley, Abraham, 215, 218
Cowper, William
    'The Diverting History of John Gilpin', 40
    'On the Death of Mrs. Throckmorton's
        Bullfinch', 148–9
    Table Talk, 2
    The Task, 163
Cox, C. B. and Schmidt, Michael, 176
Crashaw, Richard, 'Wishes to His (Supposed)
    Mistress', 220
CreateSpace, 186
creative writing courses, viii, 6, 183–5, 198
cretic foot, 97, **206**
crisis lyric, 19, **206–7**
crossed rhyme, **207**
crown, **207**
Cummings, E. E., 28–9, 32–3

dactyl, 92, **207**, 224
    dactylic metre, 92–4, 208
    and substitution, 93, 207
Daniel, Samuel, *Defence of Rhyme*, 141
Dante Alighieri, *The Divine Comedy*, 36
De la Mare, Walter, 196

Defoe, Daniel, *Robinson Crusoe*, 174
deviation, 111
diæresis, **207**
dialect, 5, 137, 149–53, 168–9
    and standard English, 168–71
Dickinson, Emily, 21, 186
diction, poetic, 5, 12, 19, 140–5, 172, **218**; *see also*
    archaism; periphrasis
dimeter, 98–100, **207**
dirge, 94, **207**; *see also* coronach; elegy; lament;
    threnody
dissonance, **207**
distich, **207**
diversity, linguistic, 137–40
Dobell, Sydney, 95
Dodgson, C. L. *see* Carroll, Lewis
doggerel, **207**
Donne, John, 108, 215
    and heroic couplet, 85–6
    'Satire iii', 85
double rhyme *see* rhyme, feminine
drama, verse, **225**
Drayton, Michael, *Polyolbion*, 100–1
The Dream of the Rood, 14, 174
dream vision, 15, **208**
dreams, 48, 197, 199
Drinkwater, John, 190
Dryden, John
    and definition of poetry, 11, 12–13
    and metre, 93
    and neoclassicism, 17
    and rhyme, 57
    and satire, 221
    Essay on Dramatic Poesy, 12–13, 145
    'Mac Flecknoe', 213
    Religio Laici, 126–7
Duffy, Carol Ann, 69–70, 184
    'Mrs Sisyphus', 70–1
Dunbar, William, 42
Dyer, John, 'Grongar Hill', 89–90, 91, 224

eclogue, **208**
    neoclassical, 17
    see also georgic; pastoral
elegy, 207, **208**
    elegiac couplet, **208**
    elegiac stanza *see* stanza, heroic
    and free verse, 107
    and occasional verse, 216
    Old English, 14
    see also graveyard poetry
Eliot, T. S., 184, 190, 214
    and definition of poetry, 8, 12, 189
    and everyday language, 145
    and expression of emotion, 198
    and free verse, 105–6
    'The Hollow Men', 30–1
    'The Love Song of J. Alfred Prufrock', 119–20,
        131
    Murder in the Cathedral, 225

The Waste Land, 20, 66–7, 105, 158–9, 164–6, 184, 193, 199
emblem poem, **208**
emotion, 12, 21, 175–9, 180, 189, 191, 194, 198
    and academic study of poetry, 2
enactment, visual, 26–8
encomium, **208**; *see also* eulogy; panegyric
end-rhyme, **208**, 210, 220
end-stop, 39, 82, 84–5, 206, **208**
Engle, Paul, 190
English
    and ethnic minority poets, 169–71
    and Latin, 139–40
    standard, 168–71
    see also Middle English; Old English
Enitharmion Press, 188
enjambement, 84–6, 206, **208**
envelope, **208**
envoi, envoy, 203, **208**, 221
epic, **208**
    and burlesque, 204
    and invocation, 213
    mock, **215**
    neoclassical, 17
    Old English, 14
    oral, 174
    Renaissance, 16
epic catalogue, **209**
epic simile, **209**
epigram, **209**
epistle, neoclassical, 17
epistrophe, **209**
epithalamion, **209**; *see also* prothalamion
epithet, compound, 148–9
epode, **209**, 216, 218
eroticism, and metonymy, 116
eulogy, **209**; *see also* encomium; panegyric
euphony, **209**
exemplum/exempla, 15, **209**
experience, personal, 180–3, 190, 194, 196
eye rhyme, **209**
ezines, 186

Faber & Faber, 186, 187
fable, neoclassical, 17
fabliau/fabliaux, 15, **209**
'Fair Isabell of Rochroyall', 212
feedback, 183–6, 187, 195
feeling *see* emotion
feet *see* foot
Ferrar, Nicholas, 27, 45
Fielding, Henry, *Tom Jones*, 11
fit, **210**; *see also* book; canto
foot, 74–5, 80–97, **210**
    catalectic, 201, 205, 225
    chroiambic, **205**
    complete *see* acatalectic
    cretic, 97, **206**
    defective *see* catalectic
    disyllabic, 75, 80, **207**, 222

ionic, **213**
    paeon, **216–17**
    trisyllabic 75, 80, **224**; *see also* amphibrach; anapaest
    see also dactyl; iamb; pentameter; pyrrhic; spondee; stress; trochee
foregrounding, 111
form, and content, 10, 23–33, 35, 39, 90, 92, 101, 106
fourteener, 102–3, **210**; *see also* heptameter
frame, 76, 78–9, 84, 91, **210**, 212, 215, 219, 224
France, cultural influence, 14–15
free verse, 3–4, 8, 10, 19, 20, 104–7, 197, **210**, 220
    and cadence, 205
    and line-length, 105–6
    and repetition, 105–7
    and rhyme, 104
    and rhythm, 107
    and visual enactment, 28
Frere, John Hookham, 43
Frost, Robert, 6, 176–7, 189, 199
    'My November Guest', 177
Fry, Christopher, 190

georgic, **210**; *see also* pastoral
'Gil Brenton', 36
Ginsberg, Allen, 191
Goldsmith, Oliver, 17
Gorski, Hedwig, 217
Gosse, Edmund, 20
graveyard poetry, **210**
Gray, Thomas, 145, 218
    'Elegy Written in a Country Church Yard', 40, 75–6, 77–8, 160–2, 165–6, **210**, 211
    'Ode on a Distant Prospect of Eton College', 141–3
    'The Progress of Poesy', 92
ground, 5, 119–23, 131, 132
Gunn, Thom, 192

haiku, 200, **210**
half-rhyme, **210**, 212
Hardy, Thomas
    and definition of poetry, 12, 176, 189
    'Thoughts of Phena at News of her Death', 172–3
    'The Voice', 110
Harrison, Tony
    'The Queen's English', 168–9
    'Them and [uz]', 73
Hazlitt, William, and definition of poetry, 8
Heaney, Seamus, 184, 192
    'Digging', 119
Hegley, John, 218
Hemans, Felicia
    'Casabianca', 109
    'Music of Yesterday', 99
hemistich, **210**
Henri, Adrian, 176
Henry VIII, and English Renaissance, 16

Henryson, Robert, 42
heptameter (septenary), 102–3, **211**
  iambic, 103, 210, 211, 219
  trochaic, 210, 211
  see also fourteener
heptasyllabics, 91
Herbert, Edward, 1st Baron Herbert of Cherbury, 38
Herbert, George, 44–5, 215
  'Denial', 45–6
  'Easter Wings', 26–8, 29, 30, 34, 217
  'Employment', 41
  'Mortification', 116–18
  'Prayer I', 133–4
heroics
  heroic couplet, 43, 59, 81–6, 90, 206, **211**, 212, 223, 225
  unrhymed, 83–4
Herrick, Robert
  Hesperides, 38
  'Julia's petticoat', 116
  'Thus I pass by', 97–8
  'To Daffodils', 98
  'To the Virgins, to make Much of Time', 40, 205
hexameter, 100–2, **211**
  and acephalous lines, 201
  dactylic, 208
  iambic, 100–1, 201, 211, 219
  trochaic, 101
Hill, Geoffrey, 193
  'The Martyrdom of Saint Sebastian', 130–1
Homer
  Iliad, 59–60, 174, 208
  Odyssey, 174, 208
Homeric simile *see* epic simile
homostrophic form, **211**
Hood, Thomas, 'The Bridge of Sighs', 93–4
Hopkins, Gerard Manley, 165–6, 222
  and metre, 19
  'Hurrahing in Harvest', 149
  The Wreck of the Deutschland, 147
  'The Windhover', 63–4
Horace (Quintus Horatius Flaccus), 17, 205
  Horatian ode, **211**
  Horatian satire, 95, **211**, 213, 221
Horowitz, Michael, 217
Housman, A. E., 189
Hudibrastics, 88, 206, **211**, 216, 223, 224
Hughes, Ted, 184, 191–2
  'The Thought Fox', 22, 149
Hulme, T. E., 175, 179
humanism, and Renaissance, 16–17
Hutchinson, F. E., 27
hymn, **211**
  and ballad stanza, 39
  and trochaic metre, 88
  see also psalm
hyperbole, **211**
hypercatalectic lines, 79, 86–7, 209, **211**
hypertext, 29–30

iamb/iambic, 76, 77, 80–8, 201, 205, 208, **211–12**, 214, 217, 220, 224
  and free verse, 106
  heptameter, 210, 211, 219
  hexameter, 100–1, 201, 211, 219
  iambic stanza, 222
  tetrameter, 87, 90–2, 224
  see also alexandrine
iambic pentameter, 42, 78, **212**, 216, 220, 222
  and blank verse, 81, 83–8, 204, 212
  and heroic couplet, 43, 81–5, **211**, 212
ictus, **212**
idyll, **212**, 217
imagery, **212**
imagination, creative, 18, 20–1
imitation, 17, 18, 164–8
inflection, and rhyme, 63–4
inspiration, 22, 194
intertextuality, 156–9, **212**
  and allusion, 156, 159–64, **202**, 212
  quotation and imitation, 164–8
  and source, 157–9, 164
inversion, 84, **212**; *see also* substitution
invocation, 141, **213**, 215; *see also* apostrophe
Italian sonnet *see* sonnet, Petrarchan
Italy, Renaissance, 15–16, 43

Johnson, Samuel, 10–11, 83, 140, 184, 189
  and neoclassicism, 17
Jonson, Ben, 16, 38
  'A Hymn to God the Father', 99
Jonzi D (David Johns), 218
Joyce, James, *Finnegans Wake*, 148
Juvenal (Decimus Iunius Iuvenalis), 213, 221

Kavanagh, Patrick, 190
Keats, John
  and heroic couplet, 84, 85
  and nonce-words, 148
  and rhyme, 57
  and Shakespeare, 175
  and sonnet form, 222
  Endymion, 198
  'La Belle Dame sans Merci', 39
  Lamia, Isabella, The Eve of St Agnes, and Other Poems, 198
  'Ode on a Grecian Urn', 128
  'To one who has been long', 163
Knights, L. C., 6

lai *see* lay
Lakoff, George and Johnson, Mark, 128–9
lament, **213**; *see also* dirge; threnody
lampoon, **213**; *see also* squib
Langland, William
  and dream vision, 208
  and standard English, 169
  Piers Plowman, 14, **202**, 217, 218, 222
language
  everyday, 5, 9–10, 57, 106–7, 139–40, 141–3,

145–7, 190
figurative, 5, 57, 111–12; *see also* metaphor;
    metonymy; simile; synecdoche
linguistic diversity, 137–40
and neologism, 147–9, **216**
poems about, 153–5
and poetic diction, 5, 12, 19, 140–5, **218**
polite/impolite, 138–9
and standard English, 168–71
see also dialect
Larkin, Philip, 191
    '*Vers de Société*', 180–1
Later Genesis, 14
Latin, influence on English, 139–40
Lawrence, D. H., 'Gloire de Dijon', 54–6
lay, 15, **213**
layout of text, 30–3
Lear, Edward, 214, 216
    'The Dong with the Luminous Nose', 165–6
Leonard, Tom, 169
    'Jist ti Let Yi No', 152–3
Lightning Source, 186
limerick, 40, 200, **213–14**
line
    acatalectic, 78, 79, 104, **201**
    acephalous, **201**
    brachycatalectic, 79
    break, 82–3, 84, **204**
    catalectic, 79, 86, 89, 91, 93, 104, 201, **205**
    and definition of poetry, 10–11
    end-stopped, 39, 82, 84–5, 206
    half-line, 50
    hendecasyllabic, **210**
    heroic, 81, 87–8, 92, 211, 217
    hyperbrachic, 84
    hypercatalectic, 79, 86–7, 209, **211**
    masculine ending, **214**
    metrical, 97–104
    octosyllabic, 62, 88, 90, 97, 211, **216**, 220
    overrunning, 84–6, 99
    regular, 77–8, 80–1, 92
    weak ending, **225**
    see also hemistich; truncation
line-ending, 24–5
    feminine, 87, **209–10**
    masculine, **214**
    and rhyme, 59–60, 65–6
    weak, 86–7, **225**
litotes, **214**
Liverpool poets, 176, 217
Longley, Michael, 177, 192, 194
Lonsdale, Roger, 161
Lowell, Amy, 189
Lowell, Robert, 176, 179
Lulu, 186
lyric, **214**
    crisis, 19, **206–7**
    trochaic, 216
    see also ballade; blazon; elegy; madrigal; ode,
        Horatian; rondeau; sonnet

macaronic verse, **214**
Macaulay, Thomas Babington, 103
MacDiarmid, Hugh, 151
McGonagall, William, 207
    'To Mr James Scrymgeour, Dundee', 86
McGough, Roger, 176
Machiavelli, Niccolò, *The Prince*, 16
MacNeice, Louis, 190, 195, 199
madrigal, **214**
magazines, poetry, 186–7, 195
Marie de France, 213
Marlowe, Christopher, 16
    Doctor Faustus, 96
    'A Passionate Shepherd to his Love', 87
Marvell, Andrew, 215
    and heroic couplet, 85
    'On a Drop of Dew', 124–6, 127, 132
    'An Horatian Ode upon Cromwell's Return from
        Ireland', 211
meaning
    and appearance, 26–8, 29
    and linguistic diversity, 138
    and punctuation, 31–3, 52
    and rhyme, 67–9
    and sound, 51–4
measure
    poulter's, 103, **219**
    short, **222**
    see also metre
medieval poetry, 14–15
    and ballad form, 36
    see also Chaucer, Geoffrey; Langland, William
metaphor, 4, 5, 112–15, 116–18, 189, **214–15**, 215
    and cliché, 129, 131–2
    dead and dying, 129–32
    orientational, 128–9
    and riddle, 132–4
    see also allegory; conceit; ground; simile; symbol;
        tenor; vehicle
metaphysical poets, 123, 206, **215**
metonymy, 4, 115–18, 142, **215**
metre, 5, 72–110, **215**
    base, 9, 72, 73, 84, 204, 212, 223
    definition, 72
    and definition of poetry, 9–11
    duple, 80–92, 97, **208**
    iambic, 80–8, 205, 208, 214, 220
    mixed, 91, 94, **215**
    regularity and variance, 77–9, 91, 98–9, 101
    triple, 80, 102, 217, **224**
    trochaic, 88–92, 208, 217
    see also analysis; anapaest; foot; frame; heptameter;
        hexameter; modulation; octameter; pentameter;
        rhythm; stress; syllable
metrics *see* prosody
Middle English, 14, 77, 144
Milton, John, 15
    and Christian humanism, 16–17
    and epic poetry, 16
    and sonnet form, **215**, 222

'Il Penseroso', 88
'L'Allegro', 90–1, 108
Lycidas, 208
Paradise Lost, 144, 180, 203, 204, 208, 209, 213;
    allusions to, 162–3; and blank verse, 83–4, 204;
    and metre, 74, 77, 93; and rhyme, 57, 88
Samson Agonistes, 97
The Minstrel, 44
Mitchell, Adrian, 176
Mitchell, Elma, 191
mock-heroic *see* epic, mock
modernism, 19–20, 175
    and free verse, 104–7
    and Romanticism, 12, 20
    see also Eliot, T. S.; Pound, Ezra
modulation, 78, 80, 83, 94–5, 96, **215**, 219, 222; *see
    also* amphibrach; anapaest; cretic foot
monologue, **215**
    dramatic, 19, 199, **207**, 208
monometer, 97–8, **215**
Moore, Marianne, 190
Moore, Thomas
    'Ballad Stanzas', 110
    'We may roam through this world', 94–5
More, Sir Thomas, 16
Morgan, Edwin, 'The Loch Ness Monster's Song',
    51–3
Motion, Andrew, 184
Muldoon, Paul, 184, 187
muse, 21–2, 213, **215**

narrative poetry, 204, **216**
    dream vision, 15, 208
    medieval, 15
    and Spenserian stanza, 44
    see also ballad; epic; fabliau; romance
nature, and Romanticism, 18
neoclassicism, 12, 17, 18, 175–7
    Renaissance, 15–16
    see also Pope, Alexander; Swift, Jonathan
neologism, 147–9, 173, **216**
Newton, John, 39
ní Chuilleanáin, Eiléan, 199
nonce-word, 148, **216**
nonsense verse, 214, **216**
North, Thomas, *Lives of the Noble Greeks and
    Romans*, 156–9

occasional verse, **216**
octameter, 97, 103–4, **216**
octave, 43, **216**, 218, 221
octet, 43, 203, **216**
ode, **216**
    Horatian, **211**
    irregular, 211, **213**
    neoclassical, 17
    and occasional verse, 216
    Pindaric, **218**
    see also antistrophe; epode; strophe
Old English, 140, 144

poetry, 13–14, 49–50, 77, 174, 202
onomatopoeia, 51–4, **216**
Orwell, George, 140
ottava rima, 43, 81, **216**
Ovid (Publius Ovidius Naso), 17
Owen, Wilfred, 217
    'Strange Meeting', 64–5
Oxford English, 169–71
Oxford English Dictionary, 8–11, 51, 82, 137–8, 149,
    165
oxymoron, **216**

paean, **216**
paeon, **216–17**
palinode, **217**
panegyric, **217**; *see also* encomium; eulogy
pararhyme, 64–5, 66, **217**
Parker, Dorothy, 62
Parnell, Thomas, 'The Hymn to Contentment', 90
parody, 156, 166, 212, **217**
    and burlesque, 204
passus, **217**
pastoral, 180, **217**
    and quatrain, 38
    Renaissance, 16
    see also eclogue; georgic
pathos, **217**
Patten, Brian, 176
pattern poetry, **217**, 225
pentameter, 97, **217**
    continuous iambic, 87, 204
    dactylic, 208
    iambic *see* iambic pentameter
    and Spenserian stanza, 222
performance poetry, 176, **217–18**, 222
periphrasis, 142–3, **218**
personification, 142, 202, **218**
Petrarch, Francesco, 15, 16, 218, 221
Philips, Ambrose, *Fable of Thule*, 161
Philips, John, 'The Splendid Shilling', 215
phonology *see* sound effects
pictograms, 24–8
Pindaric ode, **218**
plagiarism, 156–8, 162
Plath, Sylvia, 177–8, 196
    Ariel, 178
    'Balloons', 134
    'You're', 134
Poe, Edgar Allan
    'The Bells', 53–4
    'The Raven', 60–1, 104, 207
poetaster, **218**
poeticality, **218**
poetics, **218**
poetry
    definition, 4, 7–13, 20–1, 189–94
    dramatic, **208**
    English, 3
    ethnic minority, 169–71
    graveyard, **210**

medieval, 14–15
metaphysical, 206, **215**
modernist, 12, 19–20, 104–7
neoclassical, 12, 17, 18
Old English, 13–14, 77, 174, 202
oral, 13–14, 23, 49–50, 174, **216**; *see also* ballad
pattern, **217**, 225
performance, 176, **217–18**, 222
poets on, 189–94
Renaissance, 15–16, 214, 216, 221, 222
Romantic, 2, 12–13, 17–19
slam, **222**
topographic, 89–90, **224**
Victorian, 12, 19
visual appearance, 4
writing, 5–6, 174–200
Poetry Book Society, 187
Poetry Library, 187
Poetry Olympics, 217
poetry readings, 185–6, 192, 198
Poetry Society, 187
Pope, Alexander, 2, 12, 203
    and definition of poetry, 12
    and eclogue, 208
    and heroic couplet, 59, 82–3, 85, 90
    Homer's *Iliad*, 59–60
    and neoclassicism, 17, 175–6
    and rhyme, 63
    and satire, 221
    Dunciad, 193, 215
    'Eloisa to Abelard', 90, 164
    'Epistle to Dr. Arbuthnot', 95
    An Essay on Criticism, 12, 17, 82, 85, 101
    Essay on Man, 82
    Messiah, 82
    The Rape of the Lock, 82, 161, 163–4, 202, 204
portmanteau word, 148, **218**
postmodernism, 193
poulter's measure, 103, **219**
Pound, Ezra, 20, 105, 183, 199
    and free verse, 105–6
    'The Seafarer', 50
print
    and aesthetics, 23–4
    and layout and punctuation, 30–3
    and visual appearance of poetry, 4, 34, 217, 225
prosody, 5, 72, **219**, 223
prothalamion, **219**; *see also* epithalamion
Prynne, J. H., 193, 196
    'Streak~~~Willing~~~Entourage *Artesian*', 176
psalm, **219**; *see also* hymn
Psalm 23, 57–8
publication, 6, 186–9, 196
Pulci, Luigi, 43
punctuation, 31–3, 52, 60, 82
pyrrhic foot, 84, 86, 96, 213, 217, **219**

quantitative verse, 77, **219**
Quarles, Francis, *Emblems*, 36, 208
quatrain, 99, 203, **219**, 222

    and carol, 205
    heroic, 40
    iambic, 40, 211
    rhymed, 38, 67
    and Sapphics, 221
    stanzaic, 35, 38–40, 87, 224
Queen's English, 168–71
quintain/quintet, 40–1, **219**
quotation, creative, 164–8

Raine, Craig, 193
    'A Martian Sends a Postcard Home', 120–3, 127, 131, 132, 135, 181
Randolph, Thomas, 'An Ode to Mr. Anthony Stafford', 98
Raworth, Tom, 29
Read, Herbert, 20
Reading, Peter, 29
Reed, Henry, 'Naming of Parts', 153–5
refrain, **219**
    and carol, 205
    see also burden
register, 19, 137, 153–5, 171, 202
Renaissance poetry, 15–16, 214, 216, 221, 222;
    see also Jonson, Ben; Milton, John; Petrarch, Francesco; Shakespeare, William; Sidney, Sir Philip; Spenser, Edmund; Wyatt, Sir Thomas
repetend, **219**
repetition, 173
    and free verse, 105–7
    incremental, **212**
    phonological, 54–5
    see also rhyme
rhopalic verse, **220**
rhyme, 5, 15, 56–9, 197, 203, **220**
    anaphoric, 31
    and assonance, 203
    broken, **204**
    cross-rhyme, 87
    crossed, **207**
    double, 210
    end-rhyme, 59–60, **208**, 210, 220
    eye rhyme, 64, **209**
    feminine, 61, 63–4, 65, 69, 87, 88, **210**, 211, 215
    free, 66
    and free verse, 104
    half-rhyme, 66, **210**
    imperfect *see* half-rhyme *above*
    indeterminacies, 65–7
    internal, 60–1, 100, 104, 205, **212**, 213
    leonine, 212, **213**
    masculine, 63, **214**
    and meaning, 67–9
    mosaic, **215**
    orthodox, 59–60
    pararhyme, 64–5, 66, **217**
    polysyllabic, 61–2
    triple, 94, 215, **224**
rhyme royal, 42, 81, **220**, 221

rhyme scheme, 24, 43, 58, 66–7, **220**; *see also*
  scansion
rhythm, 8, 72–110, 197, **220**
  and cadence, 205, 220
  falling, 88–92, 93, **209**, 222, 224
  rising, 80, 91, 95, 201, 212, 220
  sprung, **222**
  see also metre
Rich, Adrienne, 6
  'Transcendental Etude', 179–80
Ricks, Christopher, 160
riddle poem, 132–4
rime couée, 41
Robinson, Mary
  'The Poor, Singing Dame', 109
  'Stanzas. Written between Dover and Calais', 89,
    91
romance, 14–15, **220**
  and Burns stanza, 41–2
  and *rime couée*, 41
Romanticism, 17–19, 145
  and crisis lyric, 19, 206–7
  and emotional impact of poetry, 2, 12–13, 18,
    175–6
  and modernism, 12, 20
  see also Blake, William; Byron, George Gordon;
    Coleridge, S. T.; Keats, John; Robinson, Mary;
    Shelley, Percy Bysshe; Wordsworth, William
rondeau, 19, **220**
Rossetti, D. G., 'The White Ship', 35
roundel, **220–1**
Ruskin, John
  and definition of poetry, 8
  Lectures on Art, 12

Sapphics, **221**
Sappho, 221
satire, **221**
  Horatian, 95, **211**, 213, 221
  Juvenalian, 211, **213**, 221
  neoclassical, 17
  and *ottava rima*, 218
  and parody, 217
  see also clerihew; fabliau; lampoon; squib
scansion, 5, **221**
  graphic, 76, 80, 82, 108, **210**, 221
Schmidt, Michael, 193
Scott, Sir Walter, 'He is gone on the mountain', 206
The Seafarer, 14, 50, 176
self-expression, 176–9
self-publishing, 186
separation, 82, **221**
septenary *see* heptameter
septet/septuary, 42–3, **221**
sestet
  and Burns stanza, 41–2, 204
  and Petrarchan sonnet, 41, 218, **221**
  stanzaic, 41–2
sestina, **221**
Sexton, Anne, 6, 177, 191, 196

'The Abortion', 178–9
All My Pretty Ones, 178
Shakespeare, William, 83, 216
  and everyday language, 140
  and sonnet, 16, 200, **221–2**
  Antony and Cleopatra, 156–9
  As You Like It, 217
  Hamlet, 159
  King Lear, 95–6, 147
  Macbeth, 89, 139–40
  The Merry Wives of Windsor, 11
  'The Phoenix and the Turtle', 79
  The Rape of Lucrece, 42, 81, 220
  Richard II, 68–9
  Romeo and Juliet, 203, 219
  The Tempest, 86–7
  Twelfth Night, 94
shape poems, 4, 24–8
Sharpe, Richard Scrafton, **214**
Shelley, Percy Bysshe
  and definition of poetry, 8
  Adonais, 208
  'Hymn to Intellectual Beauty', 211
  'Ode to a Skylark', 41, 110
  'Ode to the West Wind', 37
  Prometheus Unbound, 88–9
  The Revolt of Islam, 44
  'A Summer-Evening Churchyard', 41
Shew, Marie Louise, 53
Shirley, James, 'The Glories of our Blood and State',
    115
sibilance, 55, **222**
Sidney, Sir Philip, 8, 221, 222
  and pastoral, 16
  and sonnet, 16
  Arcadia, 221
  The Defence of Poesie, 11, 13
sigmatism, **222**
simile, 5, 113–15, 214, **222**
  epic, **209**
  extended, 123–7, 162
  see also metaphor
Sir Gawain and the Green Knight, 14, 202, 208, 220
'Sir Patrick Spence', 39
slam poetry, **222**
Smart, Christopher
  'My Cat Jeoffrey', 166–8
  A Song to David, 41–2
Smith, Charlotte, *Elegaic Sonnets*, 164
Smith, Stevie, 198
sonnet, **222**
  Miltonian, **215**
  Petrarchan, 41, 200, 215, 216, **218**, 221, 222
  Shakespearean, 16, 200, **221–2**
  see also crown
sound
  segmental, 47
  suprasegmental, 47
sound pattern, 4–5, 8–10, 47–71; *see also* assonance;
    consonance; dissonance; metre; onomatopoeia;

rhyme; rhythm; sibilance
sound poem, 5, 51–3
Southey, Robert, 218, 221
Southwell, St. Robert, 'The Burning Babe', 102
spelling
  and rhyme, 56
  and sound, 47–8
Spender, Stephen, 'The Pylons', 113–15, 132
Spenser, Edmund, 42, 220, 222
  and eclogue, 208
  and epic poetry, 16
  'Epithalamion', 209
  Faerie Queene, 43, 58, 66, 144, 202
  'Prothalamion', 219
  Spenserian stanza, 43–4, 58, 66, 101, 144, 201, 220, **222**
  'The Teares of the Muses', 21
spondee, 84, 86, 95–6, 213, **222**
sprung rhythm, **222**
squib, **222**; *see also* lampoon
Stafford, William, 6, 183
  'Travelling Through the Dark', 178–80
stanza, 4, **223**
  ballad, 39–40, **203**, 206, 216, 219
  Burns, 41–2, **204**
  Chaucerian, 42, 220
  heroic/elegiac, 40, **211**
  iambic, **222**
  romance, 41
  Spenserian, 43–4, 58, 66, 81, 101, 144, 201, 220, **222**
  and visuality, 33–44
  see also couplet; octave; octet; quatrain; quintain; sestet; tercet; triplet
stave, **223**
Stevens, Wallace, 190
stichic verse, **223**
Strachan, John
  'Fourteen', 200
  'Of Sunderland, and its Vicinities', 181–3
stress, 5, 75–6, 221, **223**
  and accentual analysis, 77
  sound, 59–60
strophe, 216, 218, **223**
  and antistrophe, **203**
sublimity
  and iambic verse, 92
  and Romanticism, 18
substitution, 80, 91, **223**, 224
  amphibrachic, 96–7
  anapaestic, 94
  dactylic, 93, 207
  pyrrhic, 96
  spondaic, 95
  trochaic, 78, 83, 84, 88, 91, 94–5
  see also inversion; modulation
Supergrass, 'Alright', 96–7
Surrey, Henry Howard, Earl
  and poulter's measure, 103, 219
  'Lady Surrey's Lament for her Absent Lord', 103

Swift, Jonathan
  and neoclassicism, 17, 175–6
  and rhyme, 61–2
  and satire, 221
  A Proposal for Correcting … the English Tongue, 140
  'Verses on the Death of Doctor Swift', 87
Swinburne, A. C.
  and metre, 19, 100, 102, 103
  and roundel, 221
  'A Ballad of François Villon', 203, 205
  'Ballade of the Lords of Old Time', 203
  'Choriambics', 205
  'Christmas Antiphones', 100
  'Double Sestina', 221
  'A Forsaken Garden', 222
  'Hesperia', 102
syllable, 74–5, **223**
  missing and extra, 79–80
  and quantitative verse, 219
  syllabic analysis, 77, **223**
  see also stress
symbol, 5, 56, **223**; *see also* allegory; metaphor
synecdoche, 115–18, **223**

Tennyson, Alfred, Lord, 220
  and metre, 19, 77, 93, 103
  'The Charge of the Light Brigade', 93
  'Locksley Hall', 103
  'Maud', 103
  'The Talking Oak', 40
  'Tithonus', 160
  'Ulysses', 166
tenor, 5, 118–23, 124–6, 131, 132, 214, **223**
tercet, 36–8, **223–4**
  continuous, 224
  stanzaic, 224
terza rima, 36–7, 200, 223, **224**
tetrameter, 97, 203, 222, **224**
  and ballad stanza, 39
  iambic, 87, 90–2, 224
  trochaic, 87, 89, 91–2, 205
Theocritus, and eclogue, 208
Thomas, Dylan, 64, 174, 189
  'Do not Go Gentle into that Good Night', 37, 225
  'Fern Hill', 111–12
  'The Force that through the Green Fuse Drives the Flower', 65–6
  Under Milk Wood, 149
Thomson, James
  'Autumn', 161
  The Castle of Indolence, 44, 81
  'Hymn to the Seasons', 84, 211
threnody, 179, **224**; *see also* dirge; lament
Tolkien, J. R. R., 'Song of Eldamar', 109–10
tone, **224**
tongue-twister, 48, 205
topography, topographic verse, 89–90, 224
tragedy, neoclassical, 17

transference, and figurative language, 112–13,
   115–16, 118, 129
Trapp, Joseph, *Lectures on Poetry*, 141
trimeter, 100, 203, 222, **224**
  and ballad stanza, 39
triolet, 19, **224**
triplet, 36, 223, **224**
trochee, 105, 205, 208
  catalectic, 79–80, 100, 214
  trochaic hexameter, 101
  trochaic octameter, 103–4
  trochaic substitution, 78, 83, 84, 88, 91, 94–5
  trochaic verse, 88–92, **224**
troubadour, 15, 221
truncation, 80, 91, 96, **224–5**
turn, 218, **225**; *see also* volta
Two Ravens Press, 188
typography, **225**

unreadability, 28–30
Updike, John, 191

vanity presses, 186
vehicle, 5, 118–23, 124–6, 131, 132, 214
Vendler, Helen, 21
vers libre **225**; *see also* free verse
verse
  anapaestic, 94–5
  blank *see* blank verse
  continuous, 35, **206**, 221, 223
  dactylic, 92–3
  dialect, 149–53
  iambic, 212
  macaronic, **214**
  nonmetrical *see* free verse
  nonsense, 214, **216**
  occasional, **216**
  quantitative, **219**
  rhopalic, **220**
  stichich, **223**
  topographic, 224
  trochaic, 88–92, **224**
verse (line), 34, 75
verse drama, 16, 83, **225**
verse paragraph, **225**
versification, **225**
Victorian poetry, 12, 19, 102; *see also* Arnold,
  Matthew; Browning, Elizabeth Barrett;
  Browning, Robert; Hopkins, Gerard Manley;
  Rossetti, D. G.; Swinburne, A. C.; Tennyson,
  Alfred, Lord
villanelle, 19, 37, 200, 223, **225**
Villon, François, 203
Virgil (Publius Vergilius Maro), 17
  and eclogue, 208
  Aeneid, 163
  Georgics, 210
visuality, 4, 23–46, 217, 225

and aesthetics, 23–4
and concrete poetry, 24–8
and enactment, 28–30
layout and punctuation, 30–3
and stanza, 33–44
volta, 215, 218, **225**; *see also* turn

Walcott, Derek, 184, 191
The Wanderer, 14, 176
Warton, Joseph, 17
Wasserman, Earl, 163–4
Watts, Isaac
  'The Last Judgement', 221
  'When I survey the wondrous Cross', 87
White, E. B., 196
Williams, William Carlos
  'Death', 105–7
  'This is Just to Say', 145–7, 152
Wither, George, 'Ah me! Am I the Swaine', 34
word, portmanteau, 148, **218**
word association, 199
words *see* language
Wordsworth, William, 2, 3, 19
  and Coleridge, 183, 199
  and definition of poetry, 8, 9, 11–12, 175, 195
  and poetic language, 5, 9, 145
  and rhyme, 73
  and sonnet form, 222
  'Daffodils', 113, 119, 132, 165–6
  Guilt and Sorrow, 44
  Lyrical Ballads, 11
  'Not useless do I deem', 214
  'Ode. Intimations of Immortality', 19, 207, 213
  The Prelude, 83, 160, 204
  'She dwelt among the untrodden ways', 34
  'Strange Fits of Passion I have Known', 40
  'The Thorn', 203–4
workshops, poetry, 6, 183, 184–5, 198
Wright, Charles, 184, 192
Writers' and Artists' Yearbook, 187
writers' groups, 6, 183, 184–5, 198
Writer's Handbook, 187
writing of poetry, 5–6, 174–200
  antiquity of, 174–5
  and feedback, 183–6, 187, 195
  and personal experience, 180–3, 190, 194, 196
  poets on, 189–94
  and publication, 186–9, 196
  reasons for, 175–80
Wyatt, Sir Thomas, 16
  and poulter's measure, 103, 219

Yeats, W. B., 190
  'Sailing to Byzantium', 113
Young, Edward, 210

Zephaniah, Benjamin, 218